PELICAN BOOKS · A 334

THE FILM AND THE PUBLIC

ROGER MANVELL

Roger Manvell

THE FILM

AND THE PUBLIC

PENGUIN BOOKS

PENGUIN BOOKS LTD, Harmondsworth, Middlesex
U.S.A.: Penguin Books Inc., 3300 Clipper Mill Road, Baltimore 11, Md
CANADA: Penguin Books (Canada) Ltd, 47 Green Street, Saint Lambert,
Montreal, P.Q.
AUSTRALIA: Penguin Books Pty Ltd, 762 Whitehorse Road,
Mitcham, Victoria
SOUTH AFRICA: Penguin Books (S.A.) Pty Ltd, Gibraltar House,
Regents Road, Sea Point, Cape Town

First published 1955

Made and printed in Great Britain by Hunt, Barnard and Co, Ltd,
Aylesbury
Collogravure plates by Harrison & Sons Ltd.

To ARLETTY
star of the French Cinema,
in admiration and
friendship

CONTENTS

2. A MISCELLANY OF FILMS

representing some of the different forms and styles of film-making which reveal the development of the Art

3. THE FILM AS AN INDUSTRY

SUPPLEMENT

NOTE ON THE ILLUSTRATIONS

THE purpose of the illustrations to this book is first of all to show the complete range of film-making as it has developed during sixty years. We begin with the primary forms of recording actuality, progressing through the scientific and documentary film to the main forms of fiction film, realist, theatrical, spectacular, fantastic, etc. The main styles that have been developed in the animated film are also represented, together with some illustrations of the new forms of film-making – wide-screen and three-dimensional.

Since most films are portraits of people in action, the greater part of these illustrations were selected to show the various ways in which humanity has been portrayed on the screen, either real people portraying themselves in their actual surroundings, or actors and actresses presenting fictional characters with a greater or lesser degree of realism.

The concluding section of the illustrations shows the last shots in the opening sequence of *Oliver Twist* as it was planned in advance in a series of sketches made by the Art Director, John Bryan, by whose courtesy they are reproduced, together with one of his designs for a setting in the same film.

INTRODUCTION

To write a new book on the film is not easy. Both too much and too little have been written about it already. The film can no longer masquerade as immature; there is a glamorous grey on the adolescent temples. It is certainly old enough to feel jealous of the public's interest in television.

What kind of book ought one to write as an introduction to the film in the nineteen-fifties? A dozen years ago there were scarcely a dozen books on the subject which really mattered. Now that the specialists have moved in and have begun their surveys of the holes and corners in the history and technicalities of cinematography, it is clear that we have reached a new phase in the development of true criticism of the film. The serious historians are still very few in number, but they have begun to publish the results of their research on an international scale. Writers on films can no longer get by with hazy generalizations which act as convenient padding between the marshalling of a few obvious facts. It has become a hard and responsible task, as well as a fascinating and enjoyable one, to understand fully the art and technique of the films and the problems that beset their production and exhibition within an industrial framework. The relationship of the film to television has also to be considered, and the changes which the new systems of wide-screen and three-dimensional projection will introduce to the technique of film-making.

This book, like its predecessor *Film* which I wrote originally for the Pelican Series ten years ago in 1944, is an introduction to the whole subject intended for people who have already come to feel the fascination of the film, not only as a great form of art but also as a great medium of popular entertainment. The first and second parts (which together make up about half of its length) attempt to show how rapidly and effectively the film-makers discovered the great technical and artistic capacities of their chosen medium. I have not written here a condensed history of the film; that has been done in many other books. I have tried to show the main phases of its development as an art – the expansion of its powers as a medium both for drama and the presentation of facts. What I have written is the story of the phenomenal and exciting growth of a new art, not the story of everything that was produced, good, bad, or indifferent, which makes up the total history of the cinema. To reinforce the points made in this survey, I have in the second part added a number of detailed studies of individual films, chosen because in different ways they illustrate the wide range of achievement in film-making during the past twenty-five years. Some of these studies were specially written for this book, while others have been published only abroad; I am grateful to the Editor of *Britain To-day* for permitting their re-publication. I am also very grateful to the British Film Institute for permitting me to reprint certain others I wrote for the *Records of the Film* and also for *Revaluations*, another series I undertook some years ago for *Sight and Sound*. The selection of film-stills in this present volume illustrates these films and certain others which are mentioned in some detail elsewhere in the book. I am grateful to Miss Traylen of the National Film Library for her help in making this selection.

The next two parts of the book, three and four, deal with economic and other problems affecting film production, and with some discussion of the social effects which have resulted from the great popularity of the cinema. Lastly, there is a section on television and its relationship to the film. I am very glad that Denis Forman, Director of the British Film Institute from 1948 to 1955, allowed me to include at the end of this volume a revised version of an article on the work of the Institute originally written for *The Year's Work in the Film*, published by the British Council, by whose permission it is reproduced here. I am also grateful to the Hulton Press for permitting me to base a few paragraphs in this book on two articles I originally wrote for *The Leader*.

R. M.

I: THE SILENT FILM

The Representation of Movement

IT was in the Spring of 1948 that I first saw the Lascaux cave paintings. It was an experience which set up an immediate excitement due to the shock of delight given me by their vigour and beauty. The sheer age of the work, existing for over twenty thousand years and yet there within the reach of my hands, created a new emotion, a sudden link with the far-distant past of my own race and kind.

My friend and I were lucky because we were quite alone with the guide in the caves. The guide lit up, one by one, crypt, and alcove, and corridor, and the strange animals appeared in every place on the irregular surface of the walls and the bulging contours of the ceilings, beasts painted in brown and ochre dyes, and covered with the glistening saline deposit which has preserved the colours freshly for thousands of years. It is strange that such an accident of nature has given these painters a longer run for immortality than any of the great masters are likely to achieve.

It is the suspended motion of the beasts which gives them their vigour. The splaying limbs of these figures – both the animals painted with a near realism, and those painted as formalized shapes – are almost all in a state of activity, jumping, stretching, leaping, or sinking down in death. The artists desired to capture movement, the symbol of animal life, in the static design of their paintings. They succeeded, as later artists have done with greater technical science, in catching some phase in the transition of movement which makes the painted bodies suggest there is a life within them. Nor is the desire for movement confined to the more realistic developments of representational art; the movement of life stirs just as vigorously in the embryonic shapes of Henry Moore's sculpture. Though certain kinds of formal art seem to suggest an eternity of stillness, the objects of life petrified into beautiful immobile patterns, the splendour of movement has tempted the artists equally, as the caves of Lascaux show.

The historians of the cinema, and most notably Georges Sadoul, have shown us the various technical developments which have led to the establishment of the motion picture as we know it to-day. Everyone who writes about the prehistory of the film mentions the little machines with fantastic names like prehistoric monsters, such as the zoetrope, the phenakisticope, the choreutoscope, the praxinoscope of Reynaud and the zoogyroscope of Muybridge. The sequences of photographic images of birds in flight created by Étienne-Jules Marey with his photographic gun, and the long bands of little hand-painted pictures made with such patient devotion by Émile Reynaud for his *Théâtre Optique* (both of these men working in the eighteen-eighties), are the first developments with a beauty of their own to emerge from the early years of the invention of motion pictures, except for the images of the Chinese shadow theatres of the eighteenth and nineteenth centuries, which we can now only imagine for ourselves.

The first crude little films were a delight to their inventors and to the public first privileged to see them. They were a delight because they represented an achievement which their inventors felt, for no obviously explicable reason, was a great step forward. To where? From what? The almost hysterical joy of William Friese-Greene, who devoted his life and fortune to experimenting with motion pictures, when, one night in January 1889, it is said that he showed his first few seconds of film to a passing policeman, can only be explained in the light of our later knowledge of what was to happen when the film became a great art and a great industry. The excitement for Friese-Greene lay in the conquest of motion, the reproduction of the symbol of life which had haunted the artists from times which may well have long preceded those of the painters of Lascaux.

But the men who were really excited by this new machine, which linked photography with the projection of a picture giving a satisfactory illusion of motion, were the artists. Men like Edison and Lumière did not really believe in the importance of the invention which they had done so much to promote. Contrast, for example, the enthusiasm of Georges Méliès, who was to become the first great name in the development of the French film, with the scepticism of Auguste Lumière, the business man, in the story as told by Méliès himself and quoted by Bardèche and Brasillach in their *History of the Film*:

> I rushed up to Auguste Lumière and offered to buy his invention. I offered ten thousand, twenty thousand, fifty thousand francs. I would gladly have given him my fortune, my house, my family, in exchange for it. Lumière would not listen to me. 'Young man,' said he, 'you should be grateful, since, although my invention is not for sale, it would undoubtedly ruin you. It can be exploited for a certain time as a scientific curiosity but, apart from that, it has no commercial future whatsoever.'

Edison was equally sceptical at first, and quite content to let motion pictures be shown in Kinetoscopes, which only offered a brief peep-show for the excitement of a single viewer.

The infant films soon began to discover their strength. In 1946 I went with my colleague Rachael Low (the historian of the early period in British films) to see one of the pioneers of motion pictures, George Albert Smith, at his house in Brighton. He showed us the little notebooks in which he kept his first accounts. He had been a portrait photographer who in 1897 began to make simple record films of the streets and beaches at Brighton. The account-books showed columns with small amounts in shillings and pence for outlay and receipts during the first months of his work, but he showed us that by 1900 his profit from the sale and exhibition of his films had amounted to £1,800. The public response to the early work of men like R. W. Paul, Charles Urban (who was George Albert Smith's business partner), and Cecil Hepworth was quite overwhelming. The people wanted motion pictures, however crude and simple they might be, and they wanted them permanently. The artists had been proved right. By the middle of the year 1896 the photographers and exhibitors of the Lumière staff had crossed the world from New York to Saint Petersburg, and in 1895 the brothers Skladanovsky had demonstrated their Bioscop in the Berlin Winter-Garten two months before the Lumières held their first performance in Paris on 28 December at the Grand Café in the Boulevard des Capucines. Motion pictures were established internationally, and the regular exchange of films began between Britain, France, and America.

The Quality of the Early Films

It is difficult for those of us who were brought up, as I was, to see films from a very early age, to imagine life without them, although there are plenty of people who to this day go through the year without ever seeing a film. Over a quarter of the population of Britain seldom or never goes to the pictures. It is true that films seem less necessary for day-to-day living than either newspapers or broadcasting in sound or vision, for these bring entertainment and information directly into the home. People have to take the trouble to go out to places where films are shown, unless they are enthusiastic enough to have home movie apparatus. Once this trouble has been taken and the price of admission paid, the cinema presents us with a new dimension of experience. Those who for various reasons leave the cinema out of their lives lose the chance of sharing this new dimension with those who have learned to value it.

The first films demonstrated this quality very simply. In place of the written description of the newspapers, the still photograph, the steel engraving, the woodcut, the line drawing or the representational paintings of the nineteenth century, they showed the living scene. They replaced observation by proxy with direct personal observation by the spectator. Instead of the dead picture there was the living one, with the fundamental attraction to human curiosity as to what the people in the moving picture would do next. A still picture, once seen, excites in the ordinary observer no further curiosity. Most people looking through a picture paper are content with a quick glance. But motion pictures hypnotize the beholder like the spectacle of life itself, and often with greater power, since the motion picture is selective whereas the spectacle of life is not.

The first films which won popular support were newsreels and 'actualities', as they have come to be called. Race meetings, scenes of warfare, and travelogues filled the first catalogues of films for sale to the itinerant exhibitors. The enthusiasm of the showmen in their catalogue descriptions of the films for sale reflects the enthusiasm of their audiences.

G. A. Smith: *Waves and Spray*. Fine effect. Rough sea dashing against stone groyne. (1898.)

C. Hepworth: *Express Trains*. A photograph taken in a picturesque Railway Cutting in Surrey. During the period of the picture no less than three Express Trains rush through, emitting dense clouds of steam as they pass. The trains come from the extreme distance of the view right up into the close foreground, and the effect of their rapid travelling is very fine and quite exciting. (Early 1898.)

These films were record films, and serve to remind us that motion pictures are initially, like the microphones and television cameras of broadcasting, instruments designed to demonstrate actuality. The film cameras and the negatives inside them are not any more creative in themselves than a railway engine or a linotype machine. They are instruments of service. What is recorded by camera and celluloid is the joint affair of the men who operate them and the public who patronize the results of their work.

Still, the first film-makers were rather like grown-ups playing at trains. So long as the engines went it did not matter where they went, so the operators let them whizz round and round in gradually expanding circles. The trains had not yet been constructed on a scale which enabled them to take people anywhere on a proper journey. That was to come later.

The beginning of some sort of purpose in the making of a film can be found in descriptive actualities like the country life series of films made by J. Williamson as early as 1899. These films showed quite simply some details of operations in farming. But Cecil Hepworth's film *An Alien's Invasion*, made in 1905, revealed a genuine desire to develop a social subject on the screen, as his catalogue description shows:

This is the first of a series of Political Pictures, intended to present in a graphic and convincing form the political questions of the hour which are of the highest national importance. The alien question is shown in a manner which is both highly convincing and at the same time intensely interesting.

The first scene shows the arrival of a steamer, crowded with aliens, at the London docks, and many of its passengers can be clearly seen. Among them is a typical alien, whose face becomes familiar as the picture progresses. On the quayside a female relative welcomes him gladly and takes him to the home – a single room – which is already shared by about twenty others, men, women, and children. This room is an exact reproduction of one in the East End actually visited by our Stage Manager, and is typical of thousands of others. Across it from end to end are several clothes lines, on which the occupants keep their wearing apparel, for there is nowhere else in the room to put it. A large notice in Yiddish adorns the door, and the furniture consists of two or three broken-down bedsteads, each of which contains as many occupants as it will hold; others sleep on the floor in any place where fancy dictates. It is early morning, and the first to awake is the woman whom we have previously seen upon the quay; she arouses the other sleepers and calls them to breakfast. Those who are too fastidious to sleep in their clothes retire behind a bedstead to don their working apparel. The breakfast consists of the strange viands which are purchasable in the neighbourhood of Petticoat Lane for very small money. These are the people who oust the honest British toiler from his work and this their manner of living . . .

On the other hand, no purpose beyond mere record was served by the innumerable entertainment shorts in which well-known vaudeville artists, many of them singers, gesticulated their way through some brief turn. Showmen provided various forms of sound accompaniment, usually on a piano, to make the silent image seem like a real vaudeville turn.

It will be noticed that I am not concerned at this stage with technique, with important considerations like camera position, camera movement, or cutting. These films were shot with fixed cameras, the immovable lens of the man used to taking a still photograph from a chosen vantage point. There was no living, moving relationship between the camera and the subject. One recorded while the other performed. The first films in which the camera began to perform as well as the subject were, in fact, the trick films of men like Cecil Hepworth, R. W. Paul, and Georges Méliès.

Cecil Hepworth: *Getting Up made Easy.*

What busy man does not know the difficulties attendant upon late rising? This is an amusing film which shows how such troubles are obviated. An old Gentleman, upon waking, finds the bedclothes whisked off, and the painful effort of turning out satisfactorily solved. Stepping on to the floor, a portion of his clothes quickly attach themselves, and a chair suddenly appears in the centre of the room, upon which the old gentleman seats himself. A wash basin then rolls comically along the floor, and, on being lifted, the water springs from the floor into the basin. Afterwards, a looking-glass flies into the old gent's hands, and the remainder of his garments having satisfactorily placed themselves, he quits the room well satisfied with the small amount of exertion entailed. (1903.)

When the camera came to record the first dramas it was as cold as a mirror propped up on a seat in the stalls. It caught the voiceless antics of actors fighting to make their gestures tell us everything in the plot, with the result that most of them look like ill-bred marionettes. Plainly the first stage of film development belongs to the actualities and the fantasies. These films, projected at the proper speed at which they were photographed, have at least the dignity of the subjects they record, or recall past forms of humour with something of the charm of a bygone period. The fantasies of Méliès, for all their paste-board stagecraft, show the vigorous imagination of a true pioneer, excited by what he is doing and going about it with the whole-hearted enthusiasm of an artist. Many of the individual sequences he made in his most elaborate films, like *A Trip to the Moon* (1902), *The Impossible Voyage* (1904) and *Conquest of the Pole* (1912), have a pictorial beauty of their own, but I think it is true that he seldom loses the atmosphere of the theatre in his work as a film-maker. His designs have great dash and style, and the spirit of his work could have been realized far better in the drawn film had it been in a more advanced stage at the time he was working. His films were immensely popular for many years, but he was eventually driven out of business by the fierce competition of the cinema. The episode of his re-discovery in 1928 and rescue from the obscurity of serving in a little shop in the Gare Montparnasse is one of the most touching stories in the history of the film. The industry is too ready to forget the artists who first made it rich and successful, for many of the pioneers were showmen with the qualities of gentle visionaries and unfitted to protect themselves once the harsh and go-getting business methods of the cinema had left them and their work behind. The short film *Le Grand Méliès*, made in 1953, in which the pioneer's son plays the part of his father, and in which his aged widow appears in two most moving sequences, re-creates something both of the period and of the highly individual character of Georges Méliès. He was the first considerable artist to work in the medium of films.

It is interesting to apply certain friendly tests to the few examples of the very early films which still survive in the various national libraries. Their pretensions as fiction or as documentary are so elementary that the question of their requiring much in the way of film technique to assist them is merely academic. A few tricks in camera-work sufficed at this stage. Technique in film-making in any real sense only developed with the need to tell a story with greater detail and elaboration. This was to happen soon enough.

The friendly tests that we apply to these early films should take the form of examining them for the first signs of interpretation of a story by means which belong wholly to the cinema. The very first films of all are a continuous picture-record of an action from a single camera position (like Lumière's gardener soaked by a hose-pipe) or a scene from an actual event (like a record of the Derby). It occurred very early in film history for the camera to be set near enough to people to make a medium close-shot; this happens in Lumière's scene of feeding the baby (1895), in the famous scene of the American artists May Irwin and John C. Rice kissing (1896), and in the British facial expression films (beginning 1898). But the camera was usually placed far enough away from any action to show it complete, leaving the spectator to choose which part of the action he will watch, as he does in the theatre. *One of the first tests of film-making is the degree to which the camera is used to assist the spectator to select what there is to see, that is, when the camera is used to help interpret the action.* This may be so slight as to be unnoticeable; in *The Great Train Robbery* (1903) the camera swings a very little to the left to follow the bandits as they scramble through the woods. This could scarcely be claimed as interpretation, but it does recognize that the audience will want to follow the bandits' movements, and that they should be kept as central as possible in the picture. More important by far is the low position in which the camera is put during a few scenes in Cecil Hepworth's *Rescued by Rover*; the camera is kept near the ground because the hero of the film is a dog, and the camera can make us share the *viewpoint of the dog* better from that position than from the normal one, which is four feet or so from the ground. But film-makers were on the whole slow to make the camera a lively instrument of interpretation, as distinct from a passive recorder of what there was to be seen. The days of panning, tilting, unusual camera positions and angles, tracking and crane shots were fully developed in the nineteen-twenties. Shots like D. W. Griffith's famous scene from a captive balloon pulled down slowly over the vast steps of Belshazzar's Palace in *Intolerance* were imaginative side-lines in the

23

development of the interpretative camera, rather than part of its true development. The static, immovable camera died hard in film-making.

Development came more rapidly in the other important branch of film technique – the breakdown of the action into separate shots, and its effective presentation on the screen through the editing of these shots into sequences which tell the story clearly and with good timing. *Rescued by Rover* remains a good example of a very simple action effectively presented in a series of well planned shots edited together.

This film had a genuine sense of continuity, revealing therefore an advanced form of film technique such as Griffith was to work out in his films. It employs low-camera-angle to match the height of the dog as it runs down the street. Above all, it moves rapidly from scene to scene, employs a variety of indoor and outdoor settings, and the shots of the dog running, swimming, jumping, have a forward drive of movement which is carefully matched by the cutting of the film.   (*History of the British Film*, Vol. i, p. 108.)

When one considers that the films of this period were sold internationally and shown indiscriminately whatever their national origin (chiefly British, French, or American), the first simple techniques became almost unconsciously international. What matters is that the technique of film-making developed rapidly up to a certain point; after that it depended on film-makers of verve and imagination like D. W. Griffith, Thomas Ince, Mack Sennett, and Charles Chaplin to extend the range of film-making during the next decade until it became a medium in which farce, comedy, tragedy, melodrama, and spectacle were all developed to a standard worth the serious attention of an intelligent and critical public. This was scarcely achieved in the films made by the great players of the theatre, like Le Bargy or Sarah Bernhardt, who appeared in films mostly derived from nineteenth-century plays and novels; they gesticulated with an exaggerated form of mime in the style of the theatrical acting which Bernard Shaw spent so much time attacking in *The Saturday Review* during the eighteen-nineties. Only when the screen began to produce its own actors and actresses, men like Max Linder and Charles Chaplin, did the intimacy of film-acting technique begin to be established. It is significant that when Eleanora Duse, the great pioneer actress in the naturalistic style of acting, appeared in the film *Cenere* in 1916, she gave this sentimental melodrama dignity because of the unexaggerated beauty of her performance. Shaw's description of her work on the stage, written some twenty years earlier, gives in fact the clue to the kind of acting most suitable for films.

When she comes on the stage, you are quite welcome to take your opera-glass and count whatever lines time and care·have so far traced on her. They are the credentials of her humanity; and she knows better than to obliterate that significant hand-writing beneath a layer of peach-bloom from the chemists.
. . . Duse produces the illusion of being infinite in variety of beautiful poise and motion. Every idea, every shade of thought and mood, expresses itself delicately but vividly to the eye; and yet, in an apparent million of changes and inflexions, it is impossible to catch any line at an awkward angle, or any strain interfering with the perfect abandonment of all the limbs to what appears to be their natural gravitation towards the finest grace.

In contrast, the performances of Sarah Bernhardt in the early films *La Reine Elizabeth* or *La Dame aux Camélias* set standards of artificiality which were still current in films during the nineteen-twenties, and were suitable only for the rare macabre fantasies like *The Cabinet of Doctor Caligari* or *Doctor Mabuse*, or the wonderful farces of Mack Sennett. It was Shaw again, thinking of Duse, who gave us in the days before the film was born the best definition of this branch of dramatic performance – 'the rare and costly art', he wrote, 'of being beautifully natural in life-like human acting.'

The Development of Film Technique; Georges Méliès

Certain camera techniques useful for film-making began, as we have seen, with the trick work of men like Méliès and Paul and Hepworth (the heads vanishing in a puff of smoke;

the motor-car exploding into thin air and reassembling itself from the scattered débris afterwards), and it is usual in the history books to give them some pride of place. But, in fact, they mattered little enough; they probably did as much to keep the cinema juvenile as the antics of the distinguished theatrical artists appearing in the dramas of the nineteenth century which they had helped to make famous on the stage. What really matters is to watch the growing realization of the flexibility of the new medium at their disposal shown by film-makers between the period of Edwin S. Porter's *The Life of an American Fireman* (1902) and D. W. Griffith's *Birth of a Nation* (1915).

Griffith's work is the climax of the first stage in the maturing of the technique of film-making. It is unfair to Griffith's greatness as the first true master of the cinema not to admit from the start that much of *Birth of a Nation* and even *Intolerance* is both static and boring. It is the large and magnificent scenes of action and the strong emotional feeling revealed in many scenes of intimate action which make Griffith's work the foundation of the true art and craft of film-making as we have come to understand it to-day.

Karel Reisz, in his excellent study *The Technique of Film Editing*, is at great pains to analyse what it was that happened in the early films which helped the medium to discover its real powers. The root of it lay in the development of a true principle of editing. An action is to be represented by means of pictures projected on the screen before an audience. Méliès let the camera present the audience with scenes of theatrical charades, each shot showing a scene or tableau virtually complete in itself. This at once stresses the artificiality of what is going on. But Porter, in a crude kind of way, began to establish the principle that an exciting action could be 'described' by joining together pictures of different aspects or phases of it, building it up in this way into a single, continuous event. The action, in other words, was initially broken down into moments of detail which were then presented to the audience in as effective a form of continuity as possible. Méliès, of course, was a much more entertaining and imaginative artist than Porter, but his fantasies, for all their comic *bravura*, were pushing the new art into a by-way with no outlet to it. Porter's films, though dull and pedestrian in subject, pointed the way ahead. As soon as Porter had screened *The Life of an American Fireman* and *The Great Train Robbery*, there was no further excuse for the film-maker to use the moving-tableaux technique of Méliès. For, in spite of his delightful and charming subjects, Méliès' manner of film-making was doomed. As Karel Reisz points out, in the second of these two films, Porter even introduced parallel action, which was to become one of the mainstays of the film's technique of telling a story; he followed a scene of the bandits escaping by another in which the little daughter of the railway telegraph operator discovers him bound and gagged after the train robbery and releases him so that he can give the alarm.

The over-development of the profession of criticism in our time has led to far too much comment on technical matters connected with the arts by people who only too often cannot practise them. The film in particular has suffered from this waste of comment because it is more in the public eye than the other arts. I do not want to commit the elementary sin of criticism, which is talking about technique as if it mattered in isolation. Technique is a way of putting something over, an idea, an argument, an emotional reaction, a story. Consideration of technique apart from the nature of what it is putting over is a barren occupation, except, of course, for the artist who has to hammer his way through the craftsmanship of his medium as a pianist has to practise his scales.

What matters in this survey of the expansion of the film is its *organic* growth, the flowering of its technical ability to match the needs of the artist using it. Porter's purpose was simple, a pictorial anecdote to please an audience still fascinated by the novelty of motion pictures but beginning to need, in addition to this novelty, the interest of a little story on which a few dollars could be spent. This was equally true of *Rescued by Rover*. The level of expression in the work of Méliès compared, let us say, with that in the work of Dickens, Oscar Wilde, or W. B. Yeats, may seem no more than the preoccupations of a boy with a glorified conjuring outfit, but his enthusiasm was nevertheless that of a true artist-entertainer who knew the needs of audiences during the first decade of the cinema. But it was the work of Griffith which first showed real signs of maturity.

D. W. Griffith

It was Griffith who gave status and stature to the cinema. I am just old enough to remember the local release of *Birth of a Nation* and *Intolerance* as events in the social life of the provincial English town where I was born; they were comparable to a visit to the local theatre of a great actor in an important play. People wanted to be able to say that they had seen these films. Ten years beforehand to express interest in any films other than newsreels seen incidentally at the music-halls was, socially speaking, the equivalent of being interested in low-class touring fairs or sports arcades! Griffith was an all-important technical innovator, but more than this he was a man who expanded the medium of the film to make it match the grandeur of his ideas. He used the film to express the poetry he was unable to create in words. He was a poet of the screen, although, rather naturally in the circumstances, he did not at first realize this, and wanted to be a poet and dramatist along the conventional lines of the great literary figures of the nineteenth century. After making hundreds of short films (among them a few of some significance as preludes to the two great themes to come), his devotion to the cinema became so great that, with the phenomenal strength of the powerful artist, he eventually burst the bonds of the little medium which he inherited in 1908 and emerged, Samson-like, to reveal the epic stature which the film was capable of realizing.

He was not without forerunners; *Cabiria*, large, slow, and clumsy, had been produced in Italy in 1914. The merit of *Cabiria* lay in its pictorial scale. The Italian film-makers soon realized that their country had the sunshine essential for lighting early motion picture photography and a wealth of pictorial backgrounds in its classical remains. Italy contributed a large and completely theatrical grandeur to the development of the cinema, and offered the challenge of spectacle which Griffith took up in *Birth of a Nation*.

I think that we are in a reasonable position now to measure the true stature of Griffith. Enthusiasts for the cinema are often accused of exaggerating the importance of outstanding film-makers. To many people *no* film-maker is important in the sense that Picasso, Matisse, Elgar, Shaw, and Ibsen are called important. The fault lies, probably, in the misuse of the word, which can so often seem absurd and pretentious, and unsuitable to describe the work of people concerned with art and entertainment. I believe that an artist is the better for not being made to appear too significant during his creative period – it restricts his freedom and makes him self-conscious about his position in relation to his public. Certain film-makers and film-stars are haunted by their inflated public reputation. Then they either become pseudo-messianic, or have to be photographed by batteries of cameras while doing simple domestic tasks to prove to the world that they are still human!

Nevertheless, Griffith was in any sense of the word important, and he was the first film-maker to become so in the public eye. He was given rare privileges and facilities, and, on his visit to Britain during the first World War, he was not only fêted as a celebrity but treated like an Ambassador of State. Born in 1875, it is quite true that he retained some of the worst literary traditions of the nineteenth century in much of his work. His stories were melodramatic, his sentiments often trite, and his conception of character based on simplified types of villain, hero, and heroine. He asked nothing of his leading ladies but to look coy, pert, tearful, or pathetic, or, if they had to express joy, to jump about as if they were spring lambs.

His greatness lay in other directions. The scope of his subjects was in his best films always on the grand scale (*Birth*

29

of a Nation, Intolerance, Hearts of the World, Way Down East), or undeniably human (*Broken Blossoms* and *Orphans of the Storm*). They were intended to sweep away the emotions of the audience in the same dynamic way as his own emotions were roused. He had in his nature the giant flair of a great showman, who never forgot that he must conquer his audience. He wanted his work to be overwhelming, and it was overwhelming. He failed in the nineteen-twenties because his outlook belonged to the period which the first World War destroyed; there was no place for his sentimentalities in the disillusioned self-consciousness of the post-war era, with its fashionable psychology, its 'freedom of thought', and its sexual abandonment among the intelligentsia and the people who dominated the world of entertainment. But before this happened he had taken the minor technical developments of the cinema (which he had done much to elucidate himself since he had become a director in 1908) and stretched them to match the grandeur of the pictorial showmanship of his greatest work. No one has surpassed the splendour of his Babylonian sequences in *Intolerance*, though Sergei Eisenstein, who began his film-making where Griffith had left it off, has matched them in *The Battleship Potemkin* and *October*. Once Griffith had mastered the elementary principles of silent film-making, he was ready for the grand adventure (on which he risked his fortune) of the two great films of his career.

These elementary principles can be summarized in various ways. Here is one way:

The audience can only see what goes on through the single eye of the camera. In ordinary life we shift our visual attention from the widest range about us to points of detail that attract our curiosity. So the first principle of film-making is to let the position of the film camera be varied in relation to the action and the actors in just the same way, and to present on the screen the various shots obtained from the various camera positions in an order dictated by the dramatic impact of the story and the anticipated curiosity of the audience to follow it through.

Because the camera-picture reduces some chosen aspect of the full-scale three-dimensional world to a 'flat', two-dimensional picture of rectangular shape, the problem of pictorial composition enters into the make-up of each individual shot. The composition is governed by the arrangement of the subject, the lighting, and the movements which take place. Composition can, either consciously or unconsciously, greatly affect the attitude of the audience to what is going on in the story.

Because the film as a whole takes the form of a succession of many different shots, the timing as well as the order of the shots must be considered. Just as variation of rhythm in music has a great effect on the listener, so the tempo of the cutting of a film affects the audience. The general rate of cutting, slow or fast, can at particular moments in the story be varied to create a relaxed or a tense mood in the viewer.

In summary, therefore, the action should be broken down into moments which can be photographed and presented in such a manner as to be dramatically effective in a cumulative way; the pictorial quality of the photographs should help to develop the atmosphere of the story, and the selection of shots and rhythm of the cutting be closely related to the mood of the scene.

All this Griffith knew and practised by 1914 when he began work on *Birth of a Nation*. Examples of his work have been closely analysed – for instance, the assassination of Lincoln in *Birth of a Nation* by Karel Reisz in *The Technique of Film Editing*. The following description may give some idea of one of the most daring experiments in all Griffith's work, the famous section of *Intolerance* in which Griffith tried the impossible feat of drawing together into one edited whole the four stories which he used to illustrate the cruelty of mankind – the destruction of Babylon, the crucifixion of Christ, the massacre of St Bartholomew's Day, and the last-minute reprieve of a young American workman condemned to death through a miscarriage of justice.

The siege of Belshazzar's Babylon by the Persian Emperor Cyrus is begun by the advance of great mobile towers with drawbridges to drop on to the walls. The camera watches them now from outside the city, now from the great parapets themselves. Meanwhile the colossal image of the god Ishtar is faced by desperate worshippers who invoke his ineffectual aid to save Babylon. The defenders pour down burning oil on the Persians, while the invading Emperor Cyrus commands the attack from his chariot. The besiegers' scaling ladders propped against the walls are flung down; bodies fall from the height of the parapet; a huge battering ram is swung by Persian soldiers backwards and forwards against the gates; the camera rises slowly up the side of one of the towers. Men fall and die in close-shot. Then while Ishtar's worshippers continue their supplications, the Persian catapults come into action. One of the towers collapses, and men fall alive from its structure and from the parapets. The walls are burning, and the scenes of fire are coloured purple; the camera, high above the crowds, watches the battle; then suddenly we are in the heart of the hand-to-hand fighting: a man's head is cut from his body. A tower catches fire; the worshippers of Ishtar praise the God for his apparent goodness. From the sky above the great steps the camera gradually descends to earth and hovers over the crowded steps themselves; then it mounts slowly above the throngs of the people: this is one of the greatest panoramic shots of the film. (Griffith used a captive balloon to obtain some of his most extensive shots for *Intolerance*.)

The action changes over to the Court of Charles where he is signing the death warrant of the Protestant Huguenots. Next comes the trial scene in the contemporary story; the moment of sentence arrives and the face of the innocent man's wife reveals the intensity of her passionate suffering. She weeps and bites her handkerchief: we see in close-shot the fingers of one hand crushing the flesh of the other. As sentence of death is pronounced on her innocent husband, Christ is seen on the way to Calvary. The face of the wife holds its tragic expression: the whole situation is epitomized by intense close-ups.

The Persian armies advance in great hordes in the deep blue of the night. The massacre of St Bartholomew's night fills the screen; Christ mounts Calvary; Cyrus's horsemen move along the banks of the river: the innocent prisoner in the American jail receives the last sacrament as the car carrying his wife with a reprieve rushes on to stop the execution: Babylon falls: Christ dies on Calvary: the innocent boy's life hangs on a moment of time as the executioners stand by with their knives ready to cut the tapes which will put him to death. Every action merges. When all the rest perish, symbols of the result of man's intolerance, the boy alone is saved through his wife's devotion.*

Charlie Chaplin

If the period of the nineteen-twenties saw the full maturity of the silent film, the preceding period, dominated by the war years, saw the beginning of the work of several directors such as Thomas Ince, Mack Sennett, and Abel Gance who increased the scope of the cinema, and the work of one man of genius, Charles Chaplin.

Chaplin's genius first reached its height during the nine-teen-twenties. His natural powers as mime and clown were developed in the music-hall, and he learned how to apply his unique flair for slapstick to the silent film technique established by Mack Sennett, a man who understood edit-ing for comic effect as well as Griffith did for melodrama and spectacle. Chaplin gradually enriched his slapstick with a humanity born of his early experience of poverty and suffering, and of the warmth of family affection, especially for his mother. Charlie the clown mellowed into Charlie the little man whose sympathies were always roused by the sight of oppression and suffering, and whose romantic dreams readily responded to the attentions paid him by the succession of beautiful heroines his creator discovered for him. His real character matured for the great films of 1918–31, *Shoulder Arms*, *The Kid*, *The Gold Rush*, *The Circus*, and *City Lights*. At the same time the purely dramatic aspira-tions revealed by Chaplin's serious film, *A Woman of Paris* (1923), which he both wrote and directed, developed and were to play an increasing part in his later comedies.

To make people all over the world laugh when the stories which contained the laughter were often very sad, made

*A summary of the action by the author first published in *Experiment in the Film*.

Chaplin one of the few great artists this difficult century has produced. The simplicity of his understanding puts the intellectual complexity of our time to some shame. Chaplin's romanticism may belong to a past era, but it is not so old-fashioned as to have lost its universal validity. Charlie is to some extent dateless – a figure of the eternal *commedia dell' arte*. His idealistic hatred of injustice and cruelty in any form has led him to adopt a philosophy which is not always popular, particularly in America, since he has never been ready to change it to suit the changing values of each decade. There is a close link between the humanity of the great comedies of 1918–31 and the bitterness of *Monsieur Verdoux*. When he hates, Chaplin can be violent, but not with the cold and calculated violence which makes money out of wars or organizes concentration camps.

Chaplin's films have always been of great technical simplicity. His sets are never elaborate; he uses little subtlety of camerawork. What is seen in the background is necessary, and no more. His pictorial genius resides in his own action and in the conception of each major picture, which is his own unique creation. The figure of Charlie, elaborated later into Hitler, and transformed altogether for Verdoux and Calvero, is the figure on which, in the end, all our attention is concentrated. And because Charlie mirrors so much of ourselves in his response to the evils we experience and the joys that we desire, he has gained a universality of appeal far beyond that of any other character created for the cinema. Only through the international distribution possible to motion pictures could Charlie become known everywhere by names with a common root, representing a universal endearment, like Charlot, Carlino, Carlos, and Carlitos.

Hearts and Flowers

I have been accused of an old-fashioned devotion for silent films. I have never quite understood why this impression was given. I have no nostalgia whatsoever for the silent film.

This is not to say I cannot see or re-see the many silent films which remain impressive or amusing for me. But for the most part the limitations of silent motion pictures rob them of any real capacity to hold my full attention. Their general slowness of treatment irritates me, creating a feeling of frustration which is only increased by having to wade through the jargon of printed titles when one wants to watch the faces of the actors and the scene of the action.

Nevertheless, the silent film was an art in its own right capable of achieving a limited beauty which was scarcely discovered before it was extinguished by the overwhelming powers of the sound film. The new dimension of sound made the world on the screen an extension of our own world, which the silent film never was. The essential strength of the sound film is that it can represent the face of reality while, at the same time, remaining a highly artificial form of expression which the artist can control at every point. The strength of the silent film was its other-worldliness. The miming figures seldom gave the impression of reality, and the matinée piano (playing 'Hearts and Flowers' and many themes from Becce's collection of suitable 'mood' music) or the vibrating orchestra at night seldom permitted an audience to mistake what they were seeing for a representation of life itself. Silent films always tended to be stylized, to substitute gesture and posture for speech, to use obvious symbolisms (like little statuettes of naked girls to represent the love scenes which could not be shown, or storms to reflect the tension of human relationships), and to simplify even the most melodramatic of situations so that nothing should impede the obvious development of the story.

Out of these conventions rose a form of film art which possessed its own peculiar poetry. Even many bad films undoubtedly possessed dramatic and pictorial atmosphere – pictures like *Earthbound*, a melodrama which, as a child, I was scarcely allowed to see for fear its subject of a male ghost tied to the earth until his former wife forgave him some wrong I can no longer remember might haunt my childhood dreams. Outside the cinema in the provincial town where I lived, the crowds surged to get in, and my father, a Church of England parson who loved the films, wondered quite what his professional attitude should be to this sensational picture. Years before this he took me to a crowded theatre in Blackpool to see D. W. Griffith's *Broken Blossoms*, which had just been generally released: I remember the low-key lighting and the tinted film-stock and the sweet melancholy of this sad story shown to the close-packed, tearful audience. When we went to see Charlie Chaplin's *The Kid* he was deeply upset (and, I believe, mentioned the matter in a sermon) when the audience laughed at Charlie's mime of saying his prayers. The serials – like *The Clutching Hand*, my first weekly addiction – drew me into the cinema to be absorbed into a totally unreal world of strange imaginings, a pretty world of romantic adventure, a nightmare world, a world of open spaces, of horsemen, shack-towns, unbelievably primitive railway trains, and claustrophobic houses, a strangely coloured world, too, of red and amber, green and blue according to the action, the time, and the mood. And the farces – the new *commedia dell' arte* of Mack Sennett. Wailing with laughter, I stood no higher than the back of the seat in front, or bounced on the red plush beneath me, and rocked and yelled and gesticulated like the actors in the scene. 'He made the whole place laugh,' said a grown-up friend who took me to see a programme which included a farce about comic firemen who pulled off each other's pants in their endeavours to climb a ladder to a slightly smoking window. But on one solemn occasion, the screening of *Intolerance*, I was dragged unwillingly out of the theatre as the bodies began to fall from the walls of Babylon. I could have taken it easily after *The Clutching Hand*!

No one could enter this new world unmoved. It was the same world as the novelette and the fairground with strange, hidden excitements behind the flaps of tents as well as the obvious thrills of the giant racers. It was often frightening – memories of *The Face at the Window* terrified me for weeks. But I was soon old enough to be fascinated by the provoking beauty of the actresses – the Talmadge sisters, for instance. Their photographs, printed in the seductively smelling photogravure of the fan magazines, filled my bedroom; they were goddesses of another world from that of the lively, sulky little girls with whom my mother expected me to conduct small and seemly friendships. Because it was unreal it was as powerful as I chose to make it, a world out of which to conjure limitless day-dreaming.

When Griffith faded, there were other rising artists to take his place, more sophisticated and ready to bring a more advanced and contemporary outlook to bear on the stories they made for motion pictures. But it was extremely difficult for them to bring actuality into the shadow world of the silent film. These men needed sound, and in their efforts to force more out of the silent film than it was capable of giving through picture alone they resorted to extravagances which made their work eccentric rather than expressive.

The Silent Twenties

It is, in fact, almost incredible that in less than ten years (while most films produced remained crudely melodramatic and vulgar) such a surprising variety of good films were made. My own selection from these productions is listed on pages 321–4.

Everyone with memories of the period will want to supplement this list. Since films are not books, to be read, put aside, and easily consulted again at a later date, most lovers of the cinema have to rely on recollection with all its tricks of putting a false perspective and evaluation upon the past. Films which seemed impressive, even noble at the time they were first seen, became faded and diminished in quality, like the dance-hall revisited by the middle-aged heroine of *Carnet de Bal*. I thought *Metropolis* a magnificent film when I first saw it at a grand opening of a new cinema in Leicester and put over with all the panoply of a 'specially augmented' orchestra. The films of the nineteen-twenties which bear revival and still shine as entertainment are very rare, but they exist in sufficient numbers and with sufficient variety of style and expression to give some sense of permanence to the silent film. If they survive the difficult succeeding period which we represent they will probably have an easier passage still with future generations, for whom they will possess an historical as well as an artistic value.

The Documentary Film and Robert Flaherty

Documentary, at least as we understand it in Britain to-day, with its various branches serving many different purposes, was a development of the nineteen-thirties. It required sound to bring its pictures closer to actuality and to emphasize their content by dialogue and commentary.

The documentaries of the silent period were either commercialized descriptive films of travel or other popular interests, or impressionistic studies made by young film-makers who wished to experiment with the camera. What is said in Ruttmann's *Berlin*, for example, is said entirely by the technique of the camerawork, not by the film-maker himself as a man speaking through the camera. This was a necessary phase in film-making, just as most young poets when they are developing their ease with words and rhythm are content to leave the significance of what they are saying to the way they are saying it! Though it is true in all art that how the work is done is of crucial importance, expression which involves human values needs unique qualities of experience if the final achievement is to be lasting. Ruttmann's *Berlin* is no more now than an interesting exercise in technique; it has no more significance than well-devised scales practised on a piano. Its slightly older counterpart, Cavalcanti's *Rien que les Heures*, had more value because of the feeling it showed for the poor of Paris; they were observed with sympathy and even with humour, and the film gains in stature accordingly.

It was Robert Flaherty, with his explorer's love for people living in remote parts of the world, who showed what the motion picture camera could do for human portraiture.

The still camera can give only the photographer's choice of a phase of human facial expression; the good still photographer observes his subject, endeavours to understand him, and then makes the conditions under which he exposes the camera as nearly right for his interpretation of the subject as he can; he may take a carefully posed shot, artificially lit to emphasize the characteristics of the subject's face, or a vivid, 'candid camera' study while the subject is characteristically in action. More than this cannot be done. The human face, the most expressive form of life known to us, must be arrested either in action or in that near-stillness we call repose.

Portraiture, as it was practised by Flaherty, carried the study of human beings from stillness into motion. It is well known that he lived for long periods of time with his subjects. Though he was a man capable of sharp comment and criticism, he was naturally genial, a born story-teller whose personality flowered in good company, a man who was a warm lover of his fellow-beings. In the Arctic or the South Seas, on Aran or in the Louisiana swamplands he found people whose natures had not become complicated by the conditions of industrial civilization, and there is little doubt that he idealized them; otherwise the contrast between his interpretation of Nanook, the Eskimo, and that, for example, of Father Bulliard's closely documented records of the same people in his book *Inuk* becomes too great. Yet Flaherty recognized the fundamental truth that if man is to be happy he must feel at one with his environment, using his skill to overcome the difficulties nature puts in his way. He abhorred the up-rooting of traditional ways of life when man becomes subject to machines, or when he squanders the resources of his environment. The results of these evils he showed in his film *The Land*.

Flaherty exposed extraordinary quantities of film in his search for the best, the most revealing self-portraits of the people he made his friends in the Arctic and the South Seas for his silent films *Nanook of the North* and *Moana*. He developed the use of panchromatic film stock which gave

39

new qualities of colour and texture to the black-and-white photography of the twenties. In *Nanook* he was feeling his way towards portraiture and the representation of actions like hunting, which bring out the ancient skills. Life is a struggle for Nanook, says Flaherty, a struggle to keep his family fed and clothed. Indeed, Nanook, with his ready smile, died a year after the film was finished. But Flaherty's genial portrait of an Eskimo family is completely at variance with that of Father Bulliard, who represents almost all of them as lying, deceitful, thieving, lascivious, degenerate, and cruel, practising infanticide; he gives them only two virtues, courage and the exercise of hospitality to those whom they accept on friendly terms.

Flaherty, therefore, cast the cloak of his own warm personality round the shoulders of the people he chose to put in his films. In this sense he was a romantic, seeing life as he wished it to be. For this he was frequently attacked by the men who, ten years later, were to develop the main school of documentary film-making in Britain. But they were asking Flaherty to become a film-maker other than himself. He was to remain highly individual, as considerable a personality as he was an artist; it was an unforgettable privilege to have known him. His contribution to the silent cinema during the first part of his career was the great gift of observing with sympathy and understanding the faces, not of actors, but of simple people living in the two extreme conditions of the cold wastes of the North and the idyllic warmth of the islands of the southern Pacific. His films were the first strictly personal documents that the cinema had produced.

The expression of Flaherty's feeling for the people he filmed achieved its own poetry. While it is true that we are borrowing a term from literature when we speak of the poetry of the film, the experience to be gained from the finest forms of film-making is the same as that created by the poetry of words. The difference lies in the means. The sequence of pictures possesses its own movement and rhythm, which create mood and atmosphere like the sequence of rhythms and verbal arranging of a poem. Words are richer than photographic pictures in ambiguity of meaning, for they are, in themselves, symbols, whereas a picture represents to the audience the experience of direct observation. Nevertheless, the world of the silent film was an ambiguous one, remote in its dumb show, suggestive of the real world without belonging directly to it through its absence of sound. The beautiful tones of black-and-white photography or the other-worldliness of tinted film-stock removed the silent film even further from reality. Most silent films were cheap and lurid and melodramatic, but at their best they achieved a new form of dramatic narration which was full of promise as a rich poetic art.

The nearest to actuality which the silent films got was in the work of Flaherty, in Cavalcanti's *Rien que les Heures*, in certain Westerns like *The Covered Wagon*, in Bruce Woolfe's and Percy Smith's nature films, in a few travel films like Poirier's *La Croisière Noire* and in a few documentaries like *Turksib* and *Drifters*, in certain of the rhetorical Russian propaganda films like *The Battleship Potemkin*, *The End of St Petersburg*, *Mother*, and *The General Line* and in the dramatic films of von Stroheim (in particular, *Greed*) and in Dreyer's *Passion of Joan of Arc*. In a sense none of these films were either realist or naturalist as we would use the terms to-day. They were all concerned to create a strong emotional reaction in their audience, and their presentation was moulded accordingly. But in the frank observation of the poverty of Paris in Cavalcanti's film, in the reconstruction of the trek of the American pioneers in *The Covered Wagon*, in the portraiture of the Russian peasant in *The General Line*, in the choice of railways and ships for the subject of *Turksib* and *Drifters*, in the realistic attitude to characterization in *Greed*, *La Passion de Jeanne d'Arc*, and *Mother*, and in Flaherty's understanding portraits of the Eskimos and the South Sea Islanders, the film was widening its capacity to deal seriously and maturely with the vast range of subjects and peoples ready and waiting for the film-makers to study.

The Soviet Directors

The Russians developed a special rhetorical technique for the purposes of propaganda. Before the doctrine of 'socialist realism' was adopted, Eisenstein and Pudovkin led the movement which resulted in the so-called 'symphonic' films – *The Battleship Potemkin*, *The End of St Petersburg*, *October*, *The General Line*, *Storm over Asia* – all of them celebrating Communism in films of an heroic, even an epic structure, which was essentially poetic rather than naturalistic in presentation. There is no question of the power of these silent films, with the strong march of their pictorial images on the screen. The famous sequences have so often been analysed and discussed: the Odessa steps sequence from *The Battleship Potemkin* is described in some detail by me in *Film*; the sequence of Kerensky's shattered dream of power in *October* is analysed by Karel Reisz in *The Technique of Film Editing*; the final sequence of *Mother* (in which we see the son's escape from prison to meet his mother, who dies under the hooves of the Tsar's cavalry when they charge the procession), is described by Ernest Lindgren in *The Art of the Film*; the complete films *October* and *The General Line* are summarized by Thorold Dickinson in *Soviet Cinema*; and the scenes in *Earth* of the peasants awaiting the young man Vassily's arrival with the tractor, and his assassination later in the film as he dances gaily along the road to the village at night, are reconstructed by Paul Rotha in *Celluloid*. In each case the presentation of what is happening is made with the rhythmic strength of blank verse; the action is broken down into every facet from the broad sweep and the panorama down to the telling detail, and these are then built up into a rhythmic whole by the creative process of editing.

The silent film set motion pictures on the firm basis of camerawork (including all that goes into the single shot – selection of set-up and angle, design, composition, lighting, movement, and acting), and of editing (the assembly of the film in the most effective manner to achieve mood, atmosphere, and drama through the order and tempo of the sequence of images). These two great principles of silent film-making achieved their height in films like *October*, *Moana*, or the films of Pabst. Carried too far, they became as obvious and as irritating as a poet straining after verbal effects like alliteration or over-playing the tricks of imagery. Used rightly, they established principles which were of lasting value, even when the sound track was added to the film.

With maturity of technique came the problem of maturity of subject. The Russian films were dealing with the serious subject of revolution, but they often dealt with it on the level of schoolboy heroics because this was necessary for the ill-educated audiences whom the early films had to serve. In fact, the complex mind of Eisenstein became too involved in *October*, and his work was condemned by the next generation of film-makers as over-theoretical and therefore too full of what was called bourgeois intellectualism. In the short annals of the last period of the silent films, *October* was probably the most intellectually complex film to be made, *La Passion de Jeanne d'Arc* the profoundest study of human suffering, *Earth* and *Moana* the most lyrical expression, *Greed* and Buñuel's *Un Chien Andalou* the most bitter, the films of Lubitsch and Clair the most sophisticated comedy, and the films of Chaplin the most profoundly human of all.

The German Films and G. W. Pabst

The claim to fame of the German studios was mainly in legendary, fantastic, and macabre films, the American studios in melodramas and comedies of every kind – from the hilarious adventures of Fairbanks and the beautifully conceived comedies of Buster Keaton to the sensational films of Valentino and Garbo. The silent stars were fabulous creatures, divinities who shaped our dreams, but their films seldom rose above the level of novelettes.

It was not until Pabst emerged in the silent German cinema that German melodrama deepened into tragedy. German artistic forms in films were influenced initially by

43

the expressionist movement in art and particularly in the theatre. One aspect of the post-war German outlook, so carefully analysed by Siegfried Kracauer in his book *From Caligari to Hitler*, led to the haunted film, preoccupied with masochism, sadism, and death. *The Cabinet of Doctor Caligari* was of this kind; the medieval, the Gothic, the corpse-laden, dream-laden world of legend and fantasy gave the designer rather than the actor his chance. Human beings became part of the architectural patterns conceived by the imaginative eye of directors like Fritz Lang and Robert Weine and their designers, who included Walther Reimann, Walther Röhrig, and Karl Vollbrecht. The macabre lighting of *Destiny* and *The Student of Prague*, the great architectural spectacles of *Siegfried*, *Metropolis*, and *Faust*, and the delicate theatricality of *Cinderella* were all triumphs of studio pictorialism.

Into this world moved G. W. Pabst of Vienna, the greatest artist produced by the German-speaking cinema. As Siegfried Kracauer has shown, Pabst responded to the 'new objectivity' movement in the German art of the nineteen-twenties – a movement characterized mainly by disillusion-ment, resignation, and cynicism. With Pabst the *film noir*, as distinct from the *film macabre*, was born.

Pabst's most striking films fall into two groups – the silent films of 1925–9 (of which the more important titles are *The Joyless Street*, *Secrets of the Soul*, and *The Love of Jeanne Ney*, with their themes steeped in decadence, disillusionment, and vice), and the sound films of 1930–1 (*Westfront 1918*, and *Kameradschaft*, his greatest film), in which his idealism broke through the horrors of the broken world he had so closely portrayed during his first period of film-making. He was served in his silent films by some of the greatest artists of the time, by Asta Neilsen, Greta Garbo, Fritz Rasp, and Werner Krauss. With their help he pushed the film to its limits (and sometimes from the point of view of the censorship of many countries including Britain, Italy, France, and his native Austria, beyond its limits) in the portrayal of vice and the collapse of social morale. *The Joyless Street* was set in post-war Vienna during the disastrous period of the inflation – a

44

middle-class family starves, with their daughter's prostitution depicted by Garbo. *Secrets of the Soul* introduced psychoanalysis to the popular screen in a documentary drama of a professor whose dreams are used to discover the jealous phobias which almost drive him to stab his wife to death. *The Love of Jeanne Ney* is set against the international political background of Soviet Russia and France, the French girl Jeanne Ney being in love with a young Russian Communist, a love which is thwarted by a drunken adventurer Khalibiev, who is brilliantly played by Fritz Rasp.

The plots of Pabst's silent films are melodramatic, with happy endings superimposed upon them in almost every case. His realism lies in his settings and presentation. His Germanic sense of drama, or rather of melodrama, gives his films a horrific power which frightened the censors of the period just as much as his prostitutes, brothels, and orgies. In this he was uncompromising, although he compromised almost always in letting his *films noirs* resolve happily. In the brief period of the German sound film, before Hitler's rise to power in 1933, Pabst made a brilliant and realistic exposé of the horrors of war in *Westfront 1918* (which it is inevitable to compare with Milestone's *All Quiet on the Western Front* made at almost exactly the same time), the relatively unimportant though technically interesting *Dreigroschenoper*, and *Kameradschaft*, the most important film of his career.

Abel Gance and the Early Use of Wide-Screen

Abel Gance became the Griffith of France and he was eventually to be greatly influenced by Griffith's work. During the early and significant period of his career he was a romantic with an ebullient rhetorical nature, approaching film-making like a general facing a great campaign. He wanted to be thought the Victor Hugo of the cinema. His outstanding productions were the war film *J'Accuse* (1919), *La Roue* (1919–21), dominated by railways, and *Napoléon* (1927), an unfinished biographical film which only managed

45

in four years of production to cover the earlier phases of its hero's career.

Gance was powerfully extravagant rather than imaginative in his use of the resources of the silent film. *La Roue* was made almost entirely on location; its photographic presentation of the trains as fluidly mobile machines was an attempt to match through montage Gance's claims that 'the cinema is the music of light'; the editing was at times punctuated exactly like verse. In *Napoléon* he used both a triple screen presentation and the first-person camera. He attached the camera to the breast of a singer in order to capture the physical movement of the singing of the Marseillaise. He turned the camera into a snowball for the fight in which the young Napoleon is involved at the beginning of the film, and in the editing of this he used a remarkable technique of accelerated tempo. For the triptych screen presentation he used sometimes a complete panorama stretching the full width of the triple picture, sometimes an image split up into three parts – for example, the head of Napoleon in close-up flanked by scenes of battle, or the ranks of soldiers in the central panel marching in close shot towards the viewer, while the two lateral panels showed distant shots of the columns of men marching through the fields. He believed that the multiplication of images gave him the chance to fuse in the minds of the audience ideas arising out of seeing simultaneously before them images with a cumulative significance – Napoleon seen centrally in close-up as the presiding genius, his army seen laterally in distant shots as the instrument of his power. It would be well to study his work afresh now that the wide-screen has been introduced once more to the cinema.

Behind Gance's work lay the aim in his own words 'to make the spectator an actor, to bring him into the action, to involve him in the rhythm of the images'. One is reminded of Griffith's task, which was, he said, 'above all, to make you see'. The answer, for Gance, was 'the *paroxysme de la vie*' and he saw in Napoleon a man who was a '*paroxysme dans son époque*'. This romantic symbolism betrayed him, in his most ambitious work, as the ninteenth-century romanticism of Griffith led to the cinema leaving him behind in the past so soon after the triumphant climax of his career. Gance was not the equal of Griffith, and in any case was his successor, but his courage and vigour of expression were a loss to the cinema once he turned to more conventional forms of film-making.

Fantasy in the Silent Film

The silent film was successful, however, in the creation of fantasy. The important point about films of fantasy is that they must belong naturally to motion-picture photography if they are to succeed. Like realistic films they must invite belief. The solid ghost of the stage is not normally satisfactory in a film, because it is quite natural to use the device of double-exposure in photography and so produce the transparent ghost, or for that matter the invisible man himself riding his apparently unoccupied bicycle down the road. In the old Mack Sennett comedies thirty policemen would push one after another out of one small car – a trick easy to perform with the motion picture camera but funny because it made something unreal happen in a patently real world. Difficulty begins, unless a fine taste guides the film-maker, when an attempt is made to achieve the direct photographic representation of an unreal world built in the studio. The German film designers for films like *Siegfried* and *The Student of Prague* did this so well that the unreal studio-world became real in the moving photographs so subtly created by the highly-skilled German cameramen of the time. On the other hand, certain unskilful film-makers only succeeded in creating fantasies of other places and other worlds with quite obviously artificial moving sets looking hopelessly out of place in a moving *photograph*, however well these same sets might have sustained an illusion on a theatre stage, where we know all along that the settings are artificial, and we are therefore quite prepared to accept them as being so.

Indeed, the film offers a great chance to imaginative film-makers to create special kinds of fantasy which belong only to itself. René Clair has been the most successful creator of his kind of film; in fact France, where more purely experimental films have been made than anywhere else, had bred almost all her great directors in this experimental school before they turned to actuality in their later and better known films. René Clair, however, has made almost all his films in this style – from his early curious film-ballet of strange and wholly absurd images called *Entr'acte* (including a superb mock-funeral in which the corpse finally tires of it all and eliminates the mourners by magic) to his later films like *A Nous la Liberté, I Married a Witch*, and *Les Belles de Nuit*. Fantasy has its place in the film, but it must be a fantasy one can appreciate through watching. Very few film-makers have, like Pabst and Jean Vigo, dared to explore how far the visual dream world of our subconscious minds can be brought imaginatively on to the screen, though there seems no reason at all why even this should not be done in the future by artists of sufficient taste and psychological sensibility.

The 'Avant-Garde' Film

In many of the later silent films various forms of experimental imagery were tried out, from the strange symbolic sexual imagery used by Pabst in *Secret of the Soul*, to the curious hallucinations experienced by the imprisoned Communist in the Russian film *The Ghost that Never Returns*. In many other films naturalism was partially set aside and visual imagery was introduced to add another dimension to the plain narrative of the story. Imagery could be simple, like the famous example in *Mother* of the shots of the river ice-flow breaking against the stone parapets of a great bridge, which was cut in every so often as the cavalry prepare to charge and break up the march of the workers. Or it could be provocative and complex, as in *The Seashell and the Clergyman*, where only a knowledge of Freudian symbolisms can help the viewer understand what the different phases of the action signify. Or they can be grotesque, like the mock-funeral procession in *Entr'acte*, or the result of a desire to make a savage attack on society, as in Bunuel's *Un Chien Andalou*. Imagery in films intended for wide distribution was normally fairly obvious, though that in Eisenstein's *October* which forms part of his derision of Kerensky becomes obscure and esoteric. In the *avant-garde* films made chiefly in France and Germany, however, narration by implication rather than by direct observation became the sign of subtlety. Films like *Überfall* and *Menilmontant* told their stories almost entirely subjectively, using, as it were, a first-person camera.

Imagery was used, therefore, either as a means of comment on the action, or to help the audience identify themselves with the reactions and the emotions of the leading characters. Here the subjective element is pressed home as far as it was possible in a medium which lacked spoken words, and must achieve everything by pictures. A few films like *The Last Laugh* used no titles at all, while many like *The Battleship Potemkin* and *Vaudeville*, used very few. In *Vaudeville* and *The Last Laugh*, for example, the subjective camera is used at those moments when it will help the situation; the rotating ring of laughing faces which mock the old man who has lost his beautiful uniform in *The Last Laugh*, or in *Vaudeville* the pulsating sea of eyes which reveals the nervous tension of the male trapeze artists between whom there is a savage vendetta of jealousy when one partner learns that the other has seduced his mistress. These subjective images became commonplace, particularly in the German cinema.

But the silent cinema depended a great deal on the association of human expression with the written title. Normally the artist was shown beginning to speak and was then cut off so that the audience might read the words spoken in title form before seeing the artist complete the last words of the sentence on the screen, or achieve a reaction from some other player. The face which was expressive in repose began to matter far more to the silent film, and the great dramatic artists like Charles Chaplin, Greta Garbo, Nazimova, Baranovskaia, and Falconetti, had this supreme quality. Lesser artists like Emil Jannings or William S. Hart also possessed faces from which the audience could take their cue as to thought and feeling, and so let their imaginations fill in what could not be said in so many words. But most screen acting of the silent days was a struggle to put over too much elementary emotion by means of excessive mime and excessive grimace.

In the brief span between *Birth of a Nation* (1915) and *Earth* (1930) the silent film achieved a considerable maturity of its own, one part of which belonged only to itself and passed with it, while the other became the legacy of the sound film. Its chief quality was, as we have seen, its wordless other-worldliness, leaving, like a mimed ballet, a great deal to the imagination of the audience. This veil of silent mystery was rudely torn from it by the advent of crude sound. The mute gods and goddesses fled from the temple where their devotees had worshipped, for few of them could utter a word without destroying the beautiful illusion.

Music and the Silent Film

Music and films have always worked closely together. Many people complain that there is far too much music in sound films, and this is very true when in some nondescript documentary a concert is faded up and down behind a commentator's voice, or when some florid love scene conducted in stock dialogue is inflated into a semblance of *la grande passion* by means of luscious musical vibrations in the background.

Films were born in cafés, fairgrounds, and music-halls. Music is part of the very atmosphere of these places of relaxation and entertainment, and when the films were turned on you could not expect them to be shown in silence broken only by the clatter of the projector. But the relationship of music and films goes deeper than this. Films consist of a progression of pictures which by their very movement suggest visually the same kind of rhythm that music suggests aurally. Everyone has seen films cut directly in relation to musical rhythms; the cartoonist is in an ideal position to do this, and in his documentary, *Water Birds*, Disney applies the same technique by cutting shots of birds in such a way that their movements in the individual shots, together with the rhythm of the actual cutting from shot to shot, are made to fit like a jig-saw puzzle into the rhythm of Liszt's Second Hungarian Rhapsody.

At first, music for the films consisted merely of playing popular tunes chosen to fit what was happening on the screen, though many of the earliest films linked the phonograph to the motion picture by inviting the audience both to see and hear singers and other popular artists perform, and so created a semblance of the later sound film. As the films gradually left the noisy fairgrounds and were shown in converted dance-halls, music-halls, and other buildings (the picture palaces and cinemas of forty years ago), we became used to the girl who sat during the afternoon accompanying the film on a piano with appropriate 'mood' music, while at night a little orchestra might be employed, to be 'augmented' to full size when one of the more notable films was being shown.

This kind of music was used as an emotional background. It warmed the audience up, and made them receptive to the story. While the pictures themselves flickered along, the music helped the tempo of the action as well as its mood. Even the crudest silent films managed to get a strong pictorial rhythm into their chase sequences. The music caught this pictorial rhythm, and each element, picture and music, worked together to excite the audience. But when the love scene began, what a change came over the mood of the music! 'Hearts and Flowers' took over at once. They knew exactly what they wanted – the film-makers with their pretty actresses and the audiences with their wet handkerchiefs. It was all sweet and obvious. Every character was

51

clear to type; every situation underlined. And when in some of the melodramas the audience yearned to have its blood made cold, the music became horrific, the strings vibrating with a shuddering rhythm.

The musical range and technique of the girl at the cinema piano and of the conductor of the cinema orchestra were naturally limited. A new film programme came every three days – in some cases even more frequently. Sometimes the film company provided them with a musical score. Sometimes (and far more often) they had to shift for themselves, improvising suitable selections of popular or conventional musical themes. In 1919 an Italian musician, Giuseppe Becce, came to their rescue. He compiled a library of musical extracts designed to fit all moods, carefully timed and catalogued. The conductor, sweating through the rehearsal for the latest film, could use Becce's library to help him at every conceivable turn and twist in the development of the screen story. Here are some of Becce's classifications:

General Category: TENSION – Misterioso
    1. Night – sinister mood
    2. Night – threatening mood
    3. Uncanny agitato
    4. Magic – apparition
    5. Impending Doom

Some of this material was compiled from a large range of musical scores and some was composed by Becce himself.

It soon became obvious, however, that films of any importance should have a special musical score composed for them, so that a more subtle relationship could be established between the action on the screen and the change of mood in the music. The special score also meant that the film director who valued the dramatic effect of his work could exercise control over the music that went with it, instead of leaving the choice to the crude and hurried and scarcely rehearsed selections made by individual pianists and conductors. It is interesting that the first original composition of any importance specially made for a film was composed by Saint-Saëns as early as 1908 to accompany the melo-dramatic French *film d'art* called *L'Assassinat du Duc de Guise*. Later on D. W. Griffith was careful personally to supervise the musical score for *Birth of a Nation*. One of the most famous scores of silent film days was that composed by Edmund Meisel for the Berlin screening of Eisenstein's *The Battleship Potemkin*. So powerful was the emotional effect of this music that its performance was forbidden in some countries where the film by itself was permitted. Chaplin was another director who insisted on the composition of special scores for his films.

But the great problem was the extreme variation in the standard of performance as between one cinema and another. and the exact synchronization of the music with the picture. I remember only too well the common sight of members of cinema orchestras begging in the streets when they were thrown out of work by the sudden arrival of the synchron-ized film which immediately preceded the sound film, but there was no doubt at all that the art gained immeasurably when music could be composed and recorded under the full control of the film-makers themselves.

However, the arrival of sound-on-film added to the com-plication of scoring. For the whole nature of film-making changed, and the composer was soon to find that a new and exciting form of composition was being added to the art of music.

Sound: The Great Revolution

SOUND projected the film out of the shadowy world of its initial silence into the open arena of the direct representation of actuality.*

This was a true revolution, far greater than the introduction to the motion picture of either colour or the third dimension or the wide-screen image.

We gain our main experience of the world through the exercise of our five senses. Of these, seeing and hearing are the ones most vital to us in extending the quality and range of our experience; taste, smell, and touch are older and more animal reactions, deeply necessary to our physical welfare and pleasure. The arts make use of sight and hearing, and to a lesser extent of touch, and rely very little on the other senses.

As a branch of dramatic art wholly concerned with human thought, emotion, and action, the silent film was hampered by being limited to a single sense experience. Everything which could not be implied visually (which often proved to be a slow process on the screen, retarding the

*Warner Brothers launched sound with film commercially on 26 August 1926, when *Don Juan* was shown with synchronized music on disc. This was followed by the partial sound film *The Jazz Singer* in October 1927, which gave a sensational demonstration of lip-synchronized singing. The first complete talkie from America was *Lights of New York* (1929). In Britain, *Blackmail* (1929) was the first sound film with some dialogue; it was also released silent. The first sound film to be made in France was René Clair's *Sous les Toits de Paris* (1929), though this was preceded by some indifferent French productions made in England, because the French studios were not equipped soon enough. The first partially synchronized feature film to be produced in Germany was *I kiss your Hand, Madame*, with Marlene Dietrich, shown early in 1929; the first true sound film was Ruttmann's *Melody of the World* (March 1929). The first Swedish sound film was *Säg Det i Toner* (1929). Italy followed in 1930 with *La Canzone dell'Amore*, and Russia in the same year with Kozintsev and Trauberg's synchronized film *Alone*, and the true sound film made by Nikolai Ekk, *The Road to Life*.

natural pace of human observation and communication) had to be read in the form of printed titles. The emotion behind the various scenes had to be emphasized by music, played 'live' by innumerable pianists and orchestras of very varying merit. It was plain from the start that the film, as a branch of dramatic art, needed its own means of reproducing sound, and more especially dialogue. Only then could it rank alongside the drama of the live theatre. Though it is true that much can be conveyed by the expression of the face and the eloquent movements of the body, man's most flexible form of expression is in words. Carl Dreyer told me when he visited England after the war how much he felt the need to allow the voice of Joan to answer her prosecutors and judges in *The Passion of Joan of Arc*, and he claimed that this film was an attempt to stretch the silent cinema to the very limits of its capacity for expression. The absence of the spoken word, of dialogue, forced the film to exploit the more elementary situations in drama and the more obvious kinds of characterization, because it was impossible except by indirect methods (the use of symbols, the elaborate construction of pictorial atmosphere, and the use of tricks in editing) to move nearer in to the complexities and subtleties of human thought and feeling. Many of the finest films of the silent period evolved a form of mime-acting which varied in subtlety with the artistry of the film-makers and actors, and this mime was directly related to the continuous stream of music which accompanied the film like the score of a ballet.

The fact that twenty-five years of sound-on-film has brought us only a relatively few productions which represent the highest levels of dramatic art is no argument against the introduction of sound. Nevertheless, the lists of productions given at the end of this book show that the film has made a very considerable contribution to the artistic expression of the twentieth century. It was a misfortune that sound made films more costly to produce, and so tended to discourage that boldness in the choice and treatment of subjects which is a vital part of artistic work. It was not, and is not, to be expected that many films will aim at being more than competent dramas on the same level as the commercial novel and the novelette. They will be entertainment for entertainment's sake, and their makers will be well content if they succeed in the task of making money out of their mass audiences. For this reason the first sound films neglected the pictorial side of their narration in favour of establishing every point by means of dialogue, sound effect, and music. They were a substitute for the live theatre, and dramatist-producers like Marcel Pagnol were glad to feel that they had a medium at their disposal which could extend the audience for their plays far and wide, and enable them to overcome the limitations of 'live' production night after night in the legitimate theatre. René Clair in his book *Réflexion Faite* occupies a great deal of space attacking this theatrical conception of the film as represented by the views of Marcel Pagnol.

However that may be (and plenty of films to-day are nothing but versions of stage plays adapted with little fundamental change for the motion picture medium), the first important effect of sound was to increase the representation of actuality made by the picture on the screen. When we became more used to the presence of the sound-track and readjusted the balance of our attention as between picture and sound, we found that we still went to *see* a film. The nature and quality of the *observation* resulting from the picture still made it good or bad as a film. The sound, in fact, served to sharpen our observation. It gave an added dimension and actuality to what we were seeing. The art of the sound film began at the point when the sound was used to make the picture more effective.

Just as the picture has to be selected, so the sound has to be selected too. The sound track can offer the film-maker the use of the human voice, natural sounds, artificial sounds, and music. He must choose what he thinks will make his picture most effective, and this choice often begins at the point where he reaches a decision as to what he will *exclude* from the sound track.

In real life we focus our attention on what we hear just as we focus our attention on what we see. This focusing may be based on real need or on casual curiosity. But the artificial sound track of the film can be cleared of all the extraneous noises which accompany normal human experience, and which we have to blot out by concentrating our attention on what we want to hear. And precisely because the sound-track is artificial, recorded sounds can either be distorted (by over-emphasis, for example) for dramatic effect, or added (like a heavenly choir) quite gratuitously, whether the sound belongs by nature to the scene or not. So Alfred Hitchcock lets the word 'knife' rise to a distorted scream to represent a woman's hysterical preoccupation with the breadknife in her hand for Britain's first sound film *Blackmail*, and a distant woman's voice singing wordlessly in Vaughan Williams's score for *Scott of the Antarctic* represents far more imaginatively than dialogue the lure which the South Pole represents to the explorer, the dramatic lure of the siren which draws Scott and his companions ever deeper into the wild wastes of ice and snow and wind.

Music and the Sound Film

The sound track is, in the end, a careful amalgamation of the human voice, natural sounds, and music.* After thirty years in which music had dominated the silent film as an accompaniment, it still occupies a very powerful position after a further thirty years of dialogue pictures. There is, on the whole, far too much music in films, especially in Hollywood productions, while in India the tradition is hard to break that no film can be made at all without songs threaded into its action.

The relationship of music to the sound film is a complicated one. In filmed opera (of which Gian-Carlo Menotti's production of *The Medium* is the finest example), in the

*I am most grateful to John Huntley for the help and advice I have received from him in the preparation of this section on music and the sound film.

musical proper, in the light operetta (like René Clair's *Sous les Toits de Paris* and *Les Belles de Nuit*), and in the animated cartoon, music is the key to the nature of the show; either there is music all the time or there are passages of dialogue leading up to 'numbers' which become the successive points of climax in the entertainment. In dramatic films, music is in a more subordinate position. It may occur 'realistically' – for example, the action may take us into a concert hall (as it did at the beginning of *Men of Two Worlds*, where we heard a full performance of Sir Arthur Bliss's special composition for the film, *Baraza*), or it may be used for accompanying dramatic effect, as in almost every film we see. And sometimes it is used for a kind of emotional punctuation, as in the chords struck momentarily when the soldiers in Harry Watt's war film, *Nine Men*, have their attention drawn suddenly, after a hot engagement with the enemy, to the dead body of a comrade stretched on the ground. The chords strike at the heart as the mood changes from excitement to sadness. Music is often used in this momentary fashion in films, sometimes to bridge the change of sequences (as in magazine and news films), but mostly to achieve a rapid change of emotional emphasis in the audience. For this can be done more quickly through the ear than through the eye.

Most films have brief overtures played during the sequence of credit titles at the beginning. This music can set the mood for the film, especially if it is used cleverly to anticipate the dramatic nature of the opening sequence, as in *Of Mice and Men* or *The Sound Barrier*, where the action begins behind or even before the credits themselves. The mood – whether comic, tragic, or heroic – can be set in this way, or established during the opening sequence itself, as it is by the magnificent 'seascape' music composed by Clifton Parker for *Western Approaches*, or the grim battery of sound, filled with dramatic doom, which accompanied the camera moving slowly up the iron gates of Xanadu in *Citizen Kane* at the moment of Kane's death. The opening music to films is one of the more fascinating details in film technique.

The birth of sound in America is synonymous with *The Jazz Singer* (1927). 'Come on, Ma! Listen to this,' said Al Jolson from the screen before sobbing his way through 'Sonny Boy'. The audience was spell-bound at the effect. I remember joining in the rapturous applause after Paul Robeson had sung 'Ol' Man River' in *Show Boat*, the projectionist making the walls shudder with the crescendo of emotion in that wonderful voice. The American musical was born.

The first musicals were the back-stage shows, Nacio Herb Brown's *Broadway Melody* (1929) and Yellen and Ager's *King of Jazz* (1930), with Paul Whiteman's orchestra. The songs 'Broadway Melody', 'You were meant for me', and 'A Bench in the Park' spanned the world, with the radio in full blast to help them. Some of Walt Disney's finest songs ('Who's afraid of the Big Bad Wolf?' and 'The World owes me a Living') came during the earlier thirties to help establish the American style, and underline the contemporaneousness of Broadway's and Hollywood's musical imagination. One of the first genuine film musicals was Irving Berlin's *Top Hat* (1934), with Fred Astaire and Ginger Rogers singing 'Top Hat, White Tie and Tails', and 'Isn't it a Lovely Day?'. Instead of the spectacular stage show with its hit parade of girls and its fabulous theatrical décor, a new intimacy born of the camera was developed, and the delicate patter of Astaire's toes, which had their own musical counterpoint to the orchestration, exploited the closeness of camera and microphone and the detailed effects which this closeness could achieve. Disney spent the nineteen-thirties developing the choreography of the animated cartoon, which culminated in *Snow White and the Seven Dwarfs, Pinocchio, Dumbo*, and the experimental *Fantasia*. The musicals developed their own combination of ballet, mime, and song, which was to culminate in the work of Fred Astaire and Gene Kelly in association with Arthur Freed (producer), Vincente Minnelli (director), and Stanley Donen (dance director). *On the Town* (1950), scored by Leonard Bernstein and adapted from a successful stage show, is one of the most imaginative and yet also one of the most characteristic American musicals.

The form the 'musicals' take, whether they derive from stage shows (like *Call Me Madam*) or whether they are devised especially for the film (like *The Band Wagon*), alternate between the 'rests' of plot dialogue and the key sequences of the musical 'numbers'. These can differ as widely as the title number of *Singin' in the Rain* (1952) or the fantastic melodramatic ballet of 'Slaughter on Tenth Avenue' in *Words and Music* (1948), both completely characteristic of the American style at its best. In *Singin' in the Rain* a long tracking shot shows Gene Kelly dancing alone down a lamplit street, swinging his umbrella quite carelessly in the pouring rain, which makes enormous splashes of light on the dark pavement. With a beautiful sense of abandon he jumps into the street and splashes through the puddles until eventually, at the end of the song, he sobers down into graceful caution under the curious eye of a policeman. A delightful little opening theme, like the titillation of rain, runs underneath the whole melody; it is a lovely combination of song, orchestration, dance, and colour.

'Slaughter on Tenth Avenue' (Rodgers and Hart) shows to full advantage the famous M.G.M. orchestra, which so often rings out its cataract of sound in the cinemas of the world – sometimes in the form of the triumph of showmanship over music, sometimes as the triumph of music itself. This orchestra is noisy, even savage; it has terrific vitality, stridency, and honest vulgarity. 'Slaughter on Tenth Avenue' is a ballet of gangsters, molls, and murder in New York under the girders of the elevator, danced by Vera-Ellen and Gene Kelly. It opens on a strikingly distorted back-street stage décor under the Railway; on the street is a grouping of the night-time population of loafers, prostitutes, and police. The set pulls back to reveal Kelly in an upstairs bedroom stretching and yawning. He descends with gymnastic grace to the street. There he sees a blonde streetwalker (played by Vera-Ellen) dressed in yellow and scarlet; she dances seductively for him round a lamp-post, while he stands, dressed in black trousers and a violet-coloured sweater, and watches her. They join up and set off for a basement 'dive' where the second part of the ballet is performed with violent power. A boogie-woogie theme accompanies their dance, which precedes a fight in mime started by a jealous rival. The police enter; immediately peace reigns, the moment covered by an oboe theme. When the police leave the violence bursts out afresh; the girl is shot by the rival and flung down the flight of steps from the street door to the basement level, her body falling towards the camera. The two men fight it out, using their feet in a savage struggle, in which Kelly is finally shot in the stomach. He falls and slides along the floor to the body of the girl, pulls it up and carries it to the top of the steps, where he lies embracing the dead girl in the final tumult of the music.

The scoring for most American films is completely banal; conventions in the composition of amorphous mood music have developed with the years and often seem to go back in style to the silent days, except that the orchestration is heavier and adjustment to the action on the screen tighter. A new profession has grown up of composing and arranging music for films, and this in itself discourages the originality of approach that the true composer from the concert-halls brings to the important task of scoring for films. This is provided by the fine scores Aaron Copland produced for *Of Mice and Men*, *Our Town*, and *The Red Pony*, and Virgil Thomson for *The Plow that broke The Plains* and *Louisiana Story*. This music uses superbly the rich American tradition of the folk tune – with its gaiety combined with melancholy, and its nostalgic echoes for the great days of the pioneer out West. These traditional themes were especially effective in setting the atmosphere for films like *The Oxbow Incident* or *Shane*, and establishing the sentiment of John Ford's best films. But most scores build up dramatic mood without any compromise; this can be done well as in the case of Bernard Herrmann's rhetorical music for *Citizen Kane* or Victor Young's emotional scoring in *For Whom the Bell Tolls*. The absurdities of conventional American film music are well enough illustrated in *Quo Vadis?*, which was recorded in England, heavenly BBC chorus, bagpipes, and all!

Aaron Copland reacted against the heavy orchestration of the normal Hollywood score, and employed very few instruments to achieve his effects. Light orchestration is a feature of Continental scoring for films. In French films, the theme tune and the theme song are characteristic, and these tunes haunt the memory like a recurrent dream, beginning with 'Sous les toits de Paris' itself in 1929. Maurice Jaubert composed for *Carnet de Bal* one of the most clinging of these tunes, the waltz which recurred in many different forms corresponding to the moods of the different episodes of the film. Many gay songs, like Maurice Chevalier's 'Bouquet de Paris' or Charles Trenet's 'Boom' have been heard in French films with all that delicate Gallic concupiscence which is said to be France's finest invisible export. Among the composers of note who have created scores for films are Darius Milhaud and Arthur Honegger. Honegger's score for Bartosch's animated film *L'Idée* is one of the most striking in the history of film-making. It uses for special emotional effect the electrical instrument called the Ondes Martenot, which makes the so-called ether-wave music. Georges Auric has worked on many scores for both French and British films; one of his best was for Cocteau's *La Belle et la Bête*, in which he used choral effects to represent the emotions of Beast as he pores over Belle's image in his magic mirror. The extreme of simplicity, on the other hand, was reached in *Sylvie et le Fantôme* in which the emotions of a ghost in love with a living girl were represented by a theme on a simple pipe.

Britain has done more than any country to bring the composers of distinction into the film studio. Alongside the great and established names, like Dr Vaughan Williams (*Scott of the Antarctic*, *The Loves of Joanna Godden*), Sir William Walton (*Henry V* and *Hamlet*), Sir Arthur Bliss (*Things to Come* and *Men of Two Worlds*), Sir Arnold Bax (*Oliver Twist*) and Alan Rawsthorne (*The Captive Heart*, *Burma Victory*, and *Waters of Time*) are the names of younger composers of imagination, like Doreen Carwithen (documentary films), Elisabeth Lutyens (*Eldorado* and *World without End*), Brian Easdale (*The Red Shoes*), John Addison (*Pool of London*), and Malcolm Arnold (*The Sound Barrier* and *Hobson's Choice*).

One composer of distinction, William Alwyn, has given a considerable part of his great creative talent to film music during nearly twenty years, with scores for *Fires were Started*, *World of Plenty*, *The Way Ahead*, *The Rake's Progress*, *Odd Man Out*, *Desert Victory*, and many other feature and documentary films.

The chief credit for bringing so much musical talent into film-making should go to the musical director Muir Mathieson, who has spent twenty years in the exacting task of fitting music to films and selecting the right composers for them. Other musical directors who have helped to maintain and develop the standard of British film music have been the late Ernest Irving, who worked at Ealing Studios, and Dr Hubert Clifford, who conducted for London Films.

The first people to experiment with film music were the documentary film-makers – such as the late Walter Leigh in his beautiful score for Basil Wright's *Song of Ceylon* (1934) and Benjamin Britten in his work for *Night Mail* and *Coalface* (1935). In the case of *Night Mail*, a host of now famous people worked on this film, among them the film-makers Cavalcanti, Harry Watt, and Basil Wright, the poet W. H. Auden, and Britten himself. *Night Mail* is the story of the postal express which travels every night from London to Scotland, picking up and delivering the mail-bags on its way. Straight commentary spoken by John Grierson was alternated with Auden's poetry, and the rhythmic sounds of the rushing train were sublimated by Britten's music. The film *Coalface* was regarded as very daring in its method of composition when it was first made. Both the music and the commentary were composed together so that neither of them should destroy the effect of the other, even though the commentary is sometimes spoken over the singing. At certain stages in the film a choir combining both men's and women's voices is used, and also a chorus of male voices speaking alone in recitative emphasizes particular points, sometimes purely human, sometimes statistical. At other times, too, voices interpose in dialect. The verse once more was by W. H. Auden. Towards the end of the film the natural sounds associated with mining and with industries dependent upon coal are synchronized with a drum and cymbal accompaniment to make a kind of syncopated music of their own.

In the feature film Sir Arthur Bliss was the pioneer with his score for Sir Alexander Korda's film by H. G. Wells, *Things to Come*. Muir Mathieson, writing in *Penguin Film Review* (4) about this score, said: 'This was perhaps the first occasion on which a composer worked side by side with the film-makers from the scripting to the final editing. As Wells himself remarked, "the music is part of the constructive scheme of the film, and the composer was practically a collaborator in its production. This Bliss music is not intended to be tacked on: it is a part of the design".'

Usually the composer's first contact with a film (other than a musical or a cartoon, that is) is when it has reached the stage known as the rough-cut, that is, when the action has been photographed, the dialogue recorded, the natural sounds (footsteps, car noises, and so on) added, and the whole pieced together roughly in the form and order in which it will eventually be shown to the public. By then the director will know those periods in the film when music should, in his opinion, heighten the dramatic effect or help to establish the mood of a scene. The decisions which have to be taken at this stage are often crucial from the artistic point of view. For example, Sir William Walton's stirring music for the charge of the French Knights at Agincourt was the result of second thoughts. At first it was intended that this sequence should be accompanied by natural sounds only, like the thunder of the horses' hooves on the turf. Then it was decided to add the formal beauty and excitement of music, and let it gradually merge into the natural sounds of battle. On the other hand, in David Lean's film *Great Expectations* the opposite decision was made. At the beginning of the film the fierce convict Magwitch climbs the wall of the churchyard one stormy evening and terrifies the little boy Pip when he is standing by his mother's grave. The decision to use music was given up in favour of the simple use of the natural sounds of moaning wind and creaking trees before the audience is shocked by the sudden appearance of the convict and the scream of the frightened boy. This was a case where music would have over-complicated the dramatic effect and robbed it of its starkness.

When the passages where music is to be used are finally decided by the director, the composer gets to work – forty seconds here, a minute and ten seconds there, and so on, measured with a stop watch against script and screen. Bring it up here; take it out there; hold it behind the dialogue; fade it up as she closes the door! It is an intricate affair of co-ordination between the composer, the conductor with his orchestra, and the recording engineers. It usually takes about a week of rehearsals and actual recordings to complete the music for the normal kind of dramatic film.

A simple but very good example of background music – that is, music used to create a mood, an impression, an emotional frame for the pictures on the screen – is Clifton Parker's 'Seascape' theme for *Western Approaches*, the wartime film on the hazards faced by the merchant seamen. Parker's sea music works in with the constant images of moving water, steely blue and stirring like the limbs of some hungry animal. The challenge of these seas is implicit in every note of the title music.

The true composer of film music must be prepared to work, just like an actor or a set designer, within the character of the film. William Alwyn, as I have said, has by now the largest number of film scores to his credit of any British composer. Many of these scores are impressionist, many dramatic, playing an actual and an intimate part in the action. Others are 'in character', like the Calypso in *The Rake's Progress*.

A further stage in bringing music more closely in touch with the action is the kind of composition known as 'Mickey-

Mousing', because of Disney's technique of closely interweaving music and action in his cartoons. One example is Richard Addinsell's theme for Madame Arcati in *Blithe Spirit*. It accompanies the eccentric Madame Arcati, who is a spiritualistic medium played by Margaret Rutherford, when she rides with masterful determination through the village on her bicycle. She scatters some ducks as she passes over the bridge. A vibrophone gently suggests her link to the world of the spirits, and a trumpet calls on her to ride on and do her duty. The music reflects exactly every phase of her perilous ride.

The blending of music with natural sounds is one of the more intricate technical effects required in most films, as it is in sound broadcasting. A good example occurs in the war film *Burma Victory*, scored by Alan Rawsthorne. There is a fine atmospheric sequence early on in the film when General Wingate's Chindits are landed by air in Central Burma hundreds of miles behind the Japanese lines. In the dawn the gliders which have survived the fearful, hazardous flight over mountains eight thousand feet high, land in the clearing, their only audience birds of prey waiting for the fruits of disaster. Here Rawsthorne's music combines with the animal cries from the jungle to help spread an atmosphere of tension over the dark pictures on the screen. Other examples are Malcolm Arnold's opening themes for *The Sound Barrier*, where the music reflects the flight of the soaring aircraft before the buffeting sets in, and *Hobson's Choice*, where the music plays ironically over the display of shoes on the shop counter at night before the door bursts open with a gust of wind and a titanic belch from Charles Laughton, drunk from the Masons' monthly meeting. Like William Alwyn, Malcolm Arnold understands the importance of the chameleon qualities a composer must assume when he works for films. He is part of a dramatic team – combining the effects of music with the atmospheric use of natural sounds. Not every composer of imagination is able to adapt himself to the very considerable discipline required by this new and challenging form of composition.

Lastly, there is the most advanced use of music that occurs in films – music used for dramatic counterpointing, adding another dramatic dimension to the action on the screen. Jean Cocteau has something to say about this in the book *Cocteau on the Film*. There is nothing he dislikes more than music which glissades along in happy synchronization with the action. He thinks that nothing is more vulgar. Of his film *Orphée* he writes:

> I took the most irreverent liberties with the composer. I recorded Auric's music without the images (to a chronometer) and for example put the scherzo he had composed for the comic homecoming scene into the chase through the deserted house. . . . I made a record of Katherine Dunham's band, and superimposed it on the final orchestra of *Orphée*, going as far as occasionally cutting out some of the orchestral music and leaving only the drums.

Cocteau, in other words, makes the music provoke the audience by seeming to let it run counter to the apparent atmosphere of the action. In any case, the music adds an entirely new dimension to what is being done. A fine example of this is a musical effect devised by William Alwyn for the war film *Desert Victory*. (He told me once that he felt it was the best individual piece of scoring he had ever achieved.) Before zero hour for the great assault at night on Rommel's defences, the tension of silent waiting is expressed through close-ups of the men's faces and shots of military equipment standing poised in readiness, whilst the eyes of the officers are concentrated on their synchronized watches. Alwyn uses a single persistent note which rises octave by octave until it feels like the stretched nerves of the waiting men, and snaps when the barrage breaks loose in the wild crescendo of a great storm.

A good example of music which becomes itself part of the dramatic action is William Alwyn's scoring for the tragic end to Carol Reed's film *Odd Man Out*. Johnny, played by James Mason, is a political terrorist whom the police want for theft and murder. For twenty-four hours he wanders through the snow-covered streets, a wounded and hunted man, the hours before his death striking like doom from the city clock. In the closing moments when death is very near, his girl, Kathleen, who has been searching for him, finds him at last near the docks through which she had hoped to arrange for his escape at midnight. But it is evident that he is dying, and the police are close in on them. Alwyn's deeply emotional music for these last minutes combines with both speech and natural sounds – the ship's siren, the gun shots, the chiming of the clock which counts the lonely hours of Johnny's pain and wandering. There could be no more dramatic interlocking of words and sounds and music than that which occurs on the sound track for this last sequence of *Odd Man Out*.

The Development of Realism in Film Acting

Probably the greatest change from the silent period was in the broadening and humanizing of film acting. The audience no longer had to read snatches of dialogue from the screen; they could experience the building up of character through direct speech. This allowed the fuller development of human personality as in the legitimate theatre, but with the added values which the close-up brought to the study of facial expression, with or without speech. It was the silent film which had taught these values, and shown how, on occasion, much more can be learned from a glance, or through watching the speechless face in repose, reflection, joy, or suffering. In fact, the study of the human face, alive and in motion, is one of the cinema's greatest gifts to art. We can now meet peoples of all races and all stages of development face to face, as the range of documentary and fiction films made available to us widens with the years.

Although acting for the screen can be successfully carried out by people of low as well as of high intelligence, there is no law governing who can be effective on the screen and who cannot. Hence the long process of testing which accompanies the selection of an artist, or of the people who are chosen by the directors of both fiction films and documentaries when they are working on location and require local people on the screen. The face must be responsive to the light-values of photography, and the personality must be completely at ease beneath the all-seeing eye of the camera. The artist must survive the close-up, and this requires a form of concentration which is an important part of screen acting. Celia Johnson put it this way during the course of a broadcast discussion with me on the subject:

It's the 'thing' of having to think right, and the nearer the camera gets to you the more accurate must be your thought – it's no good looking as though you're just thinking; you must think as the character must think.

Bernard Miles defined acting in another way in a paper read before the British Kinematograph Society:

Acting is making believe you are not yourself but someone else, or rather making believe that someone else is you. It is reproducing that person's thoughts and emotions and ways of expressing them, in terms of his appearance and movements and behaviour. This kind of make-believe means not so much making other people believe as making yourself believe, for if only you can bring yourself to believe, the audience and your fellow actors are bound to believe. . . .

When lovers gaze at each other from the closest possible range, they can read the thoughts in one another's eyes, and pack a world of meaning into the flicker of an eyelid or the most delicate sigh. So it is in a close-up, except that the film camera and the microphone approach you with neither love nor longing, but with merciless curiosity and an insatiable hunger for truth.

This means that the film actor has to develop a new and most untheatrical gift, an acute and delicate sense of measurement. When your face is twelve feet high on the screen you must be able to express your thoughts with a precision which would have no meaning at all in the theatre, and those thoughts must be utterly true to the character you are playing. Not only must you tell the truth, but you must be sure that it looks like the truth, or those two arch lie-detectors, the camera and the microphone, will be sure to give you away.

Once again it is largely a question of technique, and technique is governed by means of expression. In the theatre the voice is all-important, in the film studio the eye. . . .

This change of gear from voice to eyes is perhaps the biggest of all the technical differences between stage acting and film acting.

From this it can be seen that there is a double duty in screen acting; first, the duty of the director to observe what is most expressive in the face of his actor and encourage his cameramen to light and photograph their subject sympathetically, and, second, the duty of the actor to the character he is playing, to work in every possible way through his imagination to make his face and body express the nature of that person. There is room in the cinema for very great subtlety in acting, for the suggestion of 'reserves' of character which are there to be drawn upon in the more demanding scenes, for acting with that degree of concentration which enables the performance to shine as much beneath the surface as it does upon it.

This was the kind of acting we obtained from Celia Johnson in *Brief Encounter*, Jean Gabin and Arletty in *Le Jour se lève*, von Stroheim in *La Grande Illusion*, and from the Russian actors trained in the old school of Stanislavsky, which, of all theatrical traditions, is the one best adapted to acting for the screen. It is acting in *depth*, as distinct from acting on the surface.

Whatever may be said about the pressures of propaganda and of socialist realism in Soviet sound films, no one can deny the high level of acting and of the impersonation of important personalities in Russian films like the Maxim Gorki trilogy, and the biographical film studies of men like Kutusov, Pushkin, Lermontov, Glinka, and, above all, Lenin and Stalin.

This 'acting in depth', as I have called it, springs from the long tradition of training for the stage which was begun by Constantin Stanislavsky for the Moscow Art Theatre, and worked out in a system of study and self-discipline from as early as 1906. Writing of the development in theatre art in these early years long before the sound film was thought of, Stanislavsky wrote in *My Life in Art* (1924) such passages as the following, which could be said to describe the very essence of screen acting. His actors were trained in a small

Studio Theatre before being allowed on a larger stage, in order to cultivate, first of all, an intimacy in their approach to acting.

The stage itself was not even separated from the first row of seats. There were no traditional footlights, for the light came from above. The actors were separated from the public by a simple cloth curtain. This created an altogether exceptional intimacy, and it seemed to the spectators that they were sitting in the very place where the action of the play was going on, that they were not spectators, but accidental witnesses of a strange life. The intimacy of the impression created by this was one of the chief reasons for the exceptional success of the Studio. This intimacy gave the actors the possibility to appear without any dangerous strain which would have been necessary for them in a large theatre, and to begin to live their rôles, naturally developing and strengthening at the daily performances their voices, gestures, the definiteness of the interpretation of the inner orchestration of the rôle and its image (p. 534).

He seems, in the following passage, to be describing in 1924 the art of acting for the sound film.

How was the actor to display his heart to such an extent that the spectator might be able to look into it and read all that was written there? That was a hard scenic problem. It could not be solved by the use of feet and hands or any of the accepted methods of stage representation. One needed some sort of unseen rayings out of creative will, emotion, longing; one needed eyes, mimetics, hardly palpable intonations of the voice, psychological pauses. Besides, it was necessary to do away with all that might interfere with the spectator's process of entering into the souls of the actors through the eyes or from receiving through the voice and its intonations the inner essence of the feelings and thoughts of the characters in the play.

For this it was necessary again to take advantage of immovability and the absence of gesture, to do away with all crossings on the stage, and to annul all the *mises en scène* of the stage director. Let the actors sit without moving, let them feel, speak, and infect the spectator with the manner in which they live their rôles. Let there be only a bench or a divan on the stage, and let all the persons in the play sit on it so as to display the inner essence and the word picture of the spiritual lacework of Turgenev (p. 543).

Stanislavsky insisted on his actors achieving what he called 'the feeling of truth' in their creation of theatrical character, which meant that the actor must put aside the rhetorical, artificial conception of 'type' characterization normal in the theatre of the eighteenth and nineteenth centuries, prior to Ibsen and Chehov.

The theatre, other than Stanislavsky's, may or may not be a good training ground for the screen; it depends entirely on the individual artist and his attitude to his work. Personally, I believe that the theatre is the proper place in which to learn acting, because it teaches, or should teach, the actor the technique of conveying phases of character and emotion to an audience, which, at its best, involves very great self-discipline. The same self-discipline is also needed for the screen, especially in close-shot. Every great film-producing country has found in the end a number of these artists, and their work over the years has, I believe, been a great humanizing experience for us all, something the influence of which on the great numbers of people who visit the cinema we have not yet been able to measure. Some people are so busy trying to measure the harm the cinema is supposed to do that we too easily forget the great benefits it has brought to humanity.

Realism in the Sound Film

This, then, was the first development of the films of the nineteen-thirties. Dramas which before had been simplified like a ballet into a series of expressive movements and a routine of facial acting were now taken all, or part of the way, towards naturalism in films like *Tell England, The Road to Life, All Quiet on the Western Front, Westfront 1918* (1930), *The Public Enemy, The Blue Angel, Quick Millions, M, Little Caesar, Front Page, Kameradschaft,* and *La Chienne* (1931), and *Scarface* (1932).

Some of these films were melodramas with a fine surface of realism to them – excellently balanced in their casting to suggest the underworld in the American gangster-series and in the German film *M*. Others aimed more nearly at actuality without melodrama – Pabst's last productions before the accession of Hitler, Asquith's film of the landing of the British at Gallipoli and the Russian study of child delinquency in *The Road to Life*. But in whichever direction the drama was being developed (the drama of actuality or the drama of melodrama!), naturalistic character studies were soon recognized as being the stock-in-trade of the cinema.

Counterpointing Sound and Image

On the other hand René Clair's wonderful series of musical films made between 1929 and 1932 were fantasies taking delight in the absurdity of human behaviour. Made, as they were, in the very great days of the sound film, they showed at once that the imaginative use of sound would not always be realistic. Experiments such as the 'knife' sequence previously mentioned from Britain's first sound film *Blackmail* were paralleled in France by Clair. In *Sous les Toits de Paris* the fight with knives by a railway cutting was accompanied by the savage bursts of sound made by passing trains, whose smoke and steam obscured the desperate scene and helped build up its tension. In *Tell England*, Anthony Asquith reconstructed the Gallipoli landings of the first World War in sequences which, when they are seen again to-day some twenty-five years later, still have great power, and are well worth comparison with the war scenes in *All Quiet on the Western Front*, which was being made contemporaneously in the United States. Sound is employed to increase the actuality of the scenes; the short snatches of dialogue have the throw-away value of quietness and naturalism which the British documentary film-makers were to develop later in dramatic films like *North Sea* and *Target for To-night*. There is no music at all – only the natural sounds of ships at sea, the pounding of the great cannon, the infernal clatter of the machine-guns, and the moaning cries of the wounded men. The landings are shown in three phases at separate locations on the beach-head, and the film treatment gradually intensifies from the naturalness of the first two sequences to the sharply cut, rhythmic presentation of the last sequence, using the Russian style of montage which John Grierson employed in *Drifters* – the quick succession of shots of boiler-men stoking and engines driving up to full speed, alternated with quieter scenes of officers and men talking together in the hold of one of the ships as the time for landing draws near. Tension is built up in the audience as we watch the boats come inshore covered by the sights of the silent machine-guns manned by the impersonal figures of the enemy, who are hidden behind barbed wire along the rocky coast. Little ships tow in the rowing boats laden with troops; the sea gleams beautifully in the sunlight; and the machine-guns wait. Then the tornado starts, the men stagger and fall, the wholesale massacre begins. The pictures shake and flash on the screen; close-ups of machine-guns in action are superimposed on the scenes of men collapsed and dying. With an appalling understatement, a young officer arrives in one of the larger ships to report that conditions are 'unfavourable' for further landings, and the body of a dead soldier is seen on the beach slewed backwards and forwards by the tide. At the end of *The Road to Life* the young hero's body is carried in state on the cow-catcher of the first train to run the length of a newly-laid railway track. His comrades stand silently watching, their joy at the arrival of the ceremonial train drowned in their sorrow at seeing the body of their friend stretched out dead before them. The only sound is the steam slowly expiring from the engine as it comes gradually to a standstill.

These and other rare moments of experiment in the early sound films showed the way. Whether the film was realistic or fantastic in its intention, the sound track could be used to augment the emotional values, or to emphasize the dramatic tension, or, quite simply, to underline the significance of what was happening on the screen.

The Theoretical Work of Eisenstein

By the early nineteen-thirties, the film had produced many theorists. One of the first among them was Vachel Lindsay, whose *Art of the Film* was published in America in 1915; his ideas on the subject were fundamentally very sound. * Louis Delluc, René Clair, and the many contributors to the French art journals of the nineteen-twenties, and the writers of *Close-Up* (which began publication in 1927), *La Revue du Cinéma*, and *Cinema Quarterly*, all added to the analysis of the art of the film to which many European countries, including Germany and Italy, were contributing. The first books of Rudolph Arnheim and Paul Rotha appeared in the early thirties, and Pudovkin's famous *Film Technique* was translated by Ivor Montagu and published in 1929.

Sergei Eisenstein was the first considerable aesthetician the film has produced, and his writings span the period 1927 to 1948, when he died. Marie Seton's biography of him conveys most movingly both the mental triumph and the anguish of a thinker whose mind was constantly penetrating into the further recesses of film theory, but who could seldom in actual practice resolve the problems which he set himself, especially in his later years. Nor, indeed, did he live to fulfil his greatest ambition, which was to synthesize his theories in a series of ten books on such subjects as psychology and the film, painting and the film, and so forth. He was fascinated by the ranging, inventive spirit of Leonardo da Vinci, and felt a personal affinity with him. As a writer he is most difficult to read in translation; he seems to be exploring as he writes rather than giving in an orderly manner the results of his exploration. The outcome is that his published essays make him seem like a Coleridge of film aesthetics – brilliant, inspiring, diffuse. He was a passionate believer in the intellect, and this, in the end, made him virtually an outcast of both the capitalist society of America and the communist society of Soviet Russia.

*I have written about Vachel Lindsay's ideas and quoted his book extensively in *Sight and Sound* (Spring and Summer issues, 1949).

At the basis of his thought was the theory of montage, which, at its simplest, was the axiom that, in editing, one plus one equals not two, but two plus; in other words, that the total effect of a series of shots purposefully placed in sequence is the creation in the audience of an entirely new train of thought and feeling, different from anything that could arise out of those shots seen as a number of separate units. This led to his love for the Chinese language with its pictorial form of writing; for, as Marie Seton points out, in Chinese calligraphy the idea of weeping is conveyed by the combined picture of our eyes and of water. This is montage in Eisenstein's sense of the term.

His writings have so far been made available in translations by Jay Leyda in two books, *The Film Sense* and *Film Form*, and in a few translated articles, such as that embodying his ideas on the third dimensional film published in *Penguin Film Review* (*No. 8*). They cannot be summarized since most of them are exploratory, with their thought not finally resolved. In *The Film Sense* he first of all applied the synthetic process of montage to literature, with the analysis of examples from Pushkin and Milton to show the creative amalgamation of images built up in such a manner as to inspire an equally creative act in the spectator.

And now we can say that it is precisely the montage principle, as distinguished from that of representation, which obliges spectators themselves to create, and the montage principle, by this means, achieves the great power of inner creative excitement in the spectator which distinguishes an emotionally exciting work from one that stops without going further than giving information or recording events. (*The Film Sense*, p. 37.)

He next develops his ideas about audio-visual correspondences, that is, the creative relationships which can be built up between the sound track and the picture track. He investigates the psychological relationship of colour to intellectual and emotional significance, and relates the symbolisms of colour developed in medieval times to film design, and their further relationship to sound. He then analyses at great length the sequence of the battle on the ice of Lake Peipus in *Alexander Nevsky*, illustrating his points with many graphs and diagrams.

In reading Eisenstein it must be remembered that he took his theories of film form and composition to a stage beyond that of any other writer on the cinema, and that he had to invent his own technology as he went along. The reader must accept that Eisenstein admits of no compromise, and this means that although all serious students of the cinema must read Eisenstein, there is little pleasure in doing so except in following his mental adventures. He was an erudite if erratic thinker, a student of philosophy, art, politics, and philology, and the fruits of these studies are apparent throughout the essays.

Film Form, the second book of essays, was written between 1928 and 1944. The first essay explains how he graduated from the theatre to the film in the early twenties. The second takes up his favourite theme of comparing the Japanese theatre, with its highly formalized technique, to that of the cinema. The third deals with picture-writing, the ideogram, and its pictorial analysis of the object and the event, and then applies these ancient basic principles of representation to the technique of montage. The fourth essay deals with the dialectic element in film montage (illustrated by means of formulas, diagrams, and photographs). The next essay, *The Filmic Fourth Dimension*, reveals the multiplicity of meaning a film can possess through the formal implications of subtly-prepared montage. *Methods of Montage* deals with the different kinds of shot-relationship which montage can achieve in the film – a kind of grammar of film-editing. *A Course in Treatment* deals with the training necessary for a film director from the ideological point of view, and spends some time on how Eisenstein proposed when he was in Hollywood to script Dreiser's *American Tragedy* for filming. *Film Language* includes a montage analysis of the famous Odessa Steps sequence from Eisenstein's own film *The Battleship Potemkin*. *Film Form*, the essay from which the book takes its title, deals mainly with the psychological principle in art and language of the part being used to represent the whole, and the changes with which the Soviet cinema was faced when the new principles of Socialist realism became the vogue about 1915. *The Structure of the Film* is a long essay, using literature as a parallel, showing how the composition of a work derives from its psychological content; this is again illustrated by an analysis of the Odessa Steps sequence. *Achievement* is a useful analysis of the progress of the art of the film up to 1939. The last essay, *Dickens, Griffith and the Film To-day* is the longest and in some ways the best; it is a fascinating study of the cinematic qualities in Dickens's writing illustrated by many quotations; it also shows the important link of D. W. Griffith to the writers of the nineteenth century, and contains an analysis of his strength and weakness as a film-maker.

Like Coleridge, Eisenstein stands in need of an editor who will act as guide, interpreter, and compiler to his manifold articles and lecture notes. This will no doubt be undertaken one day. When it is, we shall realize even better the potentialities of the art in the service of which Eisenstein spent his sad, frustrated, and difficult life.

The Animated Film

The animated film is quite obviously a special branch of the motion picture, and its origins can be found in the early attempts to make silhouettes and jointed figures move behind an illuminated screen long before the application of photographs to the cinema. Still pictures and reliefs in series (for example, the reliefs on the Parthenon friezes) and other early forms of art celebrating the various stages of an action or the details of some historical event (like the Bayeux Tapestry), are also a part of the history of pictorial story-telling, and so lead us through directly to the animated film. The old shadow theatres are the predecessors of Lotte Reiniger's silhouette films, and the hundreds of beautifully painted little pictures designed by Émile Reynaud for his Théâtre Optique in the eighteen-eighties are the forerunners of the kind of work Paul Grimault was to create in films like *Le Petit Soldat*.

The animated film is entirely free from the need to photograph actuality or the solidly artificial world of the studio set. It is an extension of painting on the one hand and the marionette and puppet theatre on the other. It can achieve forms of plastic design unknown in terms of the natural world. It creates its own rhythms of movement – a kind of pictorial music meticulously interwoven with the sound track. For, except in a very primitive form of which the best examples were Pat Sullivan's series of films featuring Felix the Cat, the animated film could not be developed fully until the period of the sound film, since it needed to devise a relationship between music, sound effects, and picture which was more intricate technically than in any other form of film-making.

The various styles of the animated film can be divided quite simply in this way:

1. Films using drawings:
    i. Abstract design (e.g., many films made by Len Lye and Norman McLaren).
    ii. Diagrammatic films (e.g., many of the instructional films made by the Shell Film Unit).
    iii. Highly stylized design (e.g., most films made by U.P.A. and the Halas-Batchelor Units).
    iv. More representational design (e.g., Disney's *Snow White and the Seven Dwarfs*, Grimault's *Le Petit Soldat*, and Halas-Batchelor's *Animal Farm*).

2. Films using cut-out or plastic models:
    i. Silhouette films (e.g., Lotte Reiniger's *The Magic Flute*).
    ii. Films using flat cut-out figures (e.g., Bartosch's *L'Idée*).
    iii. Puppet films (e.g., the films of Starevitch, Trnka, Pal, and Ptushko).

The production of animated films requires the development of a particular kind of technical skill and patience.

This work needs a form of imagination which can keep the end in view through long periods of preparation and carefully organized detail. Hundreds of experimental sketches must suggest to their animators creatures which will show an organic, developing form of character once they spring into motion; the characterization must be both strong and fantastic at once, like Donald Duck and Mickey Mouse, or Jiminy Cricket in *Pinocchio*, the Devil in *Le Petit Soldat*, U.P.A's Mister Magoo or John Halas's Napoleon in *Animal Farm*. For there is all the difference in establishing character in a still caricature – an isolated movement of revealing expression in a cartoon by an artist as brilliant as Giles or Ronald Searle. But imagine for a moment such characters projected into action for a ten-minute story or even a full-length feature film! And nothing in front of you to start with but blank sheets of paper!

The studios which have achieved success in this difficult art are naturally few in number. There are, of course, individualists who have made a certain reputation working alone on particular films like *L'Idée* or *Joie de Vivre*, and there are the *avant-garde* film-makers who, at certain stages in their careers, have made short abstract films, like Hans Richter, Oscar Fischinger, Fernand Léger, and Len Lye, or the puppet film-makers Pal, Ptushko, and Starevitch. But the establishment of a studio with a steady output of films, whether on a large scale like Walt Disney's in America and, more recently, John Halas's in Britain, or on a smaller scale like Norman McLaren's in Canada, happens but rarely owing to the comparatively small returns, commercially speaking, from any but full-length cartoon films. Film-makers in the Communist countries, such as Trnka in Czechoslovakia, gain their livelihood through State sponsorship. John Halas has for some fifteen years kept in production in London mainly through a combination of Government and industrial sponsorship, and Norman McLaren is an artist who has for many years been on the pay-roll of the National Film Board of Canada. Disney for a long while in the nineteen-thirties kept himself in production through the profits made from undertakings linked with his cartoons (such as royalties on toys and picture books). Animated films are as complicated to produce commercially as they are technically.

There is no space here to give an adequate account of these technical complications; they are described fully in such books as *Le Dessin Animé*, by Lo Duca, *The Art of Walt Disney*, by R. D. Feild, *How to Cartoon*, by John Halas, and my own book, *The Animated Film*.

The normal procedure, with variations in each studio, is, first, to establish the main ideas for both characters and story (assuming, that is, that the characters are new ones, and not, like Donald Duck or Mister Magoo, already familiar). The next stage is that of the 'story-board', the break-down of the action into a long series of still pictures, like a strip cartoon, giving the key stages in the story, and showing the shape the film will take and the kind of pictorial design it will have. By this time, plans for the sound-track will be taking similar shape; decisions will have to be taken on how far music will control movement in the action or comment directly upon it, how far the sound effects will be interknit with pictures and music, and how far human voices will be involved (supplying character dialogue or narration).

Any well-selected commercial gramophone disc from the sound-track of a Disney film will show the care that goes into this side of the work for these animated films, and how much detail can be overlooked in a single viewing. The disc for *Mickey's Moving Day* is a good example. The orchestration of music, effects, and voices is made to respond to every phase and detail of the pictorial action until each second is accounted for in sound accompaniment or counterpoint. 'Mickey-Mousing' has become a technical term for this correspondence between sound and image, whether it occurs in an animated film or not. Special character voices have been developed in the different studios for the animated figures of Mickey Mouse (who is always spoken by Walt Disney himself) and the growing range of birds and animals in this kind of film, like M.G.M's Tom and Jerry. It is the same for all human figures, like Mister Magoo. U.P.A. and the British Larkins Studio often use a narrator speaking in verse. Very varied styles in design characterize these different studios. All use colour vividly, for the cartoon is a dramatic medium and colour is part of its impact on the audience. Stylization seems to be taken to its limits in U.P.A's *Rooty-Toot-Toot* or the Larkins' Studio film on the structure of I.C.I., called *Enterprise*. More traditional forms of representation guide the design for most of Grimault's and Disney's animated films, though Disney occasionally permits an extravagance of the imagination, as he did in some sequences of *Fantasia*. The work of John Halas and Joy Batchelor shows a considerable range of style, usually based on a lively simplicity of line and a fine sense of colour composition. This simplicity, the simplicity of the comic strip, is the basis of the Canadian cartoon design shown at its best in a film like *Romance of Transportation*.

Rhythm and continuity are the mainspring of the animated cartoon, and this is as much a matter of sound as it is of image. Pace is of great importance to the effect of most cartoons. The editing of a cartoon film is partly in the drawing itself, it is true; the calculation of the exact point of change-over from one viewpoint to another can be determined to the smallest fraction of a second on the drawing board or in the time-measurement of the music. It is the speed with which most cartoons move (especially the American cartoons) that so often makes it difficult to appreciate the detailed effects by means of which they are built up. These effects are as complex as the dance numbers of the high quality musicals like *On the Town*; indeed, there is a very close link between these two kinds of film-making. Each has created a very exact imaginative discipline of its own. Their style of design has become closely allied to the more lively forms of contemporary draughtsmanship, particularly in the field of still-cartoon and comic strip, though the influence of other artists, for example, Matisse, can be seen in the more revolutionary designs of the U.P.A. studio.

It was Gordon Craig who claimed in his books on the theatre that more could be expressed by a puppet than by a live actor. This is a paradox; more can be expressed merely because so much less is expressed than by the living personality. Puppets are figments of humanity, and they stylize human traits and so highlight the comic aspects of human nature to a fantastic degree, after the fashion of the cartoonists. This can also be done for serious ends, though caricature is usually comic or satiric. *L'Idée* is a serious, and indeed a moving film, with its simple figures like woodcuts, and its grey silhouettes dramatizing the ideological struggles of our times. So, too, is the Halas-Batchelor animated feature film *Animal Farm*, based on George Orwell's fable. But serious cartoon and puppet films are almost non-existent; their production is too expensive for their costs to be regained in the cinemas. Puppet films of any significance have been rare in comparison with the drawn film; the exceptions to this include George Pal's early advertising films, Ladislas Starevitch's *Le Roman de Renart* and *The Mascot*, Alexander Ptushko's *The New Gulliver* and the post-war films of Jiri Trnka.

The Maturity of the Film; the National Qualities of an International Art

The strength of an art is measured by its best work. That the film is a fine, well-matured, expressive medium is proved by the wealth of its product during the twenty years following 1934. No one can deny the artistic powers of a medium which, in this short while, could produce work so varied, so exciting, or so human as *Le Jour se lève*, *Stagecoach*, *Odd Man Out*, the Maxim Gorki trilogy, *Song of Ceylon*, *La Grande Illusion*, *The Little Foxes*, *Ivan the Terrible*, *Citizen Kane*, *The Grapes of Wrath*, *The Oxbow Incident*, *Fires were Started*, *Desert Victory*, *The World of Plenty*, *Brief Encounter*, *Orphée*, *Kind Hearts and Coronets*, *Le Diable au Corps*, *The Third Man*, *Frenzy*, *Louisiana Story*, *Los Olvidados*, *Rashomon*, *Bicycle Thieves*, *Umberto D*, and *Monsieur Verdoux*. And how many others would one wish to add to this almost arbitrary list to prove the worth of the cinema? Can either the novel or the drama begin to rival the film in depth as well as in wealth of creative production these past twenty years? Though one must admit that many of the great films are adaptations of plays and novels upon which they can occasionally be said to improve.

We have seen already how greatly the nature of screen acting was changed by the development of spoken dialogue. At the same time as this raised the barriers of language, it deepened the national qualities of the screen, which have been one of the great artistic factors in the later development of the film. These intimate national qualities have been made public on a wide international scale through the interchange of films in titled versions. The practice of dubbing a new sound-track on to an important film is one which I find distasteful for films of quality, except where narration rather than dialogue develops the story, as in *The Great Adventure* and *Journal d'un Curé de Campagne*. There is normally no justification for removing the voices of highly expressive actors and actresses and substituting the language, intonations, and acting qualities of another and temperamentally foreign artist. It is true that this can be well or badly done from the technical point of view, and scarcely matters at all in the case of films where action or plot are more important than character. But sub-titles are the only proper solution to the language barrier in the case of films in which the acting values are important.

One of the greatest needs of our time is for us to understand the qualities and character of the different races and nations who people the world, for both the economy and the social expansion of the twentieth century have placed us in each other's care. We are fortunate indeed to have a medium like the film through which the observation of human character and behaviour can be so subtly conducted. The best actors and actresses are the embodiment of the characteristics of their own people. Who are more American than Spencer Tracy or Henry Fonda or Marlon Brando?

Who more Italian than Anna Magnani? Who more German than von Stroheim, more French than Jean Gabin, Arletty, or Edwige Feuillère, more Russian than Cherkasov? Who more British than Michael Redgrave, John Mills, or Laurence Olivier? Yet these and so many other actors and actresses have revealed on the international screen of the world's cinemas the finer qualities of temperament and feeling and thought and spirit proper to the nations to which they belong.

Films, in common with the other arts, produce an intensification of normal experience. Since the film is a photographic art, it invites belief from its audience in the actuality of what it presents on the screen. It is, indeed, a form of art in which representational realism can play a part unique in the arts. No one need doubt the authenticity of the background location of *The Overlanders* or *Los Olvidados*. Often locations, authentic enough in themselves, have to masquerade as other less accessible territories, like the Norwegian and Swiss locations for *Scott of the Antarctic*. But some films have been made to a formula of absolute realism, with as much of the conventional rhetoric of film art dried out of them as possible, no musical flourishes, no heightened dialogue, just the bare bones, the dry crusts, the bricks and the mortar and the scarred flesh of real life. Such was the last episode of *Paisa* set in the Po valley, the mean and dusty agony of *Journal d'un Curé de Campagne*, the picture of the concentration camp in the Polish film *The Last Stage*, the unadorned dialogue of Harry Watt's war films, *Target for To-night* and *Nine Men*, the people, actors, townsmen, and villagers of the so-called neo-realistic films of the Italian and American post-war cinema, like *Ossessione*, *Sciuscia*, *The Naked City*, and *Intruder in the Dust*.

It would be academic to try to draw the line in such films as these between the exact representation of real life and the artificial world of dramatization. Dramatization must exist, to a greater and lesser extent, in these films, whether they use professional actors or not; but the dramatization is subordinated at every stage to the need to appear to be

85

exhibiting an authentic candid-camera representation of actuality.

Some films which are in fact highly artificial in their presentation, like *Citizen Kane* and *The Magnificent Ambersons*, aim at certain moments to put the mirror squarely up to nature, in Orson Welles's case by using dialogue which is full of interruptions, the fragments of sentences thrown away like the conversation of real life before it has been tidied by the dialogue-writer and given a logic in its progress so that it may present clearly the development of plot and character. Other films, like *A Walk in the Sun* and *The Oxbow Incident* (*Strange Incident*) while aiming at a certain degree of realism in location and character, give the actors highly artificial dialogue, a heightened form of speech offering a greater insight into the human significance of the action. An example of this is the last scene from *The Oxbow Incident*, when the letter to his wife written by the innocent man just before he is lynched is read aloud in the saloon to the men who have killed him.

The flow and rhetoric and music of American speech is of incalculable value to the American films. One of the main reasons why they can be so effective is this vivid, poetic quality of good American speech. Its impact on the listener is on two levels at once, the interchange of commonplace meaning (what is said) and the poetry of human character (how it is said). Highly idiomatic speech – slang, metaphor, cracks, gags, the bombast, dust, and flowers of speech pouring unhindered out of the living imagination and off the living tongue – makes wonderful screen dialogue, for it brings us closer and closer to the roots of the people speaking. It is the stuff of American dialogue at its best, the speech of a people determined to express themselves to the limits of utterance. European speech, especially British speech, is more reticent, more refined, more quiet, more conventional. Only the Italians let their dialogue fire off the cuff with a similar measure of freedom.

When *Rashomon* opened our eyes to the capacities of the Japanese in film-making, it added a new national convention to our richly developing international stock. As the different branches of the human race develop their fluency in film-making – as, for example, the African peoples – great wealth stands to be gained by us all. We shall for the first time in history see ourselves in psychological perspective to each other – see something of the real pattern of temperament which makes up the total human character. Only a medium like the film can make this possible in terms of narrative or dramatic action, in terms of real places and real people assembled on the screens of each individual country. In the past, each nation, each particular balance of human temperament created by human groups and races, has thought itself the aristocrat of humanity. The film can help us increasingly to see the other side of the Moon. I foresee a great opening up, a flourishing of such opportunity in the next half century as the cameras spread more widely over the globe, and the film-makers everywhere acquire the mystery of their profession. The film festivals of the future should not be dominated by the product of a few nations which have been film-minded for a generation or more – others must come forward with films to delight or shock us with their new validity of expression.

Most striking among the various international differences in the film is the attitude to the portrayal of love. All human beings recognize that they must love. Most countries tend to think that the attitude of other nations to love is out of tune with their own. They all make films about love, except where the restraints of social convention and censorship become so strong, as in Indian films, that truth is replaced by pretty lies about the relationship of men and women. So each nation contributes its version of one of the deepest of human experiences, partly conscious, partly unconscious in its revelation. Every nation produces its unreal and novelettish love films – the evasions we invent and tolerate about something which eats deeply into the lives of almost everyone and frequently, as our newspapers show, disturbs them beyond their emotional capacity. But some nations occasionally produce the films which do not lie, however much they sublimate the experience of love by re-creating it in the image of poetry. Such films are *Ossessione*, *Le Jour se lève*, *Brief Encounter*, *Letter from an Unknown Woman*, *Le Diable au Corps*, and *My Darling Clementine*. Nothing is more profoundly national than the love film which does not avoid the issue of love. In every vital matter – in the attitudes we reveal to war, to violence and cruelty, to family life, to social and political behaviour, to nationalism or the simple love of one's own country – films can be profoundly revealing, though a careful study of them from this point of view is still rare. Lewis Jacobs in *The Rise of the American Film* relates the content of American films to the social attitudes of the periods in which they were produced, and Siegfried Kracauer in *From Caligari to Hitler* has devoted a whole book to the analysis of the German cinema from the point of view of the growth of Nazism. He says:

It is my contention that through an analysis of the German films deep psychological dispositions predominant in Germany from 1918 to 1933 can be exposed – dispositions which influenced the course of events during that time and which will have to be reckoned with in the post-Hitler era.

Racial cross-breeding in films is also very interesting, and would repay much more study than it has received. It is commonplace to attack Hollywood for destroying the talents it absorbs from other countries, but some have flourished there. A foreign climate can fertilize the temperament – it did so strikingly in the case of Flaherty. Or it can create its own inspiration for the visitor, as it did when Renoir brought his particular sensibility to bear on America for *The Southerner* and on India for *The River*, or when Eisenstein set his genius alight for the ill-fated *Que Viva Mexico!* In the hot-house of Hollywood some temperaments (of writers, actors, directors) are naturally happy, and live to conquer the place because they respond to its particular warmth. Others have to leave or refuse what seem to be attractive offers, in order to retain their individuality as artists. Some are simultaneously attracted and repelled by Hollywood, and try dishonestly to take Hollywood's money without delivering Hollywood's goods. One is reminded of Louis B. Mayer's statement quoted elsewhere in this book from *Picture*:

'You don't want to make money! You want to be an artist! Would you work as an artist for one hundred dollars a week? *You* want to make money. Why don't you want the studio to make money? Are you willing to *starve* for your art? You want to be the artist, but you want *other* people to starve for your art!'

But cross-breeding within certain limits can be fruitful – it depends on the person and on the subject whether an Italian director flourishes on French or German soil, or whether an actor or an actress becomes, like Greta Garbo or Ingrid Bergman, a fully developed artist in the atmosphere of another country. It is easier for actors and actresses, who are the interpreters; it is most difficult for writers and directors, who are the creative initiators of subject or treatment.

The tendency since the war has been to increase the traffic from the studio to location, in order to capture the spirit of strange places in the living celluloid – the fascination of Africa, of India, of the wonderful Moon-like landscapes in the hinterland of Australia, the great fantastic stretches of the world which lie beneath the wings of aircraft and stretch beyond the keels of ships. The units trek outwards and put on the screen the wonderful 'backgrounds' of *The Overlanders*, *The Outcast of the Islands*, *Scott of the Antarctic*, or *The River*, some of them with subjects natural to these settings, some using them synthetically. But the tendency is in the right direction, to make the astonishing, unknown, unvisited world accessible to the screen.

The Observation of Character

As the film has matured, its peculiar technique of unobtrusive, subtle observation has developed very fully, and writers, directors, and actors have responded to this. Such actors and actresses as, for example, Bette Davis, Celia Johnson, Spencer Tracy, Trevor Howard, Gérard Philipe, and Montgomery Clift, permit ranges of characterization which, in the two hours' traffic of the screen, can achieve both depth and perspective. Human nature is put under the magnifying glass of the close-up, and observation is cut to essential moments of revelation. This is characteristic of films which are the lineal descendants of *La Passion de Jeanne d'Arc*, the rare uncompromising studies of character of which *Brief Encounter*, *Le Journal d'un Curé de Campagne*, and *Umberto D* are fine examples. Such films are the examination of the souls of their protagonists. In two hours we know these people better than our friends, and perhaps as well as the heroine of *Madame Bovary* and the hero of *Crime and Punishment*. Such films help substantially to extend the maturity of the cinema to its highest point.

Similarly, there are the films which have without noticeable compromise shown us a phase of contemporary society – like *Los Olvidados*, *Zéro de Conduite*, *The Childhood of Maxim Gorki*, *The Last Stage* and the tragic burlesque of *La Règle du Jeu*. Such films are of necessity rare. It is difficult to get money without compromise, for neither sponsor nor audience can be expected to find much entertainment value in character or subjects treated with such a high level of realism or individuality. At best these films become the meat of the specialized cinemas and the film societies, though even there the weakness of the flesh will deny them long runs. Only when a more romantic, a more poetic and emotional touch is introduced, as it was in *Brief Encounter*, *Bicycle Thieves*, *The Oxbow Incident*, *The Grapes of Wrath*, and *Citizen Kane*, do these finer dramas of the human spirit become more acceptable to specialized and even, on occasion, to general audiences. It is only what you would expect. But the existence of these films in however small numbers establishes the maturity of the film as a branch of dramatic art.

'Poetic Realism'

The film has, in fact, shown this artistic maturity at its widest in the development of subjects in the style known as 'poetic realism'. If this term means anything at all (which I always doubt, even though I have sometimes used it myself) it characterizes a film in which the actuality of the drama is heightened by a strongly emotional treatment. It is this dramatic heightening, giving a kind of emotional highlight to the experiences of the chief characters, which invites a response similar to that created by dramatic poetry. *Quai des Brumes*, with its strange gathering of pseudo-realistic characters full of the world-weariness fashionable before the war, is a good example. *Le Jour se lève* is a better one because it is a very much better film; both its characterization and dramatic action are more human and truthful.

It was the French film-makers who raised our hearts in this way before the war; during the war it was British films. Since the war the American, Italian, French, Swedish, Japanese, and British cinema have all helped to widen the range of the poetic drama of the film. By now a considerable range of films has demonstrated this great quality, offering us work on the level of the best plays and novels of our time. There are a number of examples of these films discussed individually in the second section of this book.

But is there a form of poetry peculiar to the sound film? I wrote as follows on this subject in *Penguin Film Review* (6):

The use of the word 'poetry' is always ambiguous, even when applied solely to the literary medium. To use it of the film is to imply that the motion picture is capable of moments of intense emotional concentration as well as prolonged periods of narrative and character presentation which are rich in human understanding and illuminate the experience of life. It implies that the medium is flexible and eloquent under the control of the artist, and that it offers him resources of expression which will win his devotion and excite his genius. It implies also that these resources are not available in the same form in the other narrative arts, and that the film becomes a speciality and the film artist a specialist. It implies that the film is not a mere substitute for the drama or the novel, but an art with its own peculiar properties to arouse the aesthetic susceptibilities of artist and audience. . . .

The film owes its power to the mobility of its images combined with the selective use of sound, and its aesthetic derives from this. Its poetry lies in the richest use of these potentialities by the artist, as the power of literary poetry derives from the potentialities of words used in the service of emotional experience. . . .

Poetry derives much of its life-blood from imagery. By means of juxtaposed comparisons, observation becomes more acute and experience is clarified and enriched.

> The fog comes
> on little cat feet.
> It sits looking
> Over harbor and city
> on silent haunches
> and then moves on.*

The purpose of Griffith – for that matter the same had he been a descriptive writer – was served if he enabled the spectator to share vividly in the experience of the fall of Babylon. The poet begins to take the place of the reporter when the emotion of imaginative participation is induced, and the spectator becomes personally involved in the action through his imagination. The highest levels of poetry are not attempted here, but it is at this point that they may well begin. The spectator watches: the emotional values of the spectacle are sensed and the imagination catches fire. Wordsworth's sonnet written on Westminster Bridge in London is the evocation of such emotion. So Griffith, directing the flow of our attention, says: 'Look here at this, and this, and this. You see now, as I select what you shall see, how it was, how I feel about it. This great wall, the men who fall from it, is it not like that hill of Golgotha, the streets of the massacre of St Bartholomew, the platform of the American gallows?' The juxtaposition is of the simplest, each enriching the significance of the other. The medium of cinema, like that of poetry, derives its strength from the comparison of images, the swift relation of ideas through the juxtaposition of human actions.

The imagery of the sound film is the foundation of its poetry. Some images are momentary in their comment on what is happening in the total action. A fine example is the climax of the bird's flight in a sequence of Basil Wright's beautiful film, *Song of Ceylon*.

A procession is seen climbing a mountain-path to take part in a Buddhistic ritual. The sense of growing anticipation is intensified

*Fog : a poem by Carl Sandburg, as visual in its impression as a film image.

by the voices of the climbers, by the atmospheric music, by the sight of the older people resting on the way while a reader prepares them for worship, and the voice we hear recites in English the beautiful words of praise of the Buddha. When dawn comes we are high up in the mountain, and the people are singing. The singing strengthens in feeling, and the impression of a rising excitement increases. The great image of the Buddha is constantly seen, and a series of bell-notes begins to echo down the mountain-side with rising intensity. The bells combine into a varied music of their own, and a bird is startled into flight over the water, the camera following it until the images of the bird, the Buddha, the mountain-side, the water and the trees are combined together, and the reson-ance of the rising bell-notes sounded at intervals culminates in a feeling of ecstasy and worship. (*Film*, p. 99.)

Some films are small lyric poems, a series of descriptive images bound together by a unity of emotion and atmo-sphere which suffuses the photography, the tempo of the editing (which achieves its own rhythms like the lines and verses of a poem) and the touches of voice and music which give ear as well as eye to the observation of the subject. Such a film is Luciano Emmer's perfect *Isole della Laguna*, a lyrical image-poem about the flat, lonely beauty of the islands in the shallow waters of the Lagoon of Venice, as perfect in its kind of description as Wordsworth's calmly passionate sonnet on the sight of London from Westminster Bridge. The films of Arne Sucksdorff are poems – the con-templative quality of *Rhythm of a City*, the savagery of *A Divided World*, the simple acceptance of the innate and inevitable struggle of life in his feature film *The Great Adventure*, in which his love of animals and acceptance of them as they are becomes the essential value of the film.

Other poets of the cinema are Jean Painlevé and Georges Rouquier. Painlevé has made many films in which the processes of life are seen with the delight of the artist who is also a scientist; Rouquier's *Farrebique* is the finest, closest observation of French rural life which has been made. In America it was Robert Flaherty, of course, who became the greatest poet of the film of natural life.

The supreme poet of the British cinema was Humphrey

Jennings. He was a writer, a painter, and a scholar who found in the film that synthesis which lies behind Eisenstein's application of montage to a wide range of artistic experience. In several of his films – *Listen to Britain*, *A Diary for Timothy*, and in *Family Portrait* – he combined highly evocative shots of ordinary people and places in Britain with the long and deep perspective given by the literary tradition of our country. The emotional impact of his films is among the strongest I have ever experienced. Basil Wright, who had worked with him, wrote of Jennings after his death:

He made films – largely, it may be, because the art of cinema provides great possibilities for synthesis and, in terms of fluid visuals and montage, speeds the expression of ideas to a degree which no one has yet satisfactorily analysed. But not even the film could keep pace with this man who wanted, in effect, to compress the life experience of a modern renaissance into a symmetrical shape prolonged in time for less than sixty minutes. He would emerge from production feeling defeated, hardly aware that what to him was a mere sketch of what he had determined to say gave to his audiences an experience rich, rare, vivid, and often disturbing. (*Sight and Sound*, December 1950.)

One cannot divorce the image from the sound in the films of these masters. The world is full of evocative sounds – bells, gongs, drums, the cries of birds and animals, the thunder of moving water, the flashing roar of trains, the beat of engines. All these and hundreds more can be woven into music or into the vacuum of silence on the sound-track to create a mood or build an atmosphere. There are bells in the *Song of Ceylon* and *Isole della Laguna* and *Ivan the Terrible*, small, lonely bells in the distance or great, melancholy, tolling bells. The deep voice of the Cantor curls echoing up into the cathedral roof at the beginning of *Ivan the Terrible*, and the cascades of coins fall in a long, showering tinkle to the feet of the newly-crowned Tsar. The wailing sirens of American police cars create their own haunted imagery of chase and tension.

Music is very quick to start the emotions, as we have seen. The form of poetry achieved by the film is often dependent on the contribution of music. Music and picture together can create a marriage unique in the arts. The lonely, distant, wordlessly-echoing voice of a woman in Dr Vaughan Williams' score for *Scott of the Antarctic* is beautiful in itself, but, combined with the image of ice and sky, it needs no dialogue or comment to reveal the call of the Pole for men dedicated to exploration.

The poetry of the film is an endless subject which leads to the massing of examples and the cumulation of comment upon them. But the subject now must rest in the experience of the reader. If he has come so far he is hardly likely to be unobservant of the rich store of poetic imagery which the sound films of many nations have offered him since they began a quarter of a century ago.

The claim of the film to have reached an artistic maturity rests, then, on such achievements as these – that is, on its national qualities, on its mature study of human character and the spirit of places and peoples, on its own unique form of visual drama, and on its peculiar powers of creating its own poetic experience. To these artistic achievements must be added its technical maturity as a means of recording and demonstrating the facts of a visual world, its value as a tool of scientific research, and its acute and sometimes dangerous service in the field of public information and propaganda. The film is an instrument of great power, and, when its use is fully extended to include international television, it will become an ever-present part of human communications and experience.

New Dimensions

Twice in the history of the cinema the international film world has been shaken by innovations from the all-powerful industry of Hollywood. In 1926 sound was introduced to the commercial cinema by America, and within five years all the other industries had to follow suit, even though silent films were produced in Eastern countries like Japan for a very long period afterwards. Now the effects of revolution are at work again. Various new forms of motion picture are being pressed upon the international film world with all the force America can muster.

There are five of these new forms. The first is giant widescreen, using three projectors simultaneously to fill a vast curved screen which completely dominates the field of vision of the audience. This is called Cinerama, and it has an aspect-ratio (that is, a proportion of screen height to width) of 1 : 2.85. It is not suitable for normal cinemas. It is essentially a new and special form of motion picture entertainment. Nevertheless, its initial impact on audiences in New York in 1952 was so strong, that it directed the main stream of the cinema into various forms of large-screen development.

The second new form is the panoramic screen, with an aspect-ratio of about 1 : 1.6 or 1.7. Screens of this kind were hastily introduced into many cinemas in 1953 as harbingers of the shape of things to come. Ordinary films can be shown on these panoramic screens with the top and bottom of the picture masked off so that the central section may be enlarged to make a wider image. The careful compositions of many a good cameraman were at first ruined on these panoramic screens, and soon films had to be made with compositions designed for potential adaptation in this way.

The third form is Vistavision, with an ideal aspect ratio of 1 : 1.85, but capable of adaptation in projection over a range of ratios varying between 1 : 1.33 and 1 : 2.00. This system promotes films which are like an expanding suitcase, and can be adapted to the individual cinema's maximum screen capacity. To achieve this adaptability the essential action has to be confined to the central parts of the picture so that nothing which really matters will be lost when the picture is projected with the minimum aspect-ratio.

The fourth form is wide-screen Cinemascope, using only one projector equipped with a special lens – the anamorphic lens invented over a quarter of a century ago by Henri Chrétien, who demonstrated it at the time in France. It is suitable for any cinema which can accommodate effectively a screen $2\frac{1}{2}$ times as wide as it is high. It creates a huge and impressive picture, but cannot produce the sensational, engulfing effect of Cinerama.

The fifth and last form, at present, is the three-dimensional or 3-D film, or, as it is variously called, the deep film, the film in space, the stereoscopic film, and so on. There are various systems of projection in use, some using two projectors working simultaneously, some, more recently, using only one. The system of photography and projection is based on the use of polarized light filters, so that the viewer must wear polaroid spectacles in order that the two images he sees may be merged into a single image with the illusion of solidity and depth. The British system is called Stereo-Techniques, and was first demonstrated to the public during the Festival of Britain in 1951. The American system, which was introduced at home and abroad about a year later, is called Natural Vision. Later came the various systems incorporating both the right and left eye images on to a single 35 mm. film, thus saving the considerable inconvenience of using two projectors simultaneously and ensuring the exact synchronization of the images, which is essential if there is to be no eye-strain in viewing.

All these forms have been accompanied by various systems of stereophonic sound. This has meant so far only sound dispersed over a number of loud-speakers placed at strategic points behind the screen (especially the wide-screen), and round the auditorium itself. These speakers are served by various sound tracks which enable the director to use now one, now another of the loud-speakers and sometimes, for moments of climax, all of them together. So far the reproduction of binaural or 'two-eared' sound, such as we experience by nature, has not been used; this much more accurately and subtly enables us to place the origin of sound in space, as distinct from recognizing that it comes from one or more of the fixed points where the loud-speakers are stationed.

The position quite simply is this: will America be able once more to revolutionize the nature of film-making throughout the world because of her need to fight with all the weapons at her command the inroads that television has made since the war upon the patronage of her mass public?

First of all, there are three influences which are continuously at work in the cinema – the economic, the inventive, and the artistic – and they are mostly out of gear with each other. From the inventor's point of view sound should have been synchronized with the film from the beginning, and films should have been coloured from the earliest period. Both Lumière and Friese-Greene were interested in developing stereoscopic films. As for wide-screen, the equivalent of Cinemascope to-day, this was, as I have said, publicly demonstrated by Henri Chrétien twenty-five years ago, while, as we have seen, Abel Gance used a triple screen with three projectors running simultaneously for his film *Napoléon*, which was first shown in France in 1925, and so demonstrated the equivalent of Cinerama to-day, though without its special effect of engulfing the audience. The story of the film as far as the inventors are concerned is a totally different one from that of the commercial cinema as it has been known to the public.

The artist, on the other hand, has normally taken the cinema as he has found it and moulded it to his purpose. Griffith changed the shape of the picture for certain dramatic effects by masking off the sides – for example, in *Intolerance* he used a tall, narrow picture in the centre of the screen to emphasize the height of the walls of Babylon from which the dead and wounded fell to the ground far below. Eisenstein, too, wrote in favour of a square screen, saying that the film-maker could create a picture any shape he liked within the square. After the violent protests made on all sides about the horrors of sound in contrast to the beauties of the silent picture, distinguished film-makers like Clair and Hitchcock and Pabst and Milestone set about developing the true art of the sound film. These men and their successors will in all probability take over either the stereoscopic or the wide-screen films (or both of them merged together for that matter) – and develop their true potentialities for screen drama – that is, if the business men of the industry decide that these new dimensions have come to stay as a result of the public response.

The business men have got to hire or buy the expensive, patented equipment needed in the studios, and decide how far they are prepared to risk capital in adapting their cinemas to show the new kinds of film. Obviously the films are of no use either to the artist or the business man unless they are exhibited widely. The United States, faced with theatres made empty by the presence in 1953 of over twenty million television sets in American homes, pressed on with the adaptation of key cinemas for one or other of the wide-screen systems. Europe slowly, almost reluctantly, followed suit, for her economic resources to experiment in this way were far more limited than those of America. But the European exhibitors recognized that their dependence on America for a high proportion of their screen entertainment would force them in the end to equip themselves to show the films which Hollywood makes, while producers realized that their audiences would expect them to make films which would match those of Hollywood in screen dimensions as well as in entertainment value.

The vital factor in the new situation, and the one which differentiates it from the revolution of 1926, is that the new systems destroy for the first time in screen history the universal nature of the film medium. Hitherto, once sound projection had been installed in the theatres, there was nothing to prevent any film made in any part of the world from being shown anywhere else. Cinema equipment carried by sledge in Siberia and by truck travelling through the forests of equatorial Africa could provide, if required, an exhibition of the same film which had been shown in London, New York or, for that matter, in Moscow. Technically speaking, the whole world of the cinema was one. Now it appears that for a considerable while, at any rate, it will be broken up according to the cinemas which can and the cinemas which cannot cope with this form or that form of wide-screen film, while non-theatrical 16 mm. exhibition may remain distinct from any of the advanced wide-screen systems for an indefinite period.

It seems likely now (writing in 1954) that there will be at least three main kinds of motion picture film in the future. The first will be the films made for television and for various non-theatrical forms of exhibition using the familiar screen dimensions corresponding to the cinema as we have known it. The second will be the new 'standard' big-screen projection as it will be evolved by such pioneer systems as Cinemascope and Vistavision. What its final aspect-ratio will be remains to be seen, but I believe it will emphasize height more than Cinemascope does at present, and that photographic quality (in colour) will be very greatly improved with time. This may need the introduction of wider film to reduce the evil effects of grain which are revealed on the greatly enlarged screens. The third film of the future will probably follow the pattern set by Cinerama, a huge engulfing image projected on to a screen which is in shape a section of a cylinder and which provides a picture approximating to the field of vision of the human eye. Side by side with these forms of film may go the development of 3–D, which may eventually, in the more distant future, be introduced to the standard wide-screen cinema when it seems of commercial advantage to do so.

Each of these kinds of motion picture will evolve their own appropriate principles of film-making, and we are likely both to lose something and to gain something by their introduction. They may well make the film as we have known it an obsolete form fit only to be revived by film societies and other cults of ancient history!

Fifty years have been spent making the normal film a very subtle and expressive medium. Photography, either in black and white or in colour, has become excellent, and of a quality which often suggests a spatial depth to the imagination of the viewer. But the dramatic emphasis of the film, its crucial power as a dramatic medium, lies in the fluid way in which picture can be cut in with picture in the important and crucial process of editing, bringing the spectator into ever-closer contact both physically and spiritually with the protagonists. Cutting, the development of the images, is the basis of film art as we have known it, combined with the emphasis of selective sound – the careful interplay of words, natural sounds, and music. The comparatively narrow bounds of the normal screen frame sharpen perception by closing it in, giving the director full control of every detail which the audience should perceive.

In place of this, Cinerama provides a powerful sensational experience, the complete answer to what is known as 'audience participation', the act of making an audience feel they are physically within the scene or the action projected on the screen. The laws of film-making for such a medium must introduce restraints which minimize rather than emphasize any dramatic impact, or it will render its audience hysterical. Cinerama is only in its first stages of development as a dramatic medium at all; it has been mainly content so far to reproduce scenery, theatrical set-pieces, and some harmless excitements like the journey on the roller-coaster included in its first programme. The British film-makers, John Halas and Joy Batchelor, have also begun experiments in animation for Cinerama.

But what of Cinemascope, the widescreen form which is being used for the dramatic film? It is admirable for the spectacular aspects of drama – the scenic panoramas of the Westerns, the great landscapes, the crowd scenes, the big dance numbers in the musicals, the battles on land and sea. It is wonderful for all scenes which require such great width by the nature of their interest and movement, like the magnificent shot in *The Robe* of four horses galloping abreast and viewed front on from a low angle. But with the intimate scenes which make up the greater part of the interplay of characters the sheer scale of Cinemascope is an embarrassment, and quick cutting for reaction shots and subtle points of detail becomes virtually impossible. The audience must be left to discover their own details while the shot is held for them to do so, or, at the worst, the play of detail must be abandoned altogether in order to keep the screen filled with the dull interest of mere action for action's sake. The sharpened perception of the normal film will be lost, and screen dramas may degenerate into the continuous pursuit of the spectacular.

Vistavision, with its adaptability to aspect ratios which begin with those of the normal screen and stretch approximately to those of the panoramic screen (1 : 1.85), uses a technical device which reduces the effects of grain in the colour image on the enlarged screen. While it lacks the spectacular pictorial 'spread' of Cinemascope, it has great advantages for the discerning audience – a pleasing, unpretentious screen shape when enlarged to its full extent and a picture which does not sacrifice intimacy to the constant need to be pictorially spacious and impressive. This means that traditional film technique can be carried forward virtually unaltered into Vistavision. It is true that at this stage in the gradual movement of cinema theatres towards the installation of wider screens, the essential action has to be confined to the central area of the picture. But the flexibility in exhibition permitted by the system makes Vistavision films adaptable to every kind of theatre during the difficult period when there is no standard form of large screen in the cinema as a whole.

In the case of 3–D, the pursuit is in the direction of greater realism, the ever-closer reproduction of actuality. It is true that popular audiences are attracted by the reproduction of actuality through mechanical means. But this is a dead end as an aesthetic policy, for art cannot develop through mere reproduction, only through the highly selective presentation of the essentials of life as they appear to an artist's imagination within the framework of an artificial medium. However, M. L. Gunzburg, one of the American protagonists of 3–D, puts the popular point of view as follows: 'We feel that the day will come, and soon, when audiences will watch a motion picture performance as though the screen were eliminated entirely, and life itself unfolded.'

This is, I believe, a false philosophy for the artistic development of the film, and audiences, however large and popular they may be, want in the end to have their imagination enticed away from actuality by the combined work of the film story-teller and the actor. For this a medium is required which liberates the imagination, not chains it down to the pedestrian solidity of real life. Once the mechanical marvels of widescreen and 3-D have been absorbed we are back where we started. The play's the thing!

Nevertheless, 3-D, like widescreen, has certain artistic advantages. The spatial recession of planes to the horizon can produce its own form of beauty, but the projection of torsos out of what is called the 'stereo window' into the auditorium until they seem to tower over the heads of the audience in the seats nearer the screen can be the ugliest of sensations and destroy the very illusion of actuality it sets out to create. Though I believe the technical advantages of 3-D will be of the greatest value in the scientific and educational film, its strictly artistic contribution to screen drama seems to me to be relatively small. It is true that it greatly increases the sense of actuality of the image through the mere fact of giving it the illusion of spatial depth and solidity, but this only makes the imaginative handling of the images more difficult. It is true again that by the use of subtle distortions of spatial values the director can introduce new forms of emphasis in the composition of individual shots to underline some dramatic point of character or situation. But I cannot forget what a cameraman once remarked to me about motion picture photography. He said that it was much more interesting to film in black and white than in colour because, as he put it, in the former case you could paint the picture with light, whereas with colour photography sheer accuracy of reproduction was normally what mattered most. Add the third dimension to this, and you put a further obstacle in the way of the imaginative treatment of a subject Nevertheless, I believe that the stereoscopic film may well prove to possess dramatic powers which film-makers of unusual imagination will discover. We need, in fact, Orson Welles or another bold and kindred spirit to produce the *Citizen Kane* of stereoscopy! Until this happens to help us loosen 3-D from the strait-jacket of the mere reproduction of actuality, the stereoscopic film is only likely to produce relatively pedestrian and unimaginative results compared with the great films of the past.

And what about the 'normal' film, the film with which we have grown up, the film which is the subject of this book? It may well for a time fall between the two stools of small-screen television and widescreen cinema, too subtle and detailed in its technique to suit either medium of exhibition. But not, I think, for ever. The lessons learned have been too valuable to be thrown aside completely. They have brought countless millions into the cinema for half a century. They have built up an entirely new relationship in a dramatic medium between writer, director, actor, and audience. And as widescreen consolidates its aspect-ratio into a satis-factory form of large-screen picture, the subtleties will begin to creep back and the drama of character take its place once more alongside the drama of spectacle. For, in the end, audiences are more interested in individuals than they are in armies and palaces and castles and landscapes, attractive though these may be as part of a wider range of entertain-ment. We shall need always the art which has been built up by the screenwriter, the film-maker, and the actor. The future is inconceivable without it.

A MISCELLANY OF FILMS

*representing some of the different forms and
styles of film-making which reveal the development
of the Art*

SIEGFRIED, 1922–4

*Production: Decla-Bioscop and UFA. Direction: Fritz Lang.
Scenario: Thea von Harbou. Photography: Karl Hoffman and
Gunther Rittau. Design: Otto Hunte, Erich Kettlehut and
Karl Vollbrecht. With Paul Richter as Siegfried,
Margarete Schoen as Kriemhild, Hans von Schlettow as Hagen,
Hanna Ralph as Brunhild.**

Siegfried, first part of *The Nibelungen*, was released in 1924
and was followed by *Kriemhild's Revenge* in the same year.
It was made in the middle period of the German silent
cinema after the first World War. Before it came *Madame
Dubarry*, *Caligari*, and *The Golem* in Germany, as well as
Lang's own films *Destiny* (1921) and *Dr Mabuse the Gambler*
(1922). The work of the Russians was not yet known in
Germany: *Potemkin* (1925) was not to be shown in Berlin
until 1926. *Siegfried*, therefore, comes early in the fuller
development of the silent film, except, of course, for Griffith's
films which had naturally not been shown in Germany until
after the War.

Dejected after her defeat and her heavy material sufferings,
Germany tended to salve her deeply wounded pride by
reviving the more imposing of her national legends. The
propaganda value of *Siegfried* for German audiences was
emphasized a few years after by Huntly Carter in *The New
Spirit in the Cinema* (1930), and later, of course, by Siegfried
Kracauer in *From Caligari to Hitler* (1947). Kracauer refers

*Everyone is in Paul Rotha's debt for his assiduity in getting the facts
about important films correctly checked. Many of the technical credits
appearing in this section are derived from those listed in his various
books.

to Lang's own objective when he writes: 'According to him *Nibelungen* had quite another mission: to offer something strictly national, something that, like the Lay of the Nibelungs itself, might be considered a true manifestation of the German mind. In short, Lang defined this film as a national document fit to publicize German culture all over the world. His whole statement somewhat anticipated the Goebbels propaganda.' Kracauer also quotes Thea von Harbou, Lang's wife at the time of the making of *Siegfried*, and his scenarist: she said the film was designed to stress 'the inexorability with which the first guilt entails the last atonement'.

Georges Sadoul in his *Histoire d'un Art – Le Cinéma* says the film foreshadows the Nazi pomp of Nuremberg and the UFA-like architecture and pageantry of the Third Reich, and Kracauer draws a parallel between Hagen and 'a well-known type of Nazi leader'.

Lang is Viennese by birth and has Jewish blood. He studied architecture and painting. When he began film-making the values of the German artistic world were in a state of chaos. Lotte Eisner comments on the German intellectuals at the time *Siegfried* was made: 'Disillusioned, the German intellectuals who would not and could not resign themselves to hard, plain reality, clung to their old reputation as a "people of poets and thinkers", and endeavoured to take refuge in a sort of subconscious world full of anguish, unrest, and a vague remorse, obsessed by the memory of a glorious past.' (*Penguin Film Review 6.*)

All criticism of Lang's earlier films stresses the architectural quality of their sets. For *Siegfried* Lang and his designers went back to the kind of stage setting Reinhardt had used before the War. *Siegfried*, therefore, is retrogressive as far as design is concerned, compared, for example, with the earlier expressionist film *Caligari*. Lang's artistic sense is very strictly architectural, and depends on the play of light on masses: this was emphasized by Arnheim in *Film* (1930), and is taken further by Lotte Eisner in the study of Lang previously quoted. She writes: 'Critics have sometimes blamed Lang for constructing his vast-scale exteriors in the studio or on the studio lot with a huge amount of plaster, stucco, and canvas. Yet the artificial forest of *Siegfried* breathes life; sunbeams weave across the dense trees and a radiant haze floats between their heavy trunks. A painting by the Swiss artist, Arnold Boecklin, inspired this vision like other scenes of the *Nibelungen Saga*, and also the Island of Death in *Destiny*. If here paintings come to life on the screen, we could, vice versa, halt the Nibelungen film any moment and find ourselves in front of a well-balanced, self-contained, and static picture.'

Looking at *Siegfried* thirty years (almost a generation) after it was made, one is aware of the outstandingly good and bad elements in it after as little as twenty minutes' screening. (The whole film lasts about two hours when it is projected at the proper speed for silent films.) The so-called 'expressionist' style in German silent cinema, which encouraged directors and designers to stylize both decor and acting, rapidly passed out of fashion. *Siegfried* seems farther away from present-day film-making than the silent films of Griffith or Eisenstein because of this excessive stylization.

First of all the action of Lang's film is taken at a pace which is much too slow for the modern viewer, so that in almost every shot one accepts the implications of the scene long before the actors complete it. Every emotion is registered with emphatic gestures and facial expression in the manner common to the films of the period, except in the work of a few of the more exceptional players in Griffith's films. The characters are, of course, larger and psychologically simpler than life in their legendary setting, so that some heroic magnification is correct, but it is interesting to see among the grotesque figures how Georg John succeeds as Alberic, King of the Dwarfs, but fails in his other part of Mime, the blacksmith who appears at the opening of the film; Mime appears simply ludicrous, not grotesque. Richter, his hair long and Wagnerian, is adequate as Siegfried, a little like Douglas Fairbanks in his athletic mime, but with no trace of Fairbanks' humour. Both the women are poor: Kriemhild, Siegfried's wife, with her long plaits and upward glances, is absolutely colourless, whereas Brunhild, the German Amazon queen, over-acts with strenuous fierceness. On the other hand, the weak King of the Burgundians and his evil Counsellor, Hagen (macabre and splendid in his black robes and towering winged helmet) are both excellent.

Human characterization, however, was not Lang's main consideration. He wanted to create a legendary atmosphere, and to create it by pictorial means. It was more important for him that Kriemhild should sit a still and statuesque figure in the archway of a window than that she should show the nervous impulses of a woman waiting for a likely prince. Siegfried and his warrior kings observe strict formation in the Burgundian court, and processions and church services alike are seen to be perfect in their pictorial symmetry. If this exact symmetry oppresses you, then the architecture of *Siegfried* with its vast, spacious walls, its balance of curved masses with angular masses, its geometrically patterned floors and its long flights of steps will soon become a visual bore. But if you like symmetry, then you will find (for a time, at least) a nobility and grandeur in these palaces and courts, and in the costumes with their equally symmetrical designs from the Reinhardt theatre.

The most impressive and beautiful scenes in the film are those in the forests, the misty glades and the caverns through which Siegfried has to travel before he reaches the Kingdom of Burgundy. After many viewings spread over nearly twenty years I still find the sequence of Siegfried's approach to the dragon through the high trees one of the most beautiful in the silent cinema, and the dragon himself (controlled by a team of men inside his framework) the most impressive of all the screen's giant monsters. The descent into the cave holding the Rhine treasure hoard is a wonderful studio spectacle, and the shot of the slowly petrifying dwarfs is completely convincing. One's memory of this long film returns in the end to these scenes, or to those of the ride of Siegfried on his horse led by Alberic through the mists, and his death at the end of the film in the little artificial glade.

The rest of the film is best projected at sound speed. This substantially quickens the intolerably slow pace of the action in the midst of architectural sets which appear increasingly cold and dead as the film develops.

GREED, 1923

Production: Metro-Goldwyn. Direction and Script: Erich von Stroheim. Assistant Direction: Eddie Malone. Photography: Ben Reynolds, William Daniels, Ernest Shoedsack.
Editing at initial stage: June Mathis. Adapted from the novel by Frank Norris. With Gibson Gowland, Zasu Pitts, Chester Conklin, Jean Hersholt.

I have heard Erich von Stroheim describe *Greed* as a cadaver. He planned it as a film to be shown in two parts, each of some $2\frac{1}{2}$ to 3 hours' duration, the audience retiring to dinner in the middle. The first version he made ran forty-two reels, about ten hours' screen time. His friends Rex Ingram and June Mathis cut the film for him until it played some four hours. The producing company then gave the film to a staff cutter, who hacked it down to its present length of just over two hours. That editor, says Stroheim, had nothing on his mind but a hat.

The film is nevertheless remarkable, though its continuity is naturally very rough, and it moves harshly from sequence to sequence. Its value lies in its uncompromisingly realistic treatment of a section of the San Francisco community of the period, and in its unglamourized portrait of a man and his wife, and her family. It is unique also for its continuous use of location shots in San Francisco, and for the acting of Zasu Pitts as the girl whose pretty innocence, conceived in the tradition of D. W. Griffith's Victorian heroines, turns to ugly calculation after marriage and the possession of money. The last sequences shot in the intolerable heat of Death Valley itself are among the most effective ever made for the cinema.

Greed is based very literally on Frank Norris's novel *McTeague*; Stroheim insists that he derived every detail from Norris's work. He was determined to produce a faithful and realistic film, though occasionally he seems to go further than realism and reaches caricature, as in the wedding sequence with its sinister collection of aged, crippled, and dwarfed guests. Stroheim claims that he anticipated the Italian neo-realists in the manner in which he used his San Francisco locations, and it is true that scenes like the café on the seafront where Marcus (Jean Hersholt) gives up Trina (Zasu Pitts) to McTeague the dentist (Gibson Gowland), have all the vitality and immediacy of real life, while from the large window of the dentist's surgery we can see the actual movement of traffic and people in the street below.

In spite, therefore, of the overacting of which Jean Hersholt and Gibson Gowland are to some extent guilty, one has the impression that one is watching real people in a situation from real life. The priest who marries the unhappy couple, for example, does not seem like an actor at all. Although many films of this period used normal street locations for the most unlikely kinds of story, Stroheim deliberately exploited the ugliness of parts of San Francisco to help establish the nature of his film – Trina and McTeague are an unimaginative couple and court each other among the great sewer-pipes leading down into the sea, and, once they are married, and decide to look for a house, the one which they are seen visiting with an agent is a typical, old-fashioned building, lit by the flat grey light of an ordinary, rather bleak day. There is no window-dressing anywhere in *Greed*.

For 1923 such absolutely faithful realism in the cinema was remarkable. In this early period of the film there is acting which equals and surpasses that of the chief characters in *Greed*, effective though Zasu Pitts is, with her concentrated pursed-up lips and her lean, active, grasping hands. Remarkable, too, is the sheer venom expressed in this film (Stroheim claims that it was all inspired by Norris). It emerges in the wedding sequence – a *danse macabre* which it is interesting to compare with the light-hearted satire of

René Clair, when he made the sequence of the bourgeois wedding party in *The Italian Straw Hat*. Only Chester Conklin as the absurd little Prussian-American father of Trina gives any relief to the hideousness of their celebration. The couple stand before the hungry-looking priest, their toes carefully placed in the chalk marks scratched on to the living-room floor. Outside, seen through the window, a funeral procession passes, offering a rather obvious form of symbolism. The young couple are photographed through a crude gauze mask to give them a touch of other-worldliness in this moment of romance. The rest of the family and guests are like ghouls, who fall on the food ravenously with their hands once the ceremony is over.

Only in one sequence does Stroheim seem to allow himself the licence of dramatic lighting and presentation – and this is the murder of Trina by her husband in the children's home where she works after their separation. The murder takes place off-screen behind double doors which are pushed back. Christmas decorations and a highly imaginative, almost theatrical lighting effect, due to only one section of the hall being lit, make the scene memorable. A cat rushing about adds to the horror of what is being done beyond our sight. Outside, two policemen exchange some casual remarks while the woman inside is being murdered.

The section of the film which achieves the strongest effect of all is the final one when the two friends, whose relationship is poisoned by their avaricious desire to get hold of the money that has been the cause of Trina's downfall, meet after some days' journey into the desert. Marcus manages to catch McTeague unawares. After violent interchanges, they are left through their own foolishness without either horses or water. One of them kills the other, and then finds himself chained to the corpse of his former friend by handcuffs to which he has no key. He can do nothing but prepare himself to die, an isolated figure in a huge waste of dried-up mud, baked hard into great cracked circles. The money which has caused all this tragedy and human failure lies strewn about the sand in the blistering glare of the sun.

Greed may be a cadaver from Stroheim's point of view, but there is sufficient of it left on the screen to establish its claim to be one of the first mature films to be made, a melodrama which constantly touches the level of tragedy.

MOTHER, 1926

Production: Mejrabpom-Russ. Direction: V. I. Pudovkin.
Scenario: N. A. Zarkhi from the novel by Maxim Gorki.
Photography: A. N. Golovnia. Design: S. A. Koslovski.
With Vera Baranovskaia as the Mother and Nikolai Batalov as the Son.

For those who wish to idealize the restricted art of the silent film – cut off in its prime by the devastating intrusion of sound – *Mother* is as good an example as any of the high degree of imaginative expression which could be achieved by the moving picture alone, aided now and then by a rare explanatory title or an odd line of dialogue. This film holds its own against time, a beautiful museum-piece belonging to a phase which could perhaps be called the pre-Renaissance of the cinema.

Critics usually classify the work of Eisenstein and Pudovkin by means of one of those neat formulas of contrast which may well show only part of the truth. Thorold Dickinson explains the nature of this contrast as follows:

While Eisenstein's films provoked discussion and respect (or the reverse), their direct appeal was to the intelligence first and only through the intelligence to the emotions. They were connoisseur's pieces in the main. But Pudovkin's films appealed directly to the emotions of the mass audience and only secondly to their intellect. They were passionately clear and simple. To Pudovkin the most important element is the story. His attitude to his subject is personal and emotional, not detached or intellectual. In these silent films he used mixed casts of actors and non-actors, the latter to bring verisimilitude in those parts where realism was more necessary than the ability to act. (*Soviet Cinema*, p. 34.)

Both these distinguished artists reveal (in Eisenstein's case unhappily only in the past) an excitement in their work which communicates itself to an audience in what was once an electrifying manner. I well remember the emotion with which I first saw films like *Potemkin*, *October*, and *Mother* some twenty years ago – a kind of artistic awe that had no conscious connexion with the social system which these films were designed to advocate. It was an excitement entirely derived from the artistic form they exemplified. After seeing a hundred ordinary films, these seemed to have the music of pure art within them. I cannot see the best of them to-day without experiencing once more something of these same feelings – such films as these trail clouds of glory, though their formal qualities, once so advanced to our admiring eyes, seem to belong now to some golden medieval period when the aesthetics of montage transcended any consideration of the principles of socialist realism which were so soon to dominate the Soviet cinema.

While Eisenstein was normally directly concerned in his films with the emotions arising out of the great mass-movements of Russian revolutionary history, Pudovkin's interests centred on the feelings of people who had to play their individual and often painful part in these conflicts. He was, and still is, an actor himself – he plays the officer who interrogates the mother in this film. His books on *Film Editing* and *Film Acting* show his desire to make full use of the actor's powers within the framework of the principles of formal montage, which were the essence of Russian film treatment during the later period of the silent cinema. He writes:

The actor should be as close to the editing as the director. He should feel that he can lean upon him at every stage of the work. Editing should be precious to him, as shaping of his performance into the ensemble is precious to the stage actor, and he should be similarly eager and anxious for its success and the final linkage of every element of his work into the whole. (*Film Acting*, p. 84.)

He showed great respect for the long tradition of naturalistic acting founded by Stanislavski in the earliest days of the Moscow Art Theatre, and he made a significant comment about it which explains a great deal of the technique of acting used in *Mother*:

Extremely interesting are those passages in Stanislavski's memoirs where he speaks of the necessity for 'gestureless' moments of immobility on the part of the actor, to concentrate on his feelings all the attention of the spectator.

Stanislavski felt that an actor striving towards truth should be able to avoid the element of portraying his feelings to the audience, and should be able to transmit to it the whole fullness of the content of the acted image in some moment of half-mystic communion. Of course he came up against a brick wall in his endeavours to find a solution to this problem in the theatre.

It is amazing that solution of this very problem is not only not impracticable in the cinema, but extreme paucity of gesture, often literal immobility, is absolutely indispensable in it. (*Film Acting*, p. 116.)

The form of acting used in *Mother* is stylized for the purpose of underlining each emotion; expressions are frequently 'held' on the screen so that their depth and significance are emphasized and re-emphasized, especially in the beautiful performance of Baranovskaia in the leading role. This acting technique is reaffirmed by the rhythmic methods of montage used by Pudovkin. Pudovkin is unique, however, in applying them so intimately to the expression of individual feeling in his characters. *

Paul Rotha in *The Film Till Now* (1930) comments on Pudovkin's methods of analysing a situation for its dramatic contents, and then reconstructing it afresh on the screen:

In *Mother*, we discovered the scientific method of the decomposition of a scene into its ingredients, the choice of the most powerful and suggestive, and the rebuilding of the scene by filmic representation on the screen. In this respect, I recall the sequence of suspense at the gate of the factory; the gradual assembly of the workers; the feeling of uncertainty as to what was to happen. This was the result of an extraordinarily clever construction of shots and of camera set-ups in order to achieve one highly emotional effect. It may, perhaps, appear the simplest of methods, the basis of all filmic representation, but it needs the creative skill of a Pudovkin

*See the analysis of the scene when the officer demands evidence from the mother of her son's revolutionary activities, in *Experiment in the Film*, p. 40.

to extract such dramatic force from a scene. I recall, also, the scene with the falling of the clock; the discovery of the hidden firearms under the floorboards; the trial, with the judges drawing horses on their blotting pads; the coming of spring; the escape from the prison, and the final crescendo ending of the cavalry charge. It is impossible to describe the emotional effect of this film. Without hesitation, I place it amongst the finest works in the history of the cinema. (*The Film till Now*, New Edition, pp. 234-5.)

Mother is fundamentally a very simple story of a woman living in Russia during the revolutionary period around 1905. Her husband is a drunken reactionary and her son belongs to the new political movement organizing the strike. After her husband has been killed in the struggle, she is tricked into thinking she is doing the best for her son by revealing to the police the secret of the weapons hidden under the floorboards of their miserable home. After a mock-trial the son is imprisoned and she realizes she must herself join the revolution. The son is freed by an organized revolt in the prison, but he is killed at the very moment he joins his mother in the great procession of the people. The cavalry breaks up the crowds and shoots them down. The mother dies holding the Red Flag in the face of the charging horses of Tsardom.

Pudovkin gives this drama every possible overtone he can, enriching each episode (the smashing of the clock, the sequence at the factory gate, the betrayal scene, the trial, and the great procession) in the process of his analysis. The audience is gripped partly by the tension which belongs naturally to each successive situation, and partly by the carefully constructed mime with which Pudovkin builds up every detail of thought and feeling. In the final episode he resorts to the now famous simile of the ice-floe breaking up against the bastions of the great bridge with a movement parallel to that of the procession of men and women marching with the Red Flag held high before them, until they are scattered and broken by the cavalry. The ice-floe intensifies the action by its strong forward movement far more than by its obvious symbolism. The purpose of Pudovkin's technique is to sublimate the action of every part of his film, so that the commonplace is raised to the level of a kind of epic poem. It is, I believe, this poetic quality, this quality of silent music, which makes the film so exciting as well as so moving to watch even now in these days of rich, smooth photography and the blandishments of a sound track used almost always without poetic imagination.

THE ITALIAN STRAW HAT, 1927

Production: Albatross-Sequana. Direction and Script: René Clair.
Photography: Maurice Désfassiaux and Nicholas Rondakoff.
With Olga Tschechowa, Albert Préjean, Jim Gerald, and
Paul Ollivier.

The Italian Straw Hat established the maturity of René Clair as a film-maker. Though the gay stage farce by Labiche and Michel, on which the story is based, is turned into a satire, a strong element of fantasy remains to lighten the attack on the social posturing of a stupid middle-class society and sweeten it with laughter which has no trace of bitterness. Successful satire is usually the mark of maturity in an artist, since he has to keep his sense of humour alive at the very moment when his desire to attack the evils of society is at its strongest. Clair's previous films, *Paris qui Dort, Entr'acte, Le Fantôme du Moulin Rouge, Le Voyage Imaginaire,* and *La Proie du Vent,* showed his versatility and, in some instances, his delicate sense of visual humour. But *The Italian Straw Hat,* which also gained Clair a certain notoriety because some sections of society found its satire objectionable, will remain one of the permanent 'classics' of the silent cinema.

The film is made up of a succession of episodes linked together by the slender story of a young bridegroom whose horse eats part of a married lady's straw hat while she is preoccupied with a lover behind a bush in the Bois de Vincennes. This incident might have been smoothed out with reasonable diplomacy, had not the bridegroom been on his way to his wedding and the young lady's safety been dependent on returning home with her hat, if not her honour, intact. Her lover is a fierce and foolish officer, intent only on revenge and immediate reparation. This pair pursue the bridegroom throughout his wedding and the subsequent celebrations. They loll in his house and send him threatening messages by means of his terrified valet; he must replace the hat before they will consent to go. There is no other plot-link to the film except the coincidence that the deaf uncle of the bride, M. Vezinet, is discovered almost at the end of the film to have brought the bride the present of an Italian straw hat. This is given to the errant wife, the bride and groom are reconciled, and the deceived but suspicious husband is tricked into a grudging belief in his wife's innocence.

Clair has a happy time with this delightful situation, which provides the motivation for his incredible collection of bourgeois characters of 1895. The realism of the film lies in the settings and in the formalities of the wedding, in all those things people do to make themselves seem important and dignified in their own eyes. The bride's father is fat and self-opinionated, a provincial market gardener in comfortable circumstances, stuffing his body into tight clothes and struggling with his boots. Everyone who arrives is kissed on both cheeks. A stupid, bearded uncle, henpecked by his tall and pretentious wife, wears a made-up tie which constantly drops loose from his collar. This drives his wife to distraction and eventually provides the funniest scene in the film. The climax of the kissing formalities comes in a shot made directly looking down upon the bald heads of the men and the monstrous feathered hats of the women, all dipping together in the movements of a mock ballet. All these social activities take place against the fussy backgrounds of the nick-nack nineties so ably assembled by the late Lazare Meerson, who was Clair's art director.

As a piece of story-telling the film moves slowly enough, but it contains so much carefully contrived humour and is so well acted by the excellently chosen cast that it survives repeated viewings, at any rate as far as I am concerned. Clair learned from Chaplin, for whom he has the greatest admiration, the value of 'building' and timing his visual gags, developing them under the scrutiny of the camera with a certain affectionate regard for their rich humour. The best of these gags, in my opinion, is the scene during the Mayor's oration after the civil wedding ceremony. The bearded uncle's made-up tie slips once more from the socket of his collar. He is leaning forward intent on the Mayor's sentimental oratory; his wife delivers him a series of nudges, but he is too stupid to take the point. He moves along to give her more room, so starting a chain-movement until the man at the end of the row nearly falls off his seat, a time-honoured subsidiary gag. But the aunt's nudges grow in violence, and she grimaces and gestures to make him understand. He does nothing, but the infection has begun; the Mayor fingers his tie, so does his Deputy, so eventually does every man in the company, though the Mayor's oration still flows on. Eventually the aunt can bear it no more, and with a great French shoulder-shrug of exasperation, she herself shoves the offending tie violently back into place. With mild annoyance her husband sinks back into a listening posture. But the Mayor's tedious oration never ceases the whole time.

All through the film episodes as carefully conceived as this are worked out with little need for captions or dialogue. That the film is both too slow and too long for popular entertainment I have no doubt, and the characters of the officer, the fainting wife, and the bridegroom's sorrowful valet become repetitive and tedious. For it is the elderly folk who distinguish this film; they are comic types, no doubt, but wickedly apt and typical in their behaviour. The deceived husband, standing upright and indignant in a foot bath, still wearing his frock-coat but without any trousers, is perhaps the funniest portrait of all. While searching the bridegroom's apartments for his lost wife he is the image of stupid suspicion, looking behind the doors where the lovers had been hiding only after he has given them every chance to escape. It is characters like these which give the film its final right to survive as one of the richest and most meticulously made comedies of the silent period of film-making, almost, in fact, without equal, except for the best work of Chaplin, Lubitsch, and Stroheim.

LA PASSION DE JEANNE D'ARC, 1928

Production: Société Générale de Films. Direction: Carl Theodore Dreyer. Scenario: Dreyer and Joseph Delteil. Historical adviser: Pierre Champion. Photography: Rudolph Maté and Kotula. Design: Hermann Warm. Costumes: Jean and Valentine Hugo. Musical Score: Léo Poufet and Victor Allix. With Falconetti, Silvain, Maurice Schutz, Ravet, André Berley, Antonin Artaud.

The first impression one gains from seeing this film is its silent cry for sound. Most of the time is occupied by five gruelling cross-examinations of Joan. The great ecclesiastical heads with their gesticulating mouths seem to require some corresponding cataclysmic uproar of the human voice. Dreyer himself says that he would prefer to have made the film with sound. But the treatment of the film as it stands is purely visual, and very often involves a carefully contrived interplay between the written dialogue and the visual action, which does not duplicate it so much as follow it through. The film, therefore, operates on two planes at once, first the hard, factual plane of the terms of the examinations, with its succession of wearying questions directed at Joan and given to the audience in the form of printed words, and, second, the stylized visual interpretation of what the trial meant emotionally and psychologically to Joan and to her persecutors, the French ecclesiastics led by Bishop Cauchon and the English occupation authorities led by the gross, overbearing military figure of the Earl of Warwick.

The process of the trial itself, which is conducted in the brutal manner of a third degree investigation, has its twentieth-century parallels, for it is essentially an ideological trial in which Joan for reasons of state must be led to condemn herself for the sake of power politics. The stylized presentation of the trial gives it a universality which goes beyond its immediate historical setting. Joan is the victim of an earthly authority which cannot allow itself to be put to question by a future saint whose integrity of vision is never deluded by its complex diplomacy. The significance of the trial of Joan of Arc will always appeal to poets who celebrate our human liberties, and the film remains almost unbearably poignant.

Falconetti, who never made another remarkable appearance in films, relives Dreyer's interpretation of Joan so intensely that one becomes completely oblivious of her as an actress. This *is* Joan of Arc, or, at any rate, *a* Joan of Arc, her face sunk and wasting, her body near collapse, her short hair matted with sweat and eventually shaved from her head before our eyes, her cheeks streaked with the tear-drops of real suffering. Her lips move, but she seldom seems to speak more than a word or a phrase. Her head, photographed in almost continuous close-up, mostly against a plain white background, turns now this way, now that. She peers round over a shoulder raised in fear; now her head sinks in profile, or lifts full face as her eyes light with the emotion of her belief that she is fulfilling the will of God. She is not Joan the Warrior, but Joan the sexless maid dressed in a poor jerkin and surrounded by towering male enemies she cannot understand but whose trickeries she evades through the great integrity of her faith. Dreyer's relentless presentation of Joan's situation is without any romantic relief. There is no way out for her except the way of recantation closed to her by her own convictions, and even that way, which she seems at one stage to be prepared to take, would undoubtedly be denied to her by the English authorities. The situation gives full play to Dreyer's passionate desire to portray on the screen the very roots of human persecution and suffering.

For the purposes of the film's dramatic structure, Joan's long trial is contracted to one day. We see her called before the ecclesiastical court which is gathered in the prison, examined later in her cell when she is presented with a forged letter seeming to come from the King of France urging her to recant, mocked by the English soldiers and given, like Christ, a mock crown and a mock sceptre, faced with instruments of torture which make her faint, bled in her cell and then taken out on a stretcher to be examined in a graveyard where, in her weakness, she signs the recantation which angers the Earl of Warwick. While the common people who side with her celebrate the recantation (shots of jugglers and contortionists give a macabre touch to this misplaced joy) her head is shaved and she realizes that the birds and the flowers, symbols of life and liberty, possess the freedom denied to her, now that she finds herself condemned to perpetual imprisonment. She renounces her recantation, receives the last sacrament and is handed over to the English military to be burnt as a witch. The film ends with the horribly violent measures used by the English soldiers to quell the riots which break out round the pyre where Joan coughs and twists in agony and finally droops to death in the smoke and flames.

The film proceeds with an unrelieved intensity, and is a great strain as well as a great experience to watch. The fact that no real change in Joan's situation is possible in the successive examinations to which she is subjected (there are five of them, all abortive, except for the last which results in her temporary recantation) means that there can be no element of dramatic development in the film. The result is that the film, considered purely as drama, sometimes seems tedious. There is no story to tell, only a situation to present in various successive phases. The beauty of the images provides a certain measure of relief, though this, of course, is insufficient in itself. The stylization often goes to extremes, when, for example, three monkish heads are arranged in the perspective of a receding pyramid, or when the instruments of torture are seen by Joan in a montage of moving wheels, spiked rollers and saw-toothed silhouettes, or when, in the final scenes of the film, soldiers and people are shot from unnecessarily impressionistic angles immediately overhead and even underfoot. But for the most part the stylization of treatment and the theatrical austerity of the settings suit the film exactly, and give it the right sense of universality, lifting it out of a particular period of the past and making it belong to all and every time. The camera, when it is not concentrating on the succession of cruel monkish heads, foxy, narrow, cadaverous, pitted, warted, gross, be-sweated and brutal, or, in the case of the young priest who helps Joan, idealistically handsome, tracks about a great deal to emphasize the patterned groupings of priests and soldiers. The acting itself is an interesting mixture of stylization and naturalism; Dreyer obviously wanted to intensify and emphasize the psychological realism of his film, and the acting as a result becomes slightly slower and slightly larger than life. He used panchromatic film to photograph his carefully chosen cast, none of whom wore make-up. The contours and markings of their faces, therefore, appear as in relief.

Critics in the past have insisted that Dreyer sacrifices true film technique in order to emphasize the separate values of individual shots. There are, however, many sections of the film which use, sometimes almost over-use, the dynamic methods of film technique implied by the word montage – some moments in the cross-examinations, for example, when the hostile faces seem to surround and even to punch forward at Joan, or the interchanges in the cell between the half-trusting girl and the foxy monk who organizes the forgery of the King's letter, or the terrible scenes in the torture-chamber and graveyard, and especially the long burning and rioting sequence which ends the film. But it is true to say that very frequently a consciously-posed image which is, in effect, a single static composition is put on the screen in a manner unrelated to the continuity of the images which precede and follow it. That is why still photographs from this film appeal so strongly to collectors and to publishers of illustrated books on the cinema.

But the compelling power of this film remains unaltered by age or criticism. Dreyer rehearsed and photographed it in the exact order of the script, treating his cast with a strict discipline, above all in the case of Falconetti. The deep suffering which marks her portrayal of Joan bears all the signs of a profound personal experience in carrying out an exacting part under the relentless direction of an uncompromising artist.

KAMERADSCHAFT, 1931

Production: Nerofilm. Direction: G. W. Pabst. Assistant Direction: Herbert Rappaport. Screen-play: Karl Otten, Ernst Vajda, and P. M. Lampel. Photography: Fritz Arno Wagner and R. Baberski. Design: Erno Metzner and Karl Vollbrecht. Editing: Hans Oser. With (German Artists) Alexander Granach, Fritz Kampers, E. Busch, Elizabeth Wendt, G. Püttjer, O. Höcker; (French Artists) D. Mendaille, G. Charlia, A. Ducret, A. Bernard, P. Louis, Helena Manson.

In this age of thickening political hides, the effectiveness of Pabst's former liberalism, which was applauded some twenty years ago when *Kameradschaft* was first being shown, has now been called in question. Siegfried Kracauer has pointed out that the simple socialist philosophy which inspired the film on the eve of Hitler's rise to ultimate power in Germany represents the essential weakness of German democracy through which Hitler's jackboots strode as if through water. The fact that many of us at the time shared the same faith in the efficacy of the liberal decencies and were proved wrong during this tragic decade, does not give back to the film the strength it formerly seemed to possess. Its special virtue is now seen to lie in the integrity of its artistic values rather than in the over-simple social philosophy that it represents.

Kameradschaft, in spite of this naiveté in its social philosophy, still remains a very important film. It is the direct predecessor of films like *Boomerang*, in which a true story illustrating directly and simply the struggle of the human decencies against graft and bureaucracy is reconstructed almost entirely on location, using a mixed cast of professional and non-professional actors. It is well-known that *Kameradschaft* is based on an actual event which took place some time before the first World War, when German miners went to the assistance of French miners just over the border after a disaster at Courrières. Pabst brought the story forward to the period immediately after the Versailles treaty, and gave it the pacifist-socialist interpretation fashionable among the liberal-minded left-wing at the time. Kracauer emphasizes this point in his book *From Caligari to Hitler:*

Comradeship advocated the international solidarity of the Workers, characterizing them as the pioneers of a society in which national egoism, this eternal source of wars, will be abolished. It is the German miners, not their superiors, who conceive the idea of the rescue action. The scene in which they urge the director to consent is the more revealing as it illustrates the omnipotence of authoritarian rule in the German mine.

While the exteriors which make up the greater part of the film were shot on location at an actual mining town, Erno Metzner, Pabst's art director, constructed all the subterranean mining scenes in a studio. Everyone agrees that these sets remain among the most effective and authentic ever to have been built artificially for the screen.

But the authenticity goes beyond the effective use of locations or the scientifically accurate reconstruction of the disaster below-ground; it extends to the characters themselves. None of them, German or French, is given special prominence. They receive just sufficient portrayal to establish themselves as decent people of a kind likely to be working in these mining communities on either side of the Franco-German frontier. The pathos of the old French grandfather, an ex-miner whose grandson is involved in the disaster on his first day below-ground, is not the pathos of an actor working up an emotional role. His suffering is an extension of the anxiety of a whole community, a channel through which Pabst is able to express the intense feeling of all the relatives of the trapped and dying men. Similarly, there is a touching scene in which a woman with a worn and sunken face runs beside the slowly moving lorry which is carrying her German husband off as a member of the volunteer rescue expedition going over the border. She holds on to her child, the symbol of her link to this man who may not come back. It is like a parting before war, a parting which belongs to the life of a community that must inevitably work and struggle.

The technique developed by Pabst derives in part from the Russian silent documentary films which he had seen, but whereas the outstanding Soviet directors of the twenties adopted certain forms of stylization to offset the realism of their subjects (as, for example, in *Potemkin* or in *The Ghost that Never Returns*), Pabst aims directly at realistic effect. The famous brief episode of hallucination, when a trapped French miner hysterical with fear sees his masked German rescuer as if he were still an enemy on the battlefront, is obviously the kind of fantasy which arises naturally out of psychological realism. But Pabst shows himself to be a film-maker of depth and imagination in the way he uses the technical capacities of the new sound-film to dramatize the key situations in this story of disaster and human courage. It is this capacity of his to dramatize these situations without any loss of realistic atmosphere which gives his film a power that the years do not diminish.

There are many examples of this imaginative handling of people and situations in the film – the scenes inside the mine immediately following the explosions, the gradual enlargement of the running crowd of people summoned by the alarm from the pithead,* the crowd scenes at the gates when the waiting women, at first so desperate and demanding, eventually break up into passively waiting groups, sitting where they can as they face the inevitable hours while the search goes on for the bodies of their men, living and dead. With a cunning montage of shots involving static cameras gathering telling details and tracking cameras identified with the running crowd, while the sound track represents the ebb and flow of human cries and the clatter of running feet, Pabst builds up a sympathetic identification between the mining community and the audience which is to watch

*This sequence is described in greater detail in my essay in *Experiment in the Film* (Grey Walls Press), p. 55.

their suffering. Working in the early, exciting days of sound, Pabst had the imagination often to impose complete silence on a scene. Often, too, he makes prolonged use of the simplest kind of natural sound, like the moaning roar which comes up from the mine-shaft when the old man climbs down to find Georges, his grandson, or the intense pulsation of an artificial respirator, or the simple echo of the old man's voice in the cavernous emptiness of the mine as he cries 'Georges ... Georges ...', an echo which emphasizes like music the piteous anxiety of his search, or the gradually quickening rhythm of the alternate tappings when the three trapped Germans are discovered by the rescuers, and finally burst into peal after peal of hysterically happy laughter when they know that they are safe. This continuous close sympathy of Pabst with the dramatic content of the situations he is handling on the screen is the result of a sensitive artistic imagination, just as his recognition of the pictorial value of including, for example, the fantastic yet realistic scene of the German miners' bath hall, with its foliage of clothes slung on chains high above the naked men, adds at the same time a fine element of authenticity to the background of life in a mining community. Indeed every important shot is composed with care, so that the realistic qualities of the film are always served by an artist's eye for the formal beauties.

Kameradschaft survives, therefore, as the work of an artist, and not as an effective example of contemporary propaganda. Now that so many films have been made recently, particularly in Italy and America, with similar qualities of realism, we should be in a good position to appreciate Pabst's achievement, and not less enthusiastically for having to re-assess it.

ZÉRO DE CONDUITE, 1933

Production: Arquis-Film. Script and Direction: Jean Vigo.
Photography: Boris Kaufman. Music: Maurice Jaubert.
With Jean Dasté, Robert le Flon, Du Veron, Delphin.

This film has a theme rather than a story. The theme is the
revolt of a number of boys against the repression of narrow
discipline and evil living conditions in a sordid little French
boarding-school. It is realistic in so far as these conditions
(the dormitory, the classrooms, the asphalt playground
with its sheds, and lavatories, and leafless trees) are faith-
fully observed. But it is non-realistic (or, more nearly,
surrealistic) in its presentation of human relations. The
masters are seen from the distorted viewpoint of the boys
themselves; the Junior Master is a 'sport', so he develops
into an acrobat who stands on his head in the classroom,
imitates Charlie Chaplin and, when he takes the boys out
for an airing, leads them in the pursuit of a girl down the
street.

The Vice-Principal is tall, darkly dressed, and elaborately
sinister in his broad-brimmed hat. He sneaks round the
school, purloining and prying. He minces round the
Principal, who is represented as a dwarf with a big black
beard and a bowler hat. He is a dwarf because the boys
despise him; but he is bearded and bowlered because they
fear him and his final authority over them. An interview
with one boy culminates in a ferocious scream and melodramatic lightning, for the Principal possesses, or seems to
possess, the magical powers of a witch-doctor.

The plan for the revolt passes through various phases or
episodes, culminating first of all in the major revolt at night
in the dormitory and then later in the shambles on Speech
Day, which is a celebration attended by local officials
dressed either like ambassadors or firemen. The dormitory
revolt has the beauty of a pagan ritual touched with imagery
which the boys have learned from the Catholic Church. It
begins with a pillow fight, then passes into a processional

phase shot in slow motion as the boys move in formation, their nightshirts looking like vestments and the feathers from their torn pillows pouring over them in ritual blessing. And it ends finally in the morning, when the ineffectual dormitory master is strapped to his bed, which is tilted on end so that he leans forward in sleep like the effigy of a saint put over an altar. The whole incident has a curious beauty which transcends the sordid surroundings of the school, and Maurice Jaubert's music is a remarkable example here of the manner in which the score for a film can enhance the emotional interpretation of a scene.

The revolt in the playground on Speech Day closes the film with a riot of schoolboy anarchy. Because of its oblique surrealist technique, aspects of school life can be presented which in the conditions affecting an ordinary realistic treatment would be censored away. The film requires great sympathy from its audience, and the desire to seek out its implications. In its way it is a masterpiece, belonging to the best in the *avant-garde* movement.

L'ATALANTE, 1934

Production: J. L. Nounez-Gaumont. Direction: Jean Vigo. Scenario: Jean Guinée. Adaptation and Dialogue: Jean Vigo, Albert Rière. Photography: Boris Kaufman. Design: Francis Jourdan. Music: Maurice Jaubert. With Dita Parlo, Jean Dasté, and Michel Simon.

Jean Vigo died in 1934, and his death was one of the greatest losses that the French cinema has ever sustained. He was a completely fearless film-maker, and a man who was determined to use the film as an artist should, for the purposes of honest expression. He made both *Zéro de Conduite* and *L'Atalante* against every possible obstacle that ill-health and inadequate budgets could produce, and if both films bear the signs of his technical inexperience, neither can be criticized, in my view, for lack of imagination or clarity of purpose. The first is filled with the artist's scorn for the petty tyrannies of life which occur at a bare and mean school for boys, and the second is a tender-bitter story of a newly-married couple who start their life together on a barge. The story begins with their marriage ('She had to be different', grumble the wedding party over the bride's choice of a husband) and ends with their reunion and reconciliation after she has run away from the barge and her self-centred, jealous husband to discover the glamorous city life in Paris of which she has dreamed so long.

In its apparently artless realism *L'Atalante* is the direct ancestor of the modern Italian realist school, exemplified by such films as Visconti's *Ossessione* and de Sica's *Bicycle Thieves*. It is not concerned with the niceties of studio lighting, the elegant use of the camera and careful montage all designed to achieve a succession of dramatic points in the development of the story – the technique which is characteristic of films like *Quai des Brumes* and *Le Jour se lève*. Yet these films are also supposed to possess the quality of realism or, as it is sometimes put, poetic realism; which only goes to show how loose our use of the term 'realism' has become, or how wide that quality is in films. The realism of *L'Atalante* is as spontaneous, as 'un-arranged' as possible; the realism of *Quai des Brumes* and *Le Jour se lève* is of a kind in which everything spontaneous is stripped away to reveal the reality beneath – the strong, harsh relationships of a particular group of people selected for their dramatic and significant contrast of character. The characterization of the hero and heroine in *L'Atalante* is quite undeveloped in this artificially dramatic way, though the naturally eccentric mate, played by Michel Simon, and the professionally eccentric travelling pedlar should, I think, be regarded as characters introduced to form a deliberate contrast to the 'normal' skipper and his young wife.

It is in this conception of his hero and heroine that the nature of Vigo's realism can best be understood. Carné's and Prévert's heroes and heroines are human symbols; though Gabin's earthy good nature may make the characters he plays appear realistic, they are in fact symbols of human goodness placed in strong dramatic contrast to the characters who incarnate evil in all the fatalistic Carné-Prévert films. But the skipper of the Atalante is as ordinary a young man as the one standing next to you on a French bus, and so is his wife, who combines a natural shyness with an innocent eagerness to regard marriage as an initiation into the adventure and glamour of travel and city life. She is typical of any simple woman rather than artificially developed in order to make a dramatic 'character'. Vigo, however, illuminates our observation of this couple in their love-making and horseplay and quarrelling by means of the so-called surrealistic interludes which he introduces into the film.

Although Vigo made his films very much as an individual artist, he was in effect one of the *avant-garde* film-makers in France. Surrealism in the French cinema either took the form of the conscious use of dream-imagery in the representation of experiences difficult or impossible to present directly (as, for example, in *The Seashell and the Clergyman*), or its use in free association (as in Buñuel's films *Le Chien Andalou* and *L'Âge d'Or*). Vigo's surrealism in *Zéro de Conduite* and especially in *L'Atalante* is obviously of the former kind. It is not strictly surrealism at all, for in surrealistic art the conscious mind should play as small a part as possible. But Vigo was well aware what he was doing. When the separation occurs after the couple's marriage, frustrated desire and remorse for what they have done combine to drive them half-crazy; the young skipper dives into the canal and swims under water while an image of his wife in her white bridal dress with its veils floating slowly turns round and round. When they reach the coast he rushes madly out to the sea verge in obedience to Freud. Over and above this deliberate use of the water imagery, the half fantastic wooing of the girl by the mate in his cramped and filthy cabin filled with mysterious and sinister relics from his travels all over the globe, and by the showman-pedlar in the little bar to which the morose, jealous, and unromantic skipper takes his wife, together represent a world which is half symbolic, half real.

Vigo is quite prepared to use these forms of partial fantasy to underline the psychological situation of his hero and heroine, who, as we have seen, are in themselves a very ordinary couple. The mingling of these two worlds – the natural, grey world of the bargee and the illuminated world of fantasy – is completely satisfying in *L'Atalante*.

There is also a rich vein of humour running through the whole film, and Michel Simon as the mate creates one of the finest comic characters to be found in the French cinema. Vigo's sense of humour entirely preserves his films from catching the disease of the *avant-garde* – a portentous seriousness about psychological matters. The music, too, composed by Maurice Jaubert, elicits the mood of many scenes, though the theme song itself, composed by Lys Gauty, is bitterly attacked by Jacques Brunius in *Experiment in the Film* when he writes about *L'Atalante*: '. . . before it was shown to the public the producer thought it necessary to soften what was too cruel in Vigo's outlook on life. Here and there a song by Lys Gauty, having nothing to do with the story, sweetened with its sugary sentiment scenes in which real emotion, veiled by irony, bursts out in brief moments of ardour and anguish. For some months the film took the title of the song, *Le Chaland qui passe* (The Passing Barge). But Vigo had left a vigorous imprint on his characters and images, and *Le Chaland qui passe* is forgotten and only *L'Atalante* remembered.' Jaubert's music constantly refreshes the film and prevents it becoming morbid or oppressive.

The main faults of this film are, curiously enough, to a certain extent assets. The photography is very rough – but how could it be otherwise unless the barge had been made artificially in a studio or every scene shot in special lighting and special weather? This is an everyday story photographed in everyday lighting, and the narrow interiors do not allow for fancy shots. The continuity is also rough, but to have made it smooth and rhythmic would have been to make it, dramatically speaking, self-conscious. Episode follows episode without any special attempts to create dramatic closing scenes or achieve significant pay-off lines;

when an episode has done its job in the story, the scene just fades and the next begins. But the main principle of such realistic films as *L'Atalante*, to achieve unity of atmosphere and faithfulness to the kind of life shown, is maintained, and the film, Vigo's main work, can always be shown as proof of the fact that his untimely death deprived us of one of the most imaginative of film-makers.

THE INFORMER, 1935

Production: RKO–Radio Pictures. Direction: John Ford.
Script: Dudley Nichols. Photography: Joseph H. August.
Music: Max Steiner. Adapted from the novel by Liam O'Flaherty.
With Victor McLaglen and Margot Grahame.

John Ford's career as a film director began early in the silent period, but his name as one of the foremost artists of the American cinema was made by his association with the script-writer, Dudley Nichols, when they made *The Informer* together in 1935. Lewis Jacobs in *The Rise of the American Film* states that Ford was in a strong position as a commercial director when after five years' pressure he managed to persuade the studios to let him make this film. Jacobs writes:

Instead of salary Ford took a percentage of the profits. The production is said to have cost $218,000, a relatively small sum; $5,000 was paid for the rights to Liam O'Flaherty's novel. The picture took only three weeks to shoot, and Ford declared it was the easiest he ever made. And no wonder: he says he dreamed of the film for five years (p. 480).

The Informer is an example of the near-perfect union of theme and structure. It has complete simplicity, unspoiled by deviations and sub-plots. Each episode is short, a constructive contribution to the carrying forward of the action from its beginning (the temptation, leading up to the betrayal of Frankie by his friend, Gypo, the brainless giant), through its middle (the foolish behaviour of Gypo deprived of the leadership of the man he has betrayed, leading up to his arrest and trial by the Rebel organization) to its end (the flight of Gypo from earthly justice and the moments that lead up to his death before the altar where Frankie's mother forgives him). The unities are observed, of action, of place (the back streets that harbour the Rebels), and of time (the action is completed over-night, from dusk to dawn). The inevitability of *The Informer* make it one of the rare tragedies so far created for the screen.

The film begins with the great figure of Gypo in the narrow streets, lamplit and misty. The street-sets are of the barest economy, their effect of realism achieved by a few details, their atmosphere created by the high-lights from the lamp-posts and doorways. With no word of dialogue until well into the first reel, the feeling of the film is created by the poster offering the £20 reward for information about Frankie McPhillip, a poster which Gypo tears down but which, blown by the wind, haunts him, clinging to his feet as he listens to the street-tenor singing 'Rose of Tralee', blowing on until it brings us to the feet of Katie, Gypo's girl-friend for whom he eventually betrays Frankie in order to buy them both a passage to the States. It is then that the first word is spoken by Katie, 'Gypo –,' like a wail, the trailing note of it caught up by the music, lonely, full of pleading. But the wind blows the poster on until it is eventually burnt before Gypo's staring eyes in the Rebel Commandant's hide-out. The close lamp-lit streets and archways, the steps and courts and alleys, the bright bar-rooms, the fish-and-chip shop and other refuges from the bleak pavements are a major part of this film, as they were of Fritz Lang's *M* made before it and Carol Reed's *Odd Man Out* made since.

Wherever he can, Ford uses visual methods of building tension. Gypo in an agony of fear after the betrayal suddenly finds himself throttling a man outside the police-station. But the man is blind and crazy. Nevertheless at the later trial scene, the camera creeps round the witnesses and comes to rest on this same mad empty face. Gypo, in funds with the reward money, enters a bar; the few people in the bar leave it just at the moment Gypo shows his cash, unconsciously ostracizing him. Gypo after the death of Frankie goes to visit the dead man's mother in an agonized attempt to appear innocent. He is already drunk, and he blunders in upon the assembled family and mourners. The women are chanting, and the great dark body of Gypo sits in the foreground like a shroud over the scene. He bursts out 'I'm sorry for your trouble, Mrs McPhillip.' The wake suddenly stops: they stare at him; he jumps up; the accusing coins drop on the floor from his pocket, and the rest of the scene is the tension of exchanged glances of suspicion. This method of timed glances shows the reactions of Commandant Gallagher and his lieutenants to Gypo as the portrait of Frankie on the poster burns in the grate. So, too, the visual rather than the aural method is used when the young Rebels draw the cuts to see who is to shoot the imprisoned Gypo. No one wants to do it, least of all the man who draws the cut for the job. The heads of his companions withdraw out of the frame of the picture; then the hand offering the last cut withdraws. The executioner is left alone, isolated with the symbol of his task.

Nevertheless, the film is rich in dialogue scenes where Victor McLaglen is seen at his best. Here the emphasis shifts from the symbolic, carefully selected visual touches just described to words and actions of complete realism and conviction. Outstanding scenes include Gypo drunk and garrulous with recriminations against Frankie's betrayer when he is summoned before the Rebel Commandant, Gypo more drunk and treating everyone in the street to fish-and-chips, Gypo in the middle of the night visiting a brothel with a buddy anxious that the cash should be spent to his advantage, the trial of Gypo, and the scene in Katie's small bedroom after his escape when he lies down like a child in front of the fire to sleep off his exhaustion. The scenes are human and right and apt; they are vigorous, crazily energetic, drunken or touching, according to the moment and the mood. They are scripted as a film should be scripted, and they are most notably directed and acted, often with the barest simplicity.

If there is a weakness in the film it comes towards the end in the scene when Katie comes to plead for Gypo's life with Gallagher, who is in love with Frankie's sister. Here the dialogue seems to leave aside what would have been said in order to dramatize the sentiment of the situation. Similarly after Gypo has been shot at close range, he manages to stagger to the church, drag himself inside and reach the altar before which Frankie's mother is kneeling. Although this end is right in terms of theme, for Gypo above all things needs to feel forgiveness from both man and God before he dies, the playing of this scene is in the exaggerated style of melodrama, and therefore is out of keeping with the treatment of the film as a whole.

Nevertheless, *The Informer* remains one of the outstanding achievements of the American screen. It bears all the marks of the artistic conviction which led Ford and those associated with him to bargain with the studio authorities to be allowed to make it, and to achieve these results with such sure economy of effort on the floor. Victor McLaglen gives a performance which remains vivid in the memory, like having met a man briefly whom one cannot somehow forget. Gypo commits a sin of the worst kind; he spends the night following in drunkenness and boasting, and yet he never ceases to command sympathy as a man incapable of responsibility for what he does. His tragedy is a sheer inability to understand; he is a fool who blunders into wisdom at the expense of his life. There are many such people in the world. *The Informer* has the universality which belongs to tragedy.

LE JOUR SE LÈVE, 1939

Production: Sigma-Frogerais. Direction: Marcel Carné.
Scenario: Jacques Viot and Jacques Prévert. Photography:
Curt Courant. Design: A. Trauner. Music: Maurice Jaubert.
With Jean Gabin, Arletty, Jacqueline Laurent, and Jules Berry.

This film probably represents the peak of the achievement of the director Marcel Carné working in association with the poet Jacques Prévert. In the subsequent films of the war and post-war years the fatalistic poetic formula of Prévert increasingly dominated Carné, who up to *Le Jour se lève* had subjected every element of his work, character, theme and dialogue, to his own penetrating sense of the needs of the film medium. The later films became more and more static, the superb presentation of Prévert's haunting but wordy scenes of dialogue between strange, half-real characters who serve the ends of his fatalistic vision in which beauty and love are defeated by the jealous forces of evil.

In *Quai des Brumes* and *Le Jour se lève* Prévert's feeling for spiritual defeat and Carné's hard sense of locality and character blended perfectly. Both these films, in spite of their contemporary setting and realistic backgrounds of works, docks, streets, and fairs, were poetic and romantic, the characters simplified and balanced so that the result was an emotional atmosphere of fatalism, the destruction of goodness and love by the wanton unaccountable evil in men's hearts. The words given to the characters of these films are always grander and simpler than the dialogue of actuality, always conceived with reference to the underlying fatalistic theme, the persecution of the fleeting beauty in the lives of men and women by evil. There is permanent happiness for no one, not even the destroyers. This theme might well be compared with that in Chehov's plays, though there the destruction of happiness is due to the social and psychological impotence of the characters, rather than the active violence of evil which Carné and Prévert introduce into their films.

Touched with a certain popular sentimentality (the

orphans in love) and the element of horror (the vaudeville artist and his treatment of his dogs), *Le Jour se lève* is grounded on real human experience of love, and beauty, and ugliness. This makes it very moving, even when it is seen as often as I have seen it; like a fine play or novel it stands the test of repetition, a test which punctures the emotional blandishments of lesser films that are effective only for one viewing.

The story of *Le Jour se lève* is simple enough. A chance meeting between an honest workman and a pretty flower-seller leads to a deeply-felt love affair. On the man's side this idealistic relationship is supplemented by the earthly attachment he has to a showman's assistant, a good-humoured, easy woman capable in her own way of great loyalty and affection; on the girl's side she is fatally fascinated by the showman himself, a half-mad representative of evil whose lust to destroy the happiness of others is so strong that he is prepared to destroy himself in the process. He is a fanatic, believing in his own lies as they pass from one distorted phase to another, fascinating the orphan Françoise with the colour of their mystery and their glimpse of unknown places, revolting the patient honesty of François until he is goaded into destroying the bestial man who seeks to destroy him. It is easy to see from this bare summary how such people and such a story slip easily into the pigeon-holes of symbolism, and once this is done how easy it is to say now that this fatalism of theme belongs spiritually to pre-war France waiting with fascinated inertia for her own destruction by war and invasion like the landowners who people Chehov's plays. It is a melancholy thought that the post-war malaise of France allowed the theme to be intensified in *Les Portes de la nuit* instead of transformed by victory into a more vital philosophy.

Technically *Le Jour se lève* is a most exciting film. By leading off with the harsh establishment of an act of violence in the middle of a scene of ordinary tenement life it might be said that Carné played a strong card anyhow, but an examination of the methods by which the tension at the beginning of the film is created in terms of good cinema

137

technique shows that he does not simply depend on the shock of the mortally wounded man reeling out of François' room to establish the effect for him. The tension is established first by Jaubert's sinister music, which has something of the same effect as that which accompanies the camera moving up the ironwork gates of Xanadu at the beginning of *Citizen Kane*. The scene is established by the briefest shots seen over the backs of two cart-horses in the foreground, with the tall tenement standing in the background of the grim little industrial *place*. Then the door at the head of the stairs is seen, shots are heard behind it, the door is wrenched open, a man in a check coat staggers out with his hands pressed to his belly. He tips and falls down the stairs to the landing below, up to which a blind man is climbing, tapping with his stick. This last touch reaches its climax with the blind man's terrified cries as he feels the body with the stick. The atmosphere is not one of mere violence; it is one of portentous violence. The difference is created by the selective, rhythmic, suggestive handling of the incident and its locality.

There are many scenes, combining a careful choice of background with an equally careful choice of character-acting, which suggest the whole significance of the theme to the viewer. This feeling for the medium as well as for the theme is the sign of artistic maturity. There is profound irony in the handling of the deployment of the small army of police and the watching crowd which is friendly to François but enjoys the spectacle of his trouble; this is in its way as subtle as the contrast of the isolated man in the high attic tower smoking his last cigarettes and putting his memories and emotions into shape to the accompaniment of low pulsations of music like the rhythms of a dying heart. Never did flashbacks emerge more necessarily from the psychology of a story than do those which François is forced to recall before our eyes: they come as naturally as the imaginary reconstructions created during a sleepless night of emotional anxiety. The music swells up to bursting-point as each memory is born. On the other hand there is great tenderness in both kinds of love scene which occur throughout this dark-toned film, the sacred love for Françoise epitomized in the simple scene in her bedroom and transfigured in the lovely scene in the greenhouse of flowers (themselves the symbols of her fresh, young beauty), and the profane love for Clara, an honest love of the body based on an easy and friendly acceptance of pleasure. The two women, united in the last attempt to protect their man at the tragic end of the film, are portrayed in fine contrast by the remote, innocent Jacqueline Laurent and the superbly casual Arletty. Gabin with his suggestion of the workman-poet who does not know his own sensitivity is equally well cast. But the outstanding performance of the film, because it is the most difficult to make really convincing, is that of Jules Berry as the fanatic masochist, the showman who must give pain for its own sake, even to himself. This terrifying characterization is completely successful: the madness is in his veins and not merely in his contract, as seemed the case with Vincent Price's portrayal of the same man in the American version of the story.

The film curves back to its beginning, the end of the last flashback re-enacting from François's side of the door the scene which was first shown from the staircase. Then the turmoil of police, crowds, and hysterical women subsides with the revolver shot of François's suicide, and then follows an unforgettable picture of the body lying on the floor as the cloud of tear-gas creeps slowly over it, and the hush is broken by the insistent little bell of the dead man's alarm-clock. The end is symbolized completely by this last perfectly-imagined device of sound and image; dawn arrives with a splendour which takes no account of the loneliness of men and women enduring the pain of love destroyed by evil.

CITIZEN KANE, 1941

Production: RKO-Radio Pictures. Direction: Orson Welles.
Script: Herman J. Mankiewicz and Orson Welles.
Photography: Gregg Toland. Design: Van Nest Polglase.
Music: Bernard Herrmann. With Orson Welles, Agnes Moorehead,
Joseph Cotten, Everett Sloan, Ruth Warwick, Dorothy Comingore.

Citizen Kane is the story of Charles Foster Kane, an American tycoon and press-lord – a man who inherited a fortune when he came of age, spent it, lost it, and made it again a hundred times over in the undisciplined pursuit of his own self-satisfaction and power.

When he is young he says he thinks 'it would be fun to own a newspaper'. His only true friend, Leland, the man he later dismisses for telling the truth about his second wife, says of him that 'he was never brutal; he just did brutal things', and that 'he had a private sort of greatness he kept to himself'. Leland also says, finally, that what Kane really needed was love, and the trouble lay in the fact that he had none to give in return.

Kane dies with a single word on his lips – 'rosebud', and lets fall a glass ball which he was clutching in his hand. Like everything connected with Kane, 'rosebud' hits the headlines. A film journalist sets out to solve the mystery of its significance to Kane, and his interviews with the men and women who had been closest to Kane during his lifetime give the film its story-line. He pieces together Kane's character in his public and private life, with all his lavish egotism, his superabundant vitality, his misplaced idealisms, and his lust for constant publicity and for power over individuals and over society as a whole. After all, he was a unique citizen, personally responsible, they say, for starting the Spanish-American war.

Orson Welles brought to this half-satiric, half-melodramatic film his own personal sense of the 'theatre' and showmanship – Kane's life was a natural subject in which he could excel as producer, writer, actor, and director, for he is himself more than life-size as an artist. He poured all his talent into this production – creating a new kind of dramatic expressionism in film terms. He is the only film-maker to have made a picture wholly in this style, though many directors have borrowed facets of it since *Citizen Kane* appeared.

Expressionism is a dangerous style to adopt, but Orson Welles is not the man to be afraid of danger. The strong currents of *Citizen Kane* constantly burst their banks; the firm flow of the narrative is occasionally stemmed by the flood of technique, by the eddies of art for art's sake. But the strength and interest of the subject is so great that these tricks and faults of style are soon forgotten as we ride the dramatic torrents downstream.

Expressionism is the use of symbolic forms of presentation to underline the universal significance of a theme. Kane is America, Kane is us, Kane is a social institution – but Kane is also flesh and blood, a man, an individual. But what is real about him is constantly on the borderland of what is unreal; such a life as this is a melodrama, a human anomaly, a monstrosity. The style of the film reflects this double view, weaving in and out of actuality like sequences in a nightmare. The realistic sequences are therefore very real – dialogue is so lifelife that people overtalk each other, leave sentences unfinished, forget words, complete their sense with gesture, cough at the wrong moment. Sequence after sequence has this almost painstaking actuality – the reception for the *Chronicle*'s staff of writers when they are bought by Kane for his *Inquirer*, for example. The unreality, on the other hand, is very unreal: the Thatcher Memorial Library, haunted by the ungenerous spirit of its founder, Kane's guardian during his minority, is like a giant morgue, echoing, vast, and empty. Kane's Xanadu is a domestic cathedral; his wife, unhappy with her puzzles, sits crouched in space beside a fireplace the size of a cottage, her querulous, pitiful voice begging for her to be taken to New York. Sometimes the expressionism shows the same excesses as the French *avant-garde* – for example, Kane's final exit between the marshalled ranks of his servants, his stricken figure reflected and re-reflected in a chain of mirror images.

The main interviews out of which Kane's life and career are reconstructed through flashbacks are, first, that with Bernstein (Kane's assistant) showing Kane during his exuberant youth as owner and editor of *The Enquirer*, and second, that with Leland (his only true friend and admirer) revealing Kane's middle years – his two marriages, the collapse of his extravagant political ambitions when his unscrupulous opponent exposes his 'love-nest' downtown, and the break with Leland over his review of Kane's second wife's deplorable performance as an opera star.

The film is extraordinarily close-packed; almost every one of its thirty or more short scenes are memorable because of the deep mark which Welles's style makes upon it. Sometimes it is a grouping of heads carefully balanced as between foreground and distance, as patterned as a frame by Eisenstein; sometimes it is a bizarre effect, like the highlights and silhouettes in the viewing room of *Life on the March*. Sometimes it is burlesque, like the Dickensian scene when Kane and his friends first invade the old-fashioned *Inquirer* office and shock the respectable staff with their modern journalistic methods; or a brilliant bit of parody, like the imitation *March of Time*, or the old and scratched newsreels of Kane's early life. There are many fine pictorial effects, like the gigantic election poster behind the desk on Kane's platform. Amid all the bombast there are moments of quiet sincerity, like Leland's expression of a real admiration for Kane when he suddenly writes down his 'Declaration of Principles' for *The Enquirer*, or Kane's own quiet, pathetic appeal to his second wife not to leave him – 'Please don't go' – the only moment of human weakness he ever shows.

After his death one watches the great column of smoke, like the cloud from an atom bomb, coming from the furnace at Xanadu as the rubbish (including Kane's boyhood sledge with the lettered name 'Rosebud') is destroyed. One hears the impersonal comments of the visitors inspecting Kane's vast storehouse of treasures, and the result is pity for the man who wanted love but could not give it, and who, in one of the most impressive scenes in the film, dismisses his best friend for destroying the particular illusion he wanted to foster – the illusion that his wife was a great singer. It is this feeling, the humanity of this study of Kane and his friends, which puts all the technical discussion – the deep focus, the expressionism – in their due place, as part of Orson Welles's imaginative presentation of a subject which completely possessed him.

As a film *Citizen Kane* is one of the richest mines of film technique yet created. For all its extravagances, it is a magnificent personal achievement, a *tour de force* which succeeds. It bears the mark of strength, even genius. The economics of the modern cinema allow very few such individual enterprises as this film and its companion-piece, *The Magnificent Ambersons*.

FIRES WERE STARTED, 1943

Production: Crown Film Unit. Producer: Ian Dalrymple.
Script and Direction: Humphrey Jennings.
Photography: Pennington Richards.
Art Direction: Edward Carrick. Music: William Alwyn.
Editor: Stewart McAllister.

This film was made by Humphrey Jennings under official sponsorship during the War. Its intention was to show the public the work of the fire service, and especially the particular human qualities of courage and endurance needed in those men and women who left their normal peace-time jobs to help fight the terrible battle of the fire-raids. Jennings decided to concentrate on twenty-four hours in the life of one of these units – a station which served a London Dock-side area. Throughout the film he reminds us that this station was part of a whole network in the fire service, linked up to the others through the Local Control Station. But the emphasis is always on this local unit, and the little group of men and women who compose it.

These men and women are quickly sketched in for us – for example, the cheerful Cockney on his knees in the backyard boxing with his small son ('I must see my manager about you'), and the husband, a small dark man, leaving his shabby street-corner shop in the charge of his wife, who says to him as he leaves, 'Don't do anything silly, dear'. These brief sequences linking up the chief characters of the film are bound together and warmed by Alwyn's music, music which sweetens in tone whenever we see shots of the Thames and the shipping. For the ships are in, loading war supplies for overseas. Jennings's very personal kind of interest, always ready to be touched off by some fragment of music, can be seen early in this film with the sudden appearance of a street musician playing a flute as he stands in a dilapidated Regency doorway, and his plaintive notes, like those of a bird singing in some tree isolated among acres of bricks, carry through on the sound track until all the men have left home and arrived at their station for morning duty. The humanity and poetry of this film are established somehow with complete authority by this single touch.

The story of the film is very simple. A new man, Barrett, an advertising copy-writer, joins the unit, and soon becomes a favourite because he can play the piano. The men service the vans and equipment, the Cockney singing 'Sweet Mystery of Life' and 'Nice to be Beside the Seaside'. Nevertheless, there is a war on, and it is full moon to-night. The greater part of the film shows the desperate struggle of these men to fight the inevitable fires with an insufficient supply of equipment and water. One man falls through the roof of a burning warehouse – the husband of the woman who had said 'Don't do anything silly'. He is killed, and it is his funeral which ends the film, while the ships pass on down the Thames.

The scenes of action at night are good and authentic, but it is the people in Jennings's films who matter far more than the action, even when they are only glimpsed by his careful but candid camera, as they are in *Listen to Britain*. Jennings always wanted to create a synthesis between the high culture and the simple human roots of his country: the man piping with a penny flute on a Regency doorstep, or the fireman Barrett strumming on the canteen piano, playing first a touch of serious music, sedate and contemplative while we look at the proud ships on the Thames, and then bursting into a vamping rhythm as the amber warning comes up, and the firemen enter through the swing door one by one, carrying their gear and joining in the verses of the song 'One Man Went to Mow, Went to Mow a Meadow' – all this somehow gives mankind his proper status, *Homo sapiens*. And after the siren has made the singing in the canteen more wild than ever, another fireman with a serious Scottish voice, and a taste for fine literature, reads momentarily from Sir Thomas Browne – 'O eloquent, just and mighty death . . .' '*Hic jacet,*' he says, as the guns outside begin to pound. Jennings never composed a finer sequence than this one, before the men go out to the fires in Swan Lane and Trinidad Street. Then the piano is left silent.

In the scenes of fire-fighting the stress is on the great technical effort involved. The fires grow whilst the frustrated men wait for the Control Station to eke out the scanty equipment and send them the water pressure which is their single weapon. It seems a tragically unequal battle, though the fires, we are told, are eventually brought under control. When relief comes with daylight and the 'all clear', the streets are awash with water and laced with the crumpled hoses, and while the exhausted men 'make up' their equipment the news passes round that 'Jacko's copped it'. His helmet is found among the debris where he crashed through the furnace of the blazing warehouse. We pass the little shop on the way back to the station; his wife is inside listening to the news and waiting for him to come back. Jennings's comment on this is to show us a tree in flower in a back-street garden, and the Scottish fireman in the Station dormitory recites Macbeth's speech on the 'valued file' of dogs and men. The ships are safe and the fires under control, though one man in the 'valued file' is lost for ever. He is given at his funeral the special honours reserved for men who die for their country. As he is lowered into his grave, the 'Last Post' sounds, but it gives way to Alwyn's triumphant music as the ships pass down the Thames.

THE OXBOW INCIDENT, 1943
(STRANGE INCIDENT)

Production: Twentieth Century-Fox. Direction: William Wellman. Script: Lamar Trotti. Photography: Arthur Miller. Music: Cyril J. Mockridge. Adapted from a novel by Walter Van Tilburg Clark. With Henry Fonda, Dana Andrews, Henry Morgan, Harry Davenport.

Since *Birth of a Nation* American films have returned again and again to the basic problem of human conduct and the establishment of law and order in a new and widely scattered society. These have often proved wonderful subjects for films – the westering of the pioneers, the dawn of the concept of justice in remote regions, and the outbreak of gang or mob violence in the rural and urban areas. Widespread corruption, lynching, and jail-breaks all testify to an unsettled society, but they enable writers and film-makers to give their work fundamental, classic themes of a kind found less often in the polite and over-sophisticated society of Western Europe, apart from the films born of the struggle against Nazism and Fascism.

The Oxbow Incident has this classic shape. It opens with two men riding into Bridger's Wells, a small and lonely cattlemen's township in Nevada. The period is 1885. The two cowboys, Gil (Henry Fonda) and Art, are occasional visitors to the place, but their function in what is to come is important, for they act as witnesses and commentators from outside the community. Neither of them is what would be called a moral man, but they instinctively stand for justice and for the practice of the common decencies. They are called on to take part in the lynching of three men on the charge of cattle rustling and murder. It is plainly the hysteria of revenge which leads a mob to go out at dusk to catch the suspected men and hang them in cold blood without trial. The lynching expedition is led by a Major Tetley, who commanded for the South in the Civil War. They carry out this expedition in the temporary absence of the Sheriff, and against the urgent advice of a small minority who wish to abide by the law. The suspected men have a good case to make for their innocence, though circumstantial evidence seems to be against them. They are a young married man, an old, simple-minded man, and a boldly impudent Mexican. As the lynching party rides away leaving the bodies swinging behind them, they meet the Sheriff and learn that there has been neither murder nor cattle rustling to avenge. The film ends with Gill reading aloud the letter written by the young American to his wife just before he died. He reads it to the line of guilty men who lean silently against the bar in the saloon. After that Gil and Art ride away up the street, empty save for a dog, in order to deliver the letter and offer help to the young woman who does not yet know she is a widow. This is an exact reverse of the opening, even to the wandering dog, and melancholy folk music touches the scene with profound emotion.

This story has the simplicity of a Greek drama. It concerns the *hubris* of those who wrongfully presume to administer justice and, as a result, commit the gravest injustice. It shows the unequal struggle between the good minority and the bad majority. The gods of justice exercise their retribution through the Sheriff who represents them. 'God had better have mercy on you,' he says, 'because you ain't gonna get any from me!'

Within the lynching mob are many kinds of men, the most fully characterized being Farnley and Tetley. Farnley is a friend of Kinkaid, the man who is thought to be murdered, and his motive is the quick exercise of savage revenge. Tetley is a bully who exploits authority under the guise of order and discipline. He forces his son Gerald to play a prominent part in the lynching, though the boy has no stomach for it; in the end he marches home with stubborn pride and shoots himself. The forces of good are led by an old man, a storekeeper called Arthur Davis, who is beautifully played by Harry Davenport. He never ceases to plead with Tetley to bring the prisoners in to stand the true course of justice.

As the action develops it intensifies from the normal realism of a good Western to the poetic concentration of a tragic drama. Music plays an important part in this strengthening emotion, the melancholy of the folk-music which opens and closes the film giving place to powerful orchestrations reflecting the sense of doom which overhangs the lynching. The vulgar joy in violence of some of the men and the raucous laughter of Ma Grier (Jane Darwell) is offset by the only representative of the Christian religion, a poor, lean Negro preacher called Sparks, who kneels and chants in a harshly rhythmic voice beneath the hanging bodies of the men. The little town and its surroundings seem spacious in comparison with the narrow confines of the camp where the lynching takes place at dawn; it is in fact a studio set, as against a location or an open-air scene filmed on a studio lot. The preparations for the lynching are a hideous parody of justice, made worse by the absence of any heroics in the victims. The young man (Dana Andrews) weeps with frustration because they will not believe in his innocence or give him fair trial; he is not ready for death, for he has a young wife and children dependent on him. The old man drools and the Mexican acts with a ferocious imitation of courage. Lamar Trotti's screen play spares us nothing in building up the final tragedy in the language of the American idiom, but the beautiful shape he gives his film relieves it of desolation. He allows the forces of retribution to take control at the end, and the light of humanity to shine in the characters of Davies and Gil.

The Oxbow Incident is an unusual Western, but it nevertheless remains one. It is profoundly American in its feeling, like the finer films of John Ford and those other Westerns which deal with the fundamental issues raised by the social life of the pioneers, such as *Shane*. It is a film which may be re-seen many times and lead to a growing appreciation of the American people who not only made it, but are also part of the life and values to which it gives expression.

IVAN THE TERRIBLE, PART ONE, 1945

*Production: Alma-Ata Studios. Direction and Script:
Sergei Eisenstein. Photography: Andrei Moskvin and
Eduard Tisse. Art Direction: I. Shrimel. Music: Sergei
Prokofiev. With Nikolai Cherkasov, Ludmilla Tselikovskaya,
Serafima Birman, A. Mgebrov, and V. I. Pudovkin.*

Ivan the Terrible, Sergei Eisenstein's sixth major film, was made during the War in the Alma Ata Studios behind the Urals in the Kazakh Soviet Republic of Central Asia. It was intended to be the first of three biographical films of the sixteenth-century Tsar Ivan IV, who was contemporary with the British Queen Elizabeth I and who was responsible for gathering under one rule the many autonomous Russian principalities, and so became the first Tsar of a united Russia. The second part of the film was completed, but subsequently banned by the Soviet authorities on the main grounds that it misrepresents the Tsar's character and does not show him as a progressive statesman. The third part was never made. On the other hand, the first part became a Stalin Prize film.

The film's structure is episodic, and divides into seven narrative sections: (i) The coronation of the young Tsar and his challenge to the Boyars and his aunt Euphrosyne in front of the ambassadors from the foreign powers gathered in the Cathedral; (ii) His wedding to Anastasia Romanovna, and his quelling of a popular riot initiated by his enemies; (iii) Ivan's seige of Kazan, and the disloyalty of the weak Prince Kurbsky; (iv) Ivan's sickness and the open disloyalty of the Boyars when they think him to be dying; (v) Ivan's power crumbles, and his beloved wife is poisoned by Euphrosyne; (vi) Ivan mourns his dead wife as she lies in state: except for a few faithful followers he is completely deserted; (vii) Ivan, in retirement at Alexandrov, receives a great procession of the common people who beg him to return to power.

Eisenstein's treatment of this large historical theme, intended to rouse the national spirit of Soviet Russia whilst she was at war with Germany, is not in the style of the normal technique of cinema. The treatment is deliberately larger than life, like that of Greek and Shakespearian tragedy. The characters speak a language which is archaic and stylized, and they act with a technique which combines simplicity with grandeur, in the very opposite tradition to the detailed naturalism of most contemporary cinema. Eisenstein is concerned with theme rather than narrative, human symbolism rather than individual characterization. Each episode is conceived like a book from an epic poem or a section from a Greek tragedy: the characters are grouped together, speak their words and, especially where speech is minimized or altogether absent, use mime to emphasize their reactions to the situation. Always the effect is both larger and simpler than actuality, and the technique has a certain parallel to that of the melodrama of the days of Griffith. Yet since the conception of *Ivan the Terrible* is poetic and epic, the intention and total design of the film is complex. The technical resemblance to melodrama is superficial only.

Since the main trend of cinema technique is realistic it may be objected that Eisenstein is retrogressive in retaining the simpler, bolder style characteristic of Russian silent cinema. The sound film, however, is a medium of the eye reinforced by the ear. Realism is only one of the methods of treatment which are all quite natural to the medium. Stylization, provided it is based on a cinematic conception and technique, is as correct on the screen as it is in the static image on a painter's canvas. What is unnatural to the true expression of the cinema is its use as a mere recording medium dominated by words or by lack of visual movement. This Eisenstein decidedly does not do. Rather does he attempt to widen the range of cinematic expression by developing new relationships and timing of sound and image, as explained rather elaborately in Chapters I and IV of his book *The Film Sense*, with reference to his previous film in a similar style, *Alexander Nevsky* (1938).

The outstanding figure in the film is that of Nikolai Cherkasov as Ivan. His appearance and voice lend themselves to the purposes of Eisenstein. He portrays the Tsar as a creature of single moods according to the needs of the situation; he is angry, happy, challenging, loving, hating, mourning. He acts on the grand scale with ease and deliberation, powerful but never melodramatic because his largest moments are born of intense feeling. He is never submerged by the almost mathematical complexity of Eisenstein's sense of design. Euphrosyne is a hawk-figure, compact of evil, bending stealthily under the low doorways, sinister and watchful. Kurbsky is handsome, empty and vacillating. Only the Tsarina seems to lack the grandeur of the symbolism implied by her position: she underplays too much in the tradition of realistic cinema.

To emphasize the great theme of Russian unification under a progressive monarch and his final triumph against the Boyars with the support of the common people, Eisenstein had the cameras of Moskvin and Tisse, and the musical score of Prokofiev. Tisse had been his cameraman since *Strike*, which they made together in 1924. Prokofiev had worked with Eisenstein on *Alexander Nevsky*. Eisenstein was his own set-designer. This team of artists produce astonishing collective results, the combined powers of photography, music and montage which merge in the all-embracing film medium. An example is the carefully constructed sequence of the coronation in which long shots of the whole cathedral are alternated with remarkable portrait close-ups, the heads of the chief actors, and the heads, framed in gigantic white ruffs, of the old and cunning ambassadors of Western Europe. Ivan is crowned without emphasis on the individual: the back of his head and his hands receiving the symbol of office are all that are shown. A bass voice of an astonishing echoing quality rises in quarter tones with a paean of thanksgiving. The Emperor turns and the ritual shower of coins is poured over his head and splashes to the ground in a stream of dancing light. The women smile, and the huge menacing heads of the Boyars threaten the young Tsar. Only after all this play with music, ritual, and symbolic portraiture does Ivan announce his challenge to the old powers in plain and ringing speech.

Throughout the film these sequences recur in which pattern and design become motifs to enlighten the theme of the film. The heavy claustrophobic Byzantine buildings with their formalized images of God and Man are the background to intense court intrigue. The marriage celebration becomes a pageant of moving designs, the crash of the huge goblets of wine seen through a perspective of ornamental curving swan-necks, the rich barbaric ceremonial shattered by the peasant invasion which calls Ivan to action as the leader of his people, and turns revolt into friendly laughter. But always there are the great shadows and all-enclosing walls to hem in the free spirit of the Tsar and bind him to the intrigues of the ancient ways. The siege of Kazan is also a matter of patterned images, like the Iliad portrayed on a Greek vase. The Tsar, the leader of his people, emerges from his rich tent on the crest of a curving hill, and he stands alone, a dark heroic figure, whilst the line of his officers is ranged in a pattern beneath him. His troops in procession march in a rhythm of moving lines. There is no realism in this portrait of an army, only the order and precision of an artist's mobile composition. Even the terrible moment of agony for the Mongolian prisoners, shot through by the arrows of their countrymen loosed from the walls of besieged Kazan, is an agony emphasized by the artistry of the close shots, the pain of death enlarged by the formal angles of the dead men's bound and twisted bodies.

The tolling of varying deep bells recurs through the film, at the coronation, at the wedding ceremony, and at the Tsar's supposed deathbed. Their religious symbolism of sound enriches the Byzantine ikons, and books of the priests, and the painted images on the walls. Life and art combine in the film. The huge heads of the actors turn slowly in significant close-up, and merge with the watchful heads and eyes in relief, or paint, which stare down on the living from the vantage ground of art. The sardonic climax of this religious ritual is when the sick Tsar peers suspiciously from under the pages of the huge illuminated Testament placed over his face by the Archbishop. Always the symbolism of objects merges into the symbolism of people. In Ivan's palatial study the shadow of the skeletal globe stands in huge relief on the wall while he discusses his foreign policy with his envoy to the British Queen Elizabeth I.

In the last scenes the symbolism of locality is uppermost. In the foreground the self-exiled Tsar stands watching the vast procession of the common people who have come to intercede with him. The procession itself spreads over a vast plain. The claustrophobia of the intriguing court is forgotten in the open sunshine which lights the great curving line of people who kneel to the Tsar. The film ends, therefore, on a note of triumph in which Ivan and his people are joined under the open skies of Russia.

LAND OF PROMISE, 1945

Production: Films of Fact for the Gas Council.
Production and Direction: Paul Rotha. Assistant Direction:
Francis Gysin. Script: Ira Calder Marshall, Miles Malleson,
Wolfgang Wilhelm, and Miles Tomalin. Music: William Alwyn.
Diagrams: Isotype Institute. With John Mills, Herbert Lomax,
Miles Malleson, Frederick Allen.

Can a film argue? A film is normally used to narrate, describe, or record, and being a photographic medium with sound it is admirably fitted for this purpose. Enacted discussion so far has tended to be an innovation of the twentieth-century theatre, though elements of it are obvious even in the Greek drama, in Sheridan's *The Critic* and in the work of Ibsen and Shaw. Dramatized discussion has in recent times involved the audience itself in such dramatic experiments as those of the British Army Bureau of Current Affairs Play

Unit and in dramas like *Exercise Bowler*, which derived from a similar elastic technique where people may arrive from anywhere (stage or auditorium) to air their views about the social problems of the moment. But can the film do this? Is it a medium for argument?

Paul Rotha claims that it is. During and since the War he has produced a number of films which have broken new ground in documentary technique, in particular *World of Plenty* (1943), *Land of Promise* (1945), and *The World is Rich* (1948). All of these films are about political and economic problems, the first and third international, the second domestic to Britain.

World of Plenty, sponsored by the Ministry of Information in the height of the War, achieved a remarkable reputation in Britain and was more widely shown, publicly and privately, than any documentary film except the most distinguished work of the Crown Film Unit (such as *Target for To-night* or *Western Approaches*). Its technical presentation caused as much discussion as its subject, which was the problems of world food production and distribution before and during the War, and the importance of proper international planning after the War to cope with the crisis which indeed followed it and which was foreshadowed in the film. *Land of Promise* deals with housing and raises issues of importance to many countries where slums have arisen through bad or selfish administration in the past, although the film concerns itself solely with the face of Britain at the end of the War. *The World is Rich* was a passionate appeal for international co-operation in the production and distribution of the world's food resources.

Every device is used in *Land of Promise* to make this 'film argument about our homes and houses' eloquent and unanswerable. Symbolic characters are used such as the grumbling enemy of progress, Know-all, played by Miles Malleson (who also helped with the scripting of the film) and the young soldier played by John Mills, who asks questions from the audience and becomes so absorbed in the discussion of the problems that he jumps up and joins the others on the screen, his shoulder coming up as a large shadow when he emerges from the sound-track (as it were) into the visual-track. Some elements in the film are voices only: there is the voice of History and the voice of *Hansard*. Real people appear in the film, such as Father John Groser, the priest of Stepney, who marched with the tenants of this slum area of London to demand a square deal for the ill-housed. The Isotype Institute, founded by the late Dr Otto Neurath, pro-vides animated diagrams to illustrate the innumerable statis-tics in the film, statistics of income, of house building, of rents, of health and mortality in relation to conditions of housing. A slum housewife appears as an enacted character who bemoans her lot but never dreams of voting because she thinks all politicians are only interested in furthering their private interests. In so far as photography with sound can be used to argue, *Land of Promise* fulfils this aim.

The film is divided into three parts, 'Homes as They Were', 'Homes as They Are', and 'Homes as They Might Be'. The first shows how the 4,000,000 houses built in Britain between 1919 and 1939 were for the most part too expensive to rent for the people who most needed them, the slum-dwellers of urban Britain and the condemned-cottage dwel-lers of rural Britain. In spite of vast slum-clearance schemes, there were in 1939 still 1,300,000 condemned houses in the country: the destruction caused by bombing, destroying good and bad property alike, aggravated the problem. The second part shows how the great evacuation scheme, when the slum children were sent at the beginning of the War to the countryside, took the lid off a social problem which most comfortably-housed people had never cared to face.

The War forced Britain to plan as never before, with the result that she revolutionized her economy and performed a miracle of production, actually improving the health of her people in the process. Housing remained an acute problem, the solution of which had to be postponed until the peace brought reconstruction to the top of the priority list. The aim of the third part of *Land of Promise* is the awakening of the national conscience. We must insist on a planned economy so that the housing problem is solved, and the hideous dwellings revealed as never before on the screen in the first section of the film are replaced by housing fit for a twentieth-century society. In spite of an overloading of statistics, this film remains one of the most courageous documentaries yet made in Britain.

BRIEF ENCOUNTER, 1945

Producers: Anthony Havelock-Allan and Ronald Neame.
Production: Cineguild. Direction: David Lean.
Script: Noel Coward. Photography: Robert Krasker.
With Celia Johnson and Trevor Howard.

Brief Encounter is one of those rare films for which one can never be sure to whom the real credit is due, one of those films one can offer to critics of the artistic integrity of the medium as an example of the unity achieved by the co-operation of many creative minds. That devoted care was given to this picture the result itself is evidence. I do not remember any more moving performance than that given by Celia Johnson. The theme and situation are perfect for so sensitive an actress, and these are the work of Noel Coward. The visual conception, the sympathetic eye that watches Miss Johnson, and relates her work to that of the other people, and to the environment of home, and street, and station which are so much part of her life, is the creative work of the director David Lean.

The theme and situation are universal. They belong to all human beings whether they have individually endured a similar love-tragedy or not. Laura Jesson is a kindly attractive woman with two children. She is married to a kindly, unimaginative husband and lives a contented, unawakened life. She visits the small town of Milford each Thursday, shops, goes to the pictures, and catches her evening train home from Milford Junction. She has a brief encounter in the station refreshment room with a doctor who removes some grit from her eye. He also visits Milford on Thursdays.

A chance tea together follows. Then lunch. Then the pictures. Their acquaintance grows into an intense and passionate love. He also is married and has children. But unlike her husband he is a man with a genuine belief in his vocation, and the vital appreciation of life and need for love which go with it, and the sight of him stirs her to her depths and turns each Thursday into a vortex of emotional anticipation. They realize the dangers and difficulties of their situation. They experience the shame of domestic evasion, and lies, and subterfuge. They decide to part.

The film begins with their parting, mercilessly ravaged by an unsuspecting garrulous woman who is one of Laura's acquaintances. We ourselves know little more than this intruder. At home again, stricken with emotional sickness, Laura tells her story in imagination to her husband, who sits trite and dull over his crossword puzzle. The story takes us back and so leads through to their parting again, with our full realization of its pain and tension. It is a brilliant piece of structure and directing. We see the same final touch of his hand on her shoulder with new eyes.

I do not remember a moment when Celia Johnson's performance falters in a part where emotional over-playing or false intonations would have turned the film from a study of life itself into another piece of cinema fiction. It is a uniquely beautiful portrait; our sympathy grows with knowledge, and Laura's beauty grows with our sympathy. The movement of the film and our relation to the character develop with the same tempo of understanding with which we all live and meet and love. It is this quality which makes the film inescapably human, and whilst we watch it we are with this other human being as with a friend.

Celia Johnson has a small pointed face with wide emotional eyes. She looks quite ordinary until it is time for her to look like what she feels. Trevor Howard plays his first considerable part in this film: he does not look ordinary, but he is not required to do so. He has strength, ease, and charm; his performance is quiet and assured. The poetry of this film, its revealing study of a man and a woman almost out of control, reveals a fine balance of their strength and weakness, now one taking the lead, now the other. It would be difficult to find a more profound study of distressed love in the history of the cinema.

Into all this complexity, Milford Junction enters as a poetic image. Its passing express trains have the rush and power of passion, its platforms and subways the loneliness of waiting lovers. Its local trains jerk and shunt with the faithful service of routine domesticity. The imagery of trains has seldom been so finely used as in that last terrifying shot when the express screams by with its windows flashing a staccato rhythm of white lights across Laura's agonized face. It is hysteria visually and aurally personified. It is the image of a moment of intended but uncommitted suicide.

Each detail of background is authentic, the streets, shops, café, and cinema. To touch the film with humour Stanley Holloway and Joyce Carey play out a grotesque love-affair in the station bar, and whilst this happens we can rest from the intense emotions of the main story in the comic casualness of their love-making. All the other characters, too, are exaggerations of reality. But this, strangely enough, does not matter, for they are all seen through the eyes of Laura, and in her suffering are as grotesquely different from herself as the close shots of Dolly Messiter's chattering lips are from Laura's pale face as she sits opposite her in the village train. The film always returns to Laura: it is her story told by herself and addressed without his knowledge to her husband. The main achievement is that of Celia Johnson, but supported throughout by the creative sympathy of her director, David Lean.

PAISA, 1946

Production: Organizzazione Films Internazionali.
Direction: Roberto Rossellini. Script: Roberto Rossellini,
Federico Fellini, Sergio Amidei, Marcel Pagliero.
Photography: Otello Martelli. Music: Renzo Rossellini.

Like all countries involved in the violent processes of liberation, Italy had to make her war films late in the day.
Rossellini started as soon as he was able on the production of
Rome, Open City, a good film but not uninfluenced by conventional melodrama. But it was in *Paisa* ('paisan' was the
American slang word for the Italians during the war) that
Rossellini showed himself capable of great artistry in film-
making. There is no melodrama here, only that kind of
observation which retains a completely objective calm as it
watches human joy, and suffering, friendliness, and hatred,
with a sympathy and understanding never marred by that
form of emotional weakness which leads to sentimentality,
and its train of ill-natured vices.

Paisa is made up of six very diverse episodes bound together by the unity of people, common and uncommon,
involved in the same distresses of war and its aftermath.
What matters is human nature, pure and simple, whether
Italian or foreign. The film is also bound by unity of artistic
treatment, a style both objective and sympathetic, calm yet
passion-loving. The six episodes are as follows: 1. Set in
Sicily, this episode shows how an Italian village girl avenged
an American G.I. member of a reconnaissance patrol killed
in a German ambush, but at the expense of her own life.
2. Naples after Liberation. A drunken American Negro
military policeman has his boots stolen by a wily street boy
left to exist on his wits. Later the American lets matters be
out of compassion when he sees the conditions in which these
orphaned children live. 3. Rome is liberated and in the happiness of the moment a young American soldier falls in love
with a pretty Italian girl. Six months later she is a whore
who picks him up drunk in the city streets. 4. Street-fighting
in Florence. An American girl somehow manages to get

herself across the city only to find her Italian partisan lover has been killed. 5. Three American army chaplains visit a monastery further north near Bologna in territory just liberated. 6. Fighting in the Northern marshlands of the Po, involving stranded RAF men, Americans, and Italian partisans: a tragic story of scattered, disorganized violence and death.

Rossellini was induced to make this film co-operatively by Rod Geiger, the G.I. who had introduced *Rome, Open City*, to America. Geiger returned to Italy with the film-stock and the American acting personnel, including Harriet White who plays the American girl in Florence, Gar Moore who plays the G.I. in Rome, and Bill Tubbs who is the Catholic Army Chaplain in the Monastery episode. Rossellini for the most part follows his usual method of picking his Italians as he finds them on location, only using professional actors and actresses for important parts here and there. The members of this mixed cast speak in their own language when they are ignorant of Italian or English, as the case may be.

All these episodes stress intimacies of one kind or another except the last, which is the broadest, most 'documentary' episode in its general treatment. The first episode, which does not possess the same quality as the others, has a long scene between the village girl and the G.I. in which he tries to talk to her, though she is dour, and evasive, and suspicious. The American Negro has a wonderful scene with the little street-boy who is trying to get him across the rubble of Naples to a quiet spot where he can rob him, which ends with the Negro singing the spiritual 'Nobody knows the trouble I've seen' and muttering 'Sh-eee-ps' when he hears the sirens in the harbour. He is full of drunken idealizations of home, but he says he does not want to go back. The scene between the G.I. and the prostitute has been compared both to Maupassant and Hemingway; however that may be, it has the touching intimacy of a camera intrusion into private experience. The urgent search of a girl for her lover through the barricades, and over the balconies and rooftops of Florence shows warfare and its indiscriminate destruction

ACTUALITY FILMS

1
Wartime
News-shot:
unposed actuality

2
Documentary;
studies from
real life.
Land of Promise
(Paul Rotha)

3
Documentary.
Canadian
Foresters in
Trees are a Crop
(Nat. Film Board
of Canada)

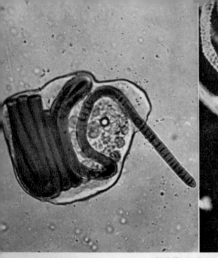

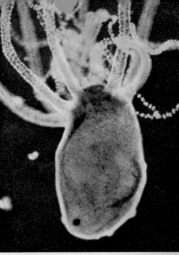

NATURE FILMS

4 Photomicrography by Jean Comandon. Amoeba absorbing algae

5 Photomicrography by Percy Smith. Hydra

6 *L'Hippocampe* (Jean Painlevé)

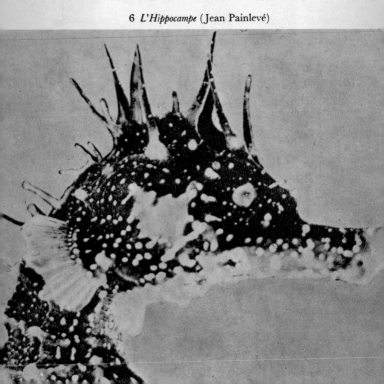

10 An African in *Dark Rapture*
(Armand Denis)

11 Old Australian Aborigine in
Back of Beyond (John Heyer)

12 A Turkmenian couple in *The Faraway Bride* (Ashchabad Studios)

13–14 The Cajun Boy in *Louisiana Story* (Robert Flaherty)

15
Early
development of
true film-acting.
Duse in *Cenere*
(1916)

16
Griffith develops
screen acting.
Lillian Gish in
Intolerance

17
Mary Pickford.
The first great
international
star

18
Greta Garbo in
Queen Christina.
Stardom at its
height

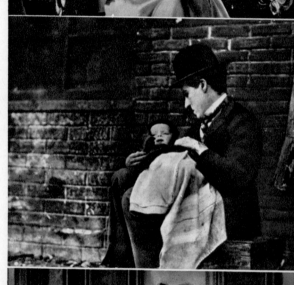

19
Charlie Chaplin
in *The Kid*.
Emergence of a
great individual
artist

20
Celia Johnson in
Brief Encounter.
The
self-effacing
portrayal of
character

THE HUMAN PORTRAIT

III: *The Spectacle of Crowds; the Grand Isolation of Great Territories*

21
Belshazzar's Palace in *Intolerance* filmed from a balloon

22
The massacre on the steps of Odessa in *The Battleship Potemkin*

23
The Pioneers' Wagon-team of the Western. *Red River* (Howard Hawks)

24
Zasu Pitts in
Greed (Stroheim)

25
Gibson Gowland
and Jean
Hersholt in
Greed

26
Non-professional
actors in fiction
film. Father
and Son in
Bicycle Thieves
(de Sica)

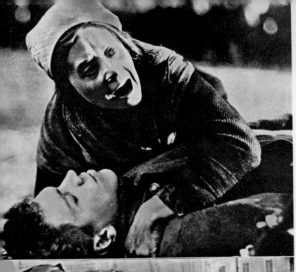

27-28
Mother and Son
(professional
actors) in *Mother*
(Pudovkin)

29
Socialist Realism
in the Soviet film.
Great Citizen
(Ermler, 1937)

30–32
Realistic study of
mining disaster.
Kameradschaft
(Pabst)

33–34
Surrealistic
imagery in a
realist setting.
Zéro de Conduite
(Vigo)

35
Compare use of
bombed sites in
London for
Hue and Cry
(Crichton)

36–37
The
non-professional
actor in wartime
documentary
drama.
Fires were Started
(Jennings)

38
The professional
actor in wartime
documentary
drama
Nine Men
(Watt)

39 Realistic reconstruction of war in Italy. Last episode in *Paisa* (Rossellini)

40 Contrast poetic use of similar landscape by Emmer in his documentary *Le Isole della Laguna*

41–42
Italian
neo-realism;
natural,
uncontrived
drama
Umberto D
(de Sica)

43
American
post-war
realism;
drama acted
in real-life
settings.
The Naked City
(Jules Dassin)

V: *The Theatrical Film*

44–45
A satiric portrait of the French bourgeoisie. *The Italian Straw Hat* (Clair)

46
Satiric attack on contemporary society. *Monsieur Verdoux* (Chaplin)

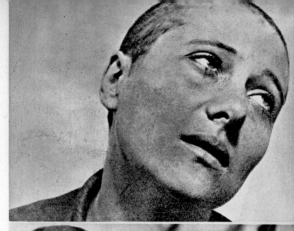

47–49
Theatrical
setting and
grouping
emphasize
Falconetti's
study of
suffering in
*La Passion de
Jeanne d'Arc*
(Dreyer)

50–52
Human drama
emphasized by
atmospheric
studio sets in
The Informer
(Ford)

56-58
The atmospheric setting of Vienna emphasized the human drama in *The Third Man* (Reed)

59–60 Both realism and expressionism used for dramatic emphasis in *Citizen Kane* (Welles)

THE
HUMAN
PAGEANT;
FANTASY
AND
DANCE

The Pictorial Film

61
Characters
become part of
the setting in
Siegfried (Lang)

62
Romantic and
heroic
characterization
in De Mille's
spectacle films.
The Crusades

63
The spectacular
presentation of
Shakespeare.
Hamlet (Olivier)

64–65
History as an
ideological
pageant.
Ivan the Terrible,
Part I.
(Eisenstein)

66–67
The dramatic
fantasy.
*La Belle et la
Bête* (Cocteau)

68
Japanese
traditional
dramatic style
in film.
Rashomon
(Kuwosawa)

69–71
Choreographic
fantasy in the
American
musical.
On the Town
(Kelly and
Donen)

**THE
ANIMATED
FILM**

*The Artist
designs a moving
Image*

72
American
animation in the
style of the
strip cartoon.
Squatter's Rights
(Disney)

73
Czech puppetry
in *Song of the
Prairie* (Trnka)

74
The French
style. *La
Bergère et le
Ramoneur*
(André Sarrut)

75
American
animation in
the non-realistic
graphic style.
*Gerald McBoing-
Boing's Symphony*
(U.P.A.)

76
Simplified
realism in
ritish animation
Animal Farm
(Halas-
Batchelor)

**THE
THIRD
DIMENSION**

77
A further step
towards realism.
(Diagram by
courtesy of
Raymond
Spottiswoode
and Brian
Borthwick)

78 CINEMA The most sensational form of widescreen image, using triple projector system invented by Fred Waller. (From *This is Cinerama*, Roller Coaster Sequence; by courtesy of Rockaways' Playland Amusement Park, New York)

THE WIDESCREEN FILM

79. Widescreen projection in triptych form first developed by Gance in *Napoléon* (1927)

80. Chrétien's anamorphic lens compresses the image, and is the basis of Cinemascope. *The Robe* (20th Century Fox)

THE FILM SEQUENCE: OLIVER TWIST

81 John Bryan's advance sketches for the last twelve shots of first sequence of *Oliver Twist*

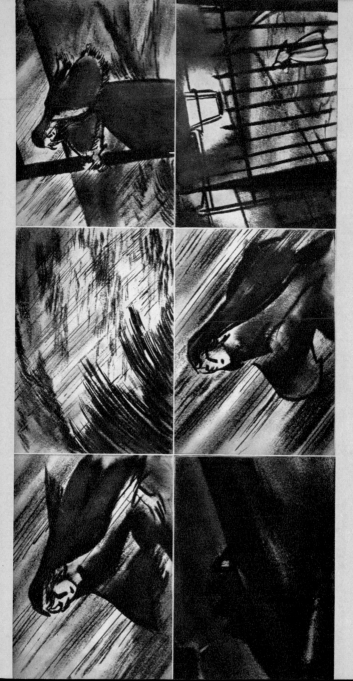

82 SET DESIGN: OLIVER TWIST John Bryan's design for a London street scene

of tender human relationships. Most delicate of all is the Monastery episode, where men divided by language, race, and creed but united by their belief in God, try to establish a relationship with each other based on the redemption of the human soul. The sincerity and simplicity of the monks endeavouring to understand why a Catholic Chaplain could feel a spiritual brotherhood with a Protestant and a Jew is somehow one of the most moving elements in the film, especially when they decide to sacrifice the little feast brought them by the Americans in a pious demonstration to save the two souls they regard as lost.

In the last episode the body of an Italian floats down the river propped up in a lifebelt and bearing the label, 'Partisano'. Two guerillas eventually pull it into the bank, and it is carried through reeds, grass, and water to burial. The rest of the action is the curious sniping warfare of such desolate open country, and the sudden comradeship of half-lost Allied soldiers and isolated partisans when they meet and join forces. There is little said and a great deal seen and done. A baby cries in a lonely house beside the dead bodies of its kinsfolk.

Eventually the Germans round up the little force of stragglers and kill them. Their death ends the film.

The collective result of these fragments of human experience during the general process of Italy's liberation, sharpened as they are by Rossellini's compassionate but ruthlessly objective observation, is to establish those values of universality which are the hallmark of true poetic feeling. Here is humanity revealed by human beings, the tragic fates seen through individual human tragedies. *Paisa* stirs the rarer emotions raised by fine imaginative film-making.

LA BELLE ET LA BÊTE, 1946

Production: André Paulvé. Direction and Script: Jean Cocteau.
Photography: Alekan. Costumes: Christian Bérard.
Décor: René Moulaert and Carré. Music: Georges Auric.
With Jean Marais, Josette Day, and Marcel André.

The two main films of Cocteau, *Orphée* and *La Belle et la Bête*, are both fantasies. The essence of legend and fairy-story is the presentation of the human struggle between good and evil, between forces contending for and against the humane values of truth, goodness, and beauty. If the humane values are destroyed, as in Cocteau's earlier film *L'Éternel Retour*, then at least the struggle should be a hard one. For legends and fairy-tales are explanations man makes for his own tribulations, or for his relation with forces he does not properly understand. If he instinctively feels them to be evil, he struggles against them. This struggle is the action of most legendary stories.

La Belle et la Bête is the story of such a struggle. It is the story of a victorious test of a girl's faith and love assailed by the powerful adverse forces of selfishness, pride, fear, weakness, diffidence, poverty, and ugliness. Belle's father is weak in both his public and domestic life; Belle's sisters are selfish and vain; her brother is diffident and lazy. When poverty threatens them the family grows chaotic and quarrelsome. Belle, alone in her devotion for her father and service to her kinsfolk, represents true faith and love. The severest test comes in the sacrifice of herself in her father's place to Beast, when the plucking of the symbolic rose from Beast's estate puts them in his power. Beast and his horrific castle are symbols of terror, but Belle by her sacrifice of herself finds all Beast's power and wealth placed in her hands. She has conquered fear. Her final test is whether her humanity is deep enough to offer love to Beast himself. This test she nearly fails, for ugliness in such a repellent and unnatural form is what she is least able to love. It is only when Beast gives her powers over his very life in a sublime gesture of faith, represented by the symbolic key to the Pavilion of his treasures, that she finally consents to marry him after nearly destroying him. Then all his ugliness and bestiality are cast aside, and his true humanity in princely form rewards her with the gift of happiness and love. That is the legendary theme behind the film.

The treatment given to this theme is a mixture of simplified realism for all scenes connected with Belle's home and its locality, and grotesque artificiality for scenes connected with Beast and his castle. The two selfish daughters are as simplified as Cinderella's sisters, and they are mocked on the sound-track by the cackling of hens and by their constant appearance in their vain high-crowned hats. Nevertheless, the domestic scenes and costumes are pictorially beautiful. The Castle is a haunted, barren place of windy corridors and live statuary. When the Father, lost in the storm, first enters the magic domain of Beast, his magnified shadow falls on the castle doors and they open without a person to touch them. He finds a black corridor lit by candles which burst spontaneously into flame and are held by the naked, impersonal arms of unseen men. The first sound after this strange encounter is the striking of a clock on the mantelpiece over a great fire, in front of which stands a small table set for two. As the Father sits down, a choir of voices sings. The stone faces inset on either side of the fireplace are alive, their eyes turning to watch his movements. Hands whose forearms grow out of the table pour out the wine. The music and voices blend in a curious song. The father falls asleep. A beast noise wakes him; the candles are out and the fire is dead. A raven cries, and the Father rushes out down the branch-strewn steps of the castle into the wild garden, past a line of stone dogs. There he plucks the Rose asked for by Belle, and Beast appears to him through parted bushes. This sequence is typical of the macabre treatment of the film at its best. But the imagination of Cocteau sometimes fails; the magic powers of the cinema become merely silly when Belle later transports herself in quickly cut flashes backwards and forwards from her home to the Castle, scrambling in and out of the glove which gives her power over space and time, or again at the end of the film when she and her Prince fly aloft through the clouds to some Paradise in shots little better than the early experiments of Méliès. Magical displays of this kind must invite, not thwart, belief.

The treatment of the leading characters is interesting. Belle represents female beauty and love, but she is presented without any touch of sexuality. Beast has the slim figure of a man, broadened by a costume with wide shoulderpieces and heightened by twin trains that fall from each shoulder to the ground. He has the great head of a bear-like animal. Yet his expression is majestic and kindly rather than terrible; his voice is gruffened, but humane. Apart from the unnatural mixture of man and beast, he is never horrific, even when at night he remorsefully paces the corridors of his castle, his gloved hands smoking after the killing of prey. It is difficult to tell whether this was compromise or intention. To Belle he is a gentle, almost abject creature. To have given him an ape-like head would have been to make him both repellent and terrible. But Cocteau's approach to this film seems to be that of the intellectual, satisfied by symbols rather than by heart-searching terrors. There is an impersonality, a contemplative element in the whole conduct of this artificial but coldly beautiful film. This robs it of either passion or conviction, pity or terror. It is rather a beautiful exercise in the macabre, depending very much on the *décor* and Christian Bérard's costumes for its final pictorial effectiveness.

Nevertheless, I would describe the film as successful within its strict limits. It is not unmoving, because of the constant beauty of its design and its ability to create real atmosphere in its key moments. But there is a curious absence of human emotion in it, of any final sense of bitter struggle between the good and evil its theme symbolizes. It is as if its maker was more interested in the technique of his fantasy than he was in its meaning.

MONSIEUR VERDOUX, 1947

Production, Direction and Script: Charles Chaplin.
Assistant Direction: Robert Florey and Wheeler Dryden.
Photography: Roland Totheroh. Design: John Beckman.
With Charles Chaplin, Martha Raye, Isobel Elsom,
Marilyn Nash, and Robert Lewis.

In the complex art and technique of the film, Chaplin is actor, writer, chief director, and musical composer of his work, which means that his films of necessity must take a long while to germinate and produce. But Chaplin's films do not bear the signs of years of deliberation, as, for example, do the films of Eisenstein, each shot and each sequence of which form a complex of deliberately calculated effects. If Chaplin is to be granted the title of genius, then it is more on account of his universal humanity, the least sophisticated aspect of his nature.

Genius, in the end, is an unusually deep-rooted concern for being human, combined with an overwhelming need to express that concern. Chaplin's wistful clown, using his superb pantomimic skill to indicate in passing a thousand sly comments on human weakness, is a sentimental symbolism of a simple, kindly man living in an involved and wicked world. I do not think Chaplin's philosophy is complicated. It is rather so deeply-felt that it has at times become almost messianic. He hates profoundly all cruelty, vice, misery, and the destructive orgies of warfare. After the pathos of his clown in the face of human greed (*The Gold Rush*), of loneliness amid gaiety (*The Circus*), and of poverty (*City Lights*), Chaplin in the later stage of his work turned his attention to what he conceived to be the greatest evils of out time, soulless industrialization (*Modern Times*), fascism (*The Great Dictator*), and callousness towards human life and security (*Monsieur Verdoux*).

Chaplin's ideal is always symbolically simple, the little flowered cottage which is man's universal dream of home, the pretty, loving wife, and the kindliness of domesticity. These things alone can foster in humanity its finest qualities.

165

Deny mankind these things, and the acid enters his soul. He becomes cruel, squalid, defeatist, violent. He becomes Monsieur Verdoux, because society has brought him to so low a pass in order that he may be able to survive at all. No film made by Chaplin in his last twenty years has been without this serious sentiment, to which his clowning is the bitter comment of the professional jester, Lear's shadow. These films are laments for the human soul lost in the devil's politics of our time.

Monsieur Verdoux is the most bitterly satiric of Chaplin's films. Dean Swift in the bitterness of his view of human kind turned to the simplicity of the kingdom of the horses for a purge to sweeten his imagination. Swift took his satire to the very boundaries of ugliness: his art overbalanced into the pit of hatred. Chaplin in *Monsieur Verdoux* shows a keener edge to his satire than in any previous film. There is almost no pathos except in the revealing relationship between Verdoux and the lost girl whom he cannot bring himself to kill because she is at once too like himself and too unlike the human beings with whom he is at war. It is this satire, this comedy of murders as Chaplin calls it, which makes the action of the film as symbolic of Chaplin's state of mind as *Gulliver's Travels* was of Swift's. If you take the action of the film at its face value it is merely puzzling, a perverse story which seems to suggest that murder is funny, provided the women destroyed are eccentric types. The film has been unpopular with reviewers (I will not say with critics), and it has undoubtedly confused the public who know Chaplin only as a rather old-fashioned and sentimental funny-man who used, if they are old enough, to make them laugh in their youth by the dexterity of his clowning. Why, they say, does he now ask us to laugh at murder? Why, they ask, does he come out of character, as it were, and pose awkward questions *at* the audience (in the closing speech of *The Great Dictator*) or make what appear to be deeply-felt remarks about the world before his execution at the end of *Monsieur Verdoux*? This is wrong, they assume, in a comedian.

The answer to these questions is not so much that Chaplin

himself has changed, as that the desperateness of these times has fortified him to make his art an outspoken challenge to the aggressiveness of humanity. It is no longer a secret that Chaplin himself, British-born, became an isolated figure in America, unpopular as a person and persecuted within certain limits. His refusal to participate in any war-work accentuated the opposition to him. It is the old story; the artist is acknowledged but his point of view disliked. Provided he will just entertain, well and good, but his social criticism is unwelcome and invites such reprisals and ostracism as can conveniently be brought to bear. He has now left the States for ever.

Monsieur Verdoux reflects all this. Verdoux is at war with society. He is an ordinary man, simple in his tastes, married to a crippled wife to whom he is devoted and living in an idealized little country cottage. His mysterious 'business' in the city does not rouse his wife's curiosity: he is a most respectable citizen, reproving his son for cruelty in some trifling offence. This is his true life, the life open to him only so long as his security as a bank-clerk remained. But the misfortunes of our ill-organized and acquisitive society rob him of that security, throw him permanently out of work, and force him to live on the black market of his wits. He 'marries' a series of women all of whom are distasteful to him, and who pass their time living parasitic lives of the kind which brought him face to face with his own insecurity as a wage-earner. He murders them in turn and takes the spoils, returning always to support his little family in the country.

In his criminal conduct he is always disciplined, meticulous, and practical. He is at war, as much a craftsman as a general, killing with as little compunction and taking the resulting booty to support life as he thinks it should be ordered. Here the satire of the central theme is lightened into comedy, and the gay tricks of Chaplin's clowning, always more perfect in the rhythm of their timing than anything of the kind yet known upon the screen, take over. But not for long. The incinerator smokes at the bottom of the garden, or the moon shines while Chaplin stands poised with delicate hands outstretched to kill, his pantomime on the verge of becoming a macabre ballet.

Verdoux is therefore the natural man dehumanized by the unnatural cruelties which are slowly strangling the civilized world. He bears the comic exaggeration of the satiric form, like Swift's characters or those of Molière. Two women soften his hard attitude to the world – his wife and the lost girl played by Marilyn Nash. Although the girl is destitute she retains an unquestioning belief in the goodness of human nature. Chaplin shows that Verdoux cannot resist the appeal of such a faith when she so openly expects him to share it. It is notable that while Verdoux is still in doubt whether he will use the girl as a human test for the strength of his poisoned wine, there is only conversation and the tension of action in silence; when the appeal to his kindliness has succeeded and the threat to her is removed, then music is introduced. The harmony of nature is restored, the balance of humanity achieved.

Chaplin could have redeemed Verdoux from this point had he so wished, and had the Hays Code allowed him to do so. But Chaplin did not choose to redeem him. By a fortuitous blow Verdoux loses his family in some outburst of social violence which Chaplin does not trouble to explain but which is due to the economic and political crises of the thirties. He is left to shift for himself, alone and more deeply embittered than ever. When he meets the lost girl once more he finds she is the kept woman of a rich manufacturer of munitions. Beauty and faith have been sold to the destroyer. Verdoux is aged and poverty-stricken: he sees no reason for prolonging life or humanity. Her faith, however, is not yet destroyed. 'Life is beyond reason,' she tells him, 'that's why we must go on.' But Verdoux allows himself to be arrested.

The last section brings to a head the philosophy of the film. No stress is laid on the process of the trial except Verdoux's last remark after his death-sentence: 'I shall see you all very soon.' Society is merely destroying him just in advance of destroying itself. In his prison cell he is interviewed by the press; now that he is notorious space in the newspapers is at his disposal. He tells the reporter that 'crime does not pay in a small way', that robbery and murder are the natural expression of 'these criminal times'. 'That's business,' he says. War is the outcome of it all. 'One murder makes a villain, millions a hero.'

To the priest who comes to escort him to the place of execution he declares, 'I am at peace with God, my conflict is with man.' When the priest prays that God have mercy on his soul, he replies lightly, 'Why not; after all it belongs to him.' He hesitates over a glass of rum and decides to have it, as he has never tasted rum before. There is something superb about this moment before death, elemental like the loosening of Lear's button. It unites the soul with the body for the last time. Then with the curious ritual which attends all scenes of death, he goes out, a small man with sloping, aged shoulders walking into the prison courtyard to heavy music. This time there is no long road to the horizon, no pretty girl for companion, no pathetic fatalism. It is a stark march to death.

In most criticism of *Monsieur Verdoux* this essential philosophy of the film has been overlooked or avoided. Reviewers have said the film is unequal, that it is not very funny, that its comedy is spoilt by the intrusion of Chaplin's personal point of view, or that it is a film of many brilliant and inimitable moments, mostly moments of superb pantomime with such skilful players as Martha Raye. The general impression is that what respect has been accorded to *Monsieur Verdoux* is a respect born of the traditional praise of Chaplin the comedian. No film which attempts so much double meaning could probably escape some faults; the comic pantomime at times seems pushed to the point of irrelevance, like the overbalanced by-play of a Lenten holiday. There are episodes such as the long action of Verdoux's avoidance of one wife who turns up at the reception held before his marriage to another, where the delicate touch of Clair would have been more appropriate. That almost all the aphorisms are kept for the end of the film is appropriate to the scene in the death cell, but robs the last sequences of some emotion; Verdoux becomes one with his creator. But these are small faults compared with the courageous achievement of the work as a whole, which is the most serious of all Chaplin's films. It points ahead to an even more important film should Chaplin care to develop and perfect his messianic style in another profoundly-felt social satire.

LOUISIANA STORY, 1948

Production and Direction: Robert Flaherty. Story: Frances and Robert Flaherty. Associate Producers: Richard Leacock and Helen van Dongen. Photography: Richard Leacock. Editing: Helen van Dongen. Music: Virgil Thomson.

Since the days of *Nanook of the North* and *Moana* various national schools of documentary cinema have developed with their policies of public service and social interpretation. Flaherty remained an interpreter of humanity rather than of social phenomena. Some critics and documentary film-makers criticized him for concentrating his superb imaginative art on people so remote from the main activities and problems of the world as to be, they say, of little consequence. This seems to me to be unfair both to Flaherty and his subjects. When an artist forces himself to be different from what he is by temperament the results may be disastrous. Flaherty was an explorer among simple humanity, a kind of poetic anthropologist, a man whose very nature required him to make films by living happily among people whose lives are governed by the basic traditions of an isolated existence in natural surroundings of ice, sea, rock, or swamp. Since Flaherty and his work are unique in the sphere of documentary, the films he made with such care should be judged primarily within their own scheme of values.

Louisiana Story is, then, a study in the Flaherty tradition, its significance arising out of his observation of a shy boy whose heart is absorbed in the activities of fishing and hunting down the sunlit waterways and through the creepered woods of the Louisiana bayous. Suddenly he is brought face to face with the outer world of industry when an oil-boring operation is carried out in his neighbourhood. It is typical of Flaherty that he keeps rigidly to the boy's-eye view of this operation. There is no question of explaining the social significance of oil in the economy of this waste land or of the change in the fortunes of the Latour family with whom the contract to carry out the operations is signed. They simply make friends of the engineers who arrive with a floating derrick, which looks like a vast electric power pylon towering over the water.

The boy is a romantic child; he has names which link him to the adventurers and conquerors of the past, Alexander Napoleon Ulysses Latour. He has skill and cunning in his own world, but is very shy in the new world of the engineers. His father is friendly but old and slow of speech, with his mixture of French and English. The oil is tapped after a terrible battle with an escape of gas and steam which silts the area with slippery mud and leads to a period of despondency in which both the Latour family and the engineers share. Then the boy lets his superstition overcome his fear, and secretly empties down the empty shaft the little bag of salt that he always carried with him for luck, and then spits after it for good measure. When the oil is actually tapped he feels his belief is justified. The story ends in happiness. The rest is hunting and fishing, and the engineers depart leaving behind a sealed pump which they call a Christmas tree. The Latours get a few simple domestic utensils, and the boy a new gun. That is all.

The film somehow has the atmosphere of a Chehov short story. Its shape lies in its continuity of atmosphere. It certainly has a beginning and an end in the coming and going of the engineers, but these are incidents and not ingredients of the true story. This story is the boy himself and the Petit Anse bayou country where he lives. The opening of the film is just photographic magic, with the sun glistening on a huge umbrella-leafed plant looking like gossamer floating above the rain-speckled water. An alligator appears. We see the boy himself, standing in his little boat and drifting carefully down the over-hung waterway with the sun flashing through the trailing creepers and making tall shafts of light in the trees. The huge umbrella-shaped leaves stand out of the water; bubbles rise up, perhaps from the green-haired mermaids who the boy believes live below the water; an eel traces its shape in liquid on the surface, all to the rich music of Virgil Thomson's score based on American folk melodies. The whole sequence is full of visual emotion underlined by music. The boy levels his gun, but his shot is superseded by a holocaust of sound and the sweep of wheeling birds; a machine like a great animal is levelling down the tall grasses and reeds. The boy pushes off in his boat for home. Here his father is telling the oil prospecting agent the story of an alligator-hunt; his speech is slow, but continuous and self-qualifying with a natural and unscripted effect. When the boy returns there is a trim little motor launch by the bank; silence follows the music. He enters home awestruck. This long introductory sequence gives us every relevant quality in the boy's character and surroundings; there only remains to show his reactions to the huge oil-boring machine and the men who work it. The motor launch comes and goes, its wash rocking and even swamping his little boat. The huge derrick is towed slowly and carefully to the place where a solitary white stick marks the spot in the water where the boring is to begin. The new world of pulsing engines arrives, while the boy watches shyly from his boat and turns away with his pet racoon (who is the comedian of the picture) to hunt an alligator single-handed. This battle gives Flaherty one of his great chances for a natural hunting sequence, which is wonderfully handled, even though the wily alligator is lost in the duel.

As far as action is concerned, the climax of the film is not the tapping of the oil so much as the explosion which follows the first stage of the boring process. The huge machine, which propels great lengths of piping into the earth after each stage of boring is completed, is not explained by anyone. Like the boy we just watch it fascinated and deafened by the crashing and clanking sounds it produces with a ringing whirl of twisting chains. The editing here by Helen van Dongen is superb. Then, after all this, the well blows off its gas and steam like a great tumult of mire, filling the sky with darkness.

It is easy to say what this film is not, less easy to say what it is. The finest character is the father. The boy himself, though he is the pivot of the film since its general treatment is conducted from his point of view, is shy to the point of being rather colourless, compared, for example, to young Moana or the fisherman's son on Aran. The film structurally is somewhat thin, a simple linking together of episodes. Yet it stands or falls on its creation of an atmosphere of place and people. Here I think it succeeds, supported by fine photography, fine editing, and a fine musical score by Virgil Thomson, who wrote the music for *The Plow that broke the Plains* and *The River*. Flaherty never lost his feeling for the job during nearly thirty years of film-making.

ON THE TOWN, 1949

Production: M.G.M. Producer: Arthur Freed.
Direction: Gene Kelly and Stanley Donen. Script: Adolph Green and Betty Comden. Photography: Harold Rossen. Editor: Ralph E. Winters. Art Directors: Cedric Gibbons and Jack Martin Smith. Music: Leonard Bernstein. With Gene Kelly, Frank Sinatra, Betty Garrett, Ann Miller, Jules Munshin, Vera-Ellen.

Many American musicals are glorified stage-shows, quickened in tempo by the resources of editing and the possibilities of spectacular presentation available in the studios. But ever since Fred Astaire and Ginger Rogers first appeared in *Top Hat* (1935), the film musical has gradually taken on a shape of its own which has to some extent drawn away from the theatre and made it, at its best, a special kind of art belonging exclusively to the cinema. The Broadway successes are still turned into films, sometimes most engagingly as, for example, in the case of *Call Me Madam*. But the most interesting form of American musical has been the line of succession from *Top Hat* to *On the Town* (which was adapted from a stage production on Broadway), *An American in Paris*, and *The Band Wagon*. The chief names connected with these musicals have been Arthur Freed, Vincente Minnelli, Stanley Donen (a dance director), and Gene Kelly, with Irving Berlin, George Gershwin, Nacio Herb Brown, and Leonard Bernstein as the composers. *On the Town* has been the most 'advanced' musical to date, as well as the most indigenously American example of this very American form of art.

Technically, the Hollywood musical combines American forms of ballet (ranging from delicate and graceful mime to ballroom dancing, tap-dancing, and sheer acrobatics) with contemporary comic and romantic opera. To these it adds the full resources of décor in colour, which has come to be used with restraint and subtlety by designers like Cedric Gibbons, who was in charge of the décor for *On the Town*, *An American in Paris*, and *The Band Wagon*.

But the essence of the American musical is the spirit it evokes – the mystique of the American way of life. The best musicals have the vitality of a nation which has no inhibitions when it comes to singing about the heartaches and happiness of contemporary life, or laughing at its own absurdities or glamourizing the sheer love of sex and material success. It is this vitality and rich sense of contemporary showmanship which make the musicals unique and, indeed, inimitable outside the States. The musicals are to America to-day what the Gilbert and Sullivan operas were to Victorian England, and this comparison is more than a superficial one in a number of respects.

On the Town is the most advanced American musical to date. The story is simple enough: three sailors, whose ship has docked in Manhattan, arrive 'on the town' at dawn to discover for the first time the strange city of New York. They spend their twenty-four hours' leave with three pretty girls, and return to their ship at dawn the next day, with no future domestic entanglements as far as one can see (which has its point in a musical!). The form this story takes ranges from presentation in real New York locations during the sailors' sight-seeing tour to extremes of choreographic colour and design which have no relation to actuality at all. Only a public well-educated in the imaginative versatility of the film could take these admirable transitions in its stride. In the manner of Gilbert and Sullivan, short sections of witty dialogue intersperse the featured 'number' and dance-routines, which range from simple lyric duets to the most elaborate combinations of dance, song, and orchestration. There is also considerable use of recitative. Although there are one or two rather weak 'numbers' in the commercial style (like 'You're awful – awful good to look at'), the film aims at establishing orchestral colour rather than would-be popular tunes, and it is unique in its manner of combining the realism of dancing in the New York streets (and in studio sets made to match) with sets as colorfully artificial as those for stage ballet.

There are plenty of good-humoured satiric touches; one of the girls is Miss Turnstiles-for-June on the New York Subway, and there is fun at the expense of the American love for gaining fame by chance. There are odd, quick moments of satire, like the little girl who passes Gene Kelly in the Symphonic Hall and says 'But I don't want to be like Margaret O'Brien'. The nasal chorines of the American night clubs are nicely done to a turn when the sailors and their girls go on a round of the cabarets. But the beauty of the film lies in the charm and high spirits of the three couples, which reach their climax in the best of the song-and-dance routines.

A lovely recitative launches the film after the camera has played over the Manhattan skyline, and shown us the sailors' ship in dock. A sleepy cranedriver arrives for work singing that he feels he is still in bed where everything is peaceful 'asleep in your lady's arms'. A slowly fading repeat of this is followed immediately by a blast from the ship's siren and the rush of the sailors on shore leave. A contingent of three dash up to the camera – the heroes of the film – and burst into the theme song 'New York, New York – it's a wonderful town!' The three work as a trio, marching, leaping, galvanizing into action as they pass through a city montage which culminates in a 360-degree turn of the camera as it follows their movements sight-seeing on the roof of the R.C.A. Building. The finale of the sequence is a highly disciplined routine in front of the fountains in the basin of the Rockefeller Plaza.

Another dance with a similar vitality and magnificent editing technique is the cine-ballet idealizing Miss Turnstiles – who is seen in a quick succession of actions played against a plain yellow-coloured background. She flashes on and off in an appropriate series of costumes and with the barest number of properties to support her in every role she assumes, from the moment she is picked from a line of lovely straphanging subway girls to the culmination of her prowess in sport, when she knocks a pile of he-men cold with her fists. The 'Prehistoric Man' song in the Museum, where one of the girls has taken refuge to study anthropology so that she may avoid the inevitable attractions of contemporary man, includes a fantastically elaborate montage of primitive costumes and musical instruments. There is also an example of the long, swinging march by the six dancers in unison, which is so characteristic of this film and of the choreographic technique of many American musicals – simple enough, but so perfect rhythmically as to be a delight to both eye and ear. Forty or fifty camera set-ups are devoured by the editor in a few vital moments on the screen. In contrast to this terrific speed of cutting is a single, long restful shot half-way through the film covering the song (not a good one musically) 'You're awful – awful good to look at'. The vitality returns soon afterwards with the dance in leap-frog style (with camera movement interplaying) in which the trio of men and the trio of girls begin the song 'We're going on the Town' on the top of a skyscraper and end by leap-frogging on to the side-walk of the street below, after entering and leaving the elevator. The recapitulation ballet, traditional in this kind of film towards the end of the picture, features Gene Kelly and Vera-Ellen (Miss Turnstiles), the girl he has lost in the Cinderella-like turn of the plot at that stage of the action. It is as artificial as a stage-ballet, with the dancers picked out by coloured spotlights and performing against a cut-out silhouette of the Manhattan skyline. The film comes full circle at the close, twenty-four hours later, with the sleepy cranedriver going on duty once more, and, as the three girls wave good-bye to their tired boy-friends, a fresh batch of men on shore leave rush off the boat and leap into the theme song 'New York, New York, it's a wonderful town!'

I do not know of any musical which pays higher dividends to anyone who sets out to enjoy it in detail. It bears seeing and re-seeing for its speed, its subtlety, and its beautiful design, and for that particular kind of captivating American charm which it possesses in almost every sequence.

THE THIRD MAN, 1949

Production: London Films. Production and Direction: Carol Reed.
Script: Graham Greene. Photography: Robert Krasker.
Zither Music: Anton Karas. Design: Vincent Korda,
John Hawkesworth, Joseph Bato. With Joseph Cotten,
Trevor Howard, Orson Welles, Alida Valli, Bernard Lee,
Paul Hoerbiger, Ernst Deutsch, Siegfried Breuer, Erich Ponto,
Wilfred Hyde-White.

With *Bank Holiday* (1938) and *The Stars Look Down* (1939), Carol Reed gained his maturity as a film-maker. He began his career in the theatre, and for a considerable period worked with Edgar Wallace. In the theatre he learned, as everyone must, how the actor controls the responses of an audience by himself responding to them. He learned from Edgar Wallace how to use the resources of the stage to build up dramatic effects on the audience. When he went over to films he knew that two things mattered most to a director – to get the maximum dramatic effect out of his actors and to use the technical resources of the film to help achieve this. He has always needed first-class scripts. In those films where he has had particularly good scripts – like *The Way Ahead* (scripted by Eric Ambler), *Odd Man Out* (scripted by F. L. Green and R. C. Sherriff), *The Fallen Idol*, and *The Third Man* (both scripted by Graham Greene), he has proved that he belongs to the first rank of screen directors. Like David Lean, he does not claim to be more than a skilled interpreter of a script. Neither appears to desire to become a screenwriter, originating his own subjects. Like men who have a supreme talent for producing plays on the stage but are not themselves dramatists, neither Carol Reed nor David Lean have gone further than to adapt a subject for the screen, and even in this case they prefer to have the assistance of a screenwriter. They know that the genius of their imagination works in the field of interpretation, not original creation.

Graham Greene went to Vienna to write the story for *The Third Man*, and this was subsequently published after the film had been released. The story is a good one, but it is, in fact, little more than the action-treatment for the main story behind the film, and in the process of film-making considerable changes and additions were made to the story before the film itself was evolved. A great deal was shot on location in Vienna, which Carol Reed used as a city 'possessed' by that particular atmosphere of post-war decay necessary for the dramatic background to the film. In the night sequences the beautiful wet streets and shadowed façades shine seductively. The dramatic conflict in *The Third Man* is between the boyish innocence of Martins, the visiting American writer of simple adventure stories, and the subtle corruption of a post-war European city, which sucks him into its intrigues and duplicities. The city becomes a monster of evil against which he can only pit his innocent desire to put things right before going back to the States. His mild attempt at a love affair with Anna, the Austrian actress, fails because she is still obsessed by the memories of her affair with Harry Lime, Martins' former friend at whose request he originally came to Vienna, only to find his friend has supposedly died by accident. In the corruption of this broken world only Calloway, the British Military Police Officer, seems able to keep his head, and to fight with weapons capable of uncovering such intrigue. Martins' idealism does not always take readily to these methods. Even Harry Lime himself, when he eventually enters the story in person, attempts to justify his own evil among the shadowy values of corruption.

Graham Greene's script provides the international cast in the film with dialogue which is beautifully ambiguous. The exactness of Calloway and the honest ordinariness of his Sergeant, Payne, offset the insinuating, mocking elusiveness of the Austrian characters. Orson Welles plays him in the same way, but insolently, boasting of evil as the journey in the great Wheel of the Prater seems to carry Martins and himself round the full circle of his terrible philosophy. Only the end of the film loses the universal subtlety of the rest – the chase through the sewers where Lime has his hiding-place and the nod of consent with which he acquiesces in his own execution at Martins' hands may have had some symbolic value for Graham Greene, but the film loses its atmosphere in the crudity of this violent action. Even the famous last shot, in which Anna finally rejects Martins as the betrayer of the man she loved, quite fails to recapture this atmosphere, even though the scene is held on the screen for a striking length of time.

The Third Man is, nevertheless, a fine example of the unity of Carol Reed's best work – his ability to make every aspect of a production serve the final dramatic effect of the film. He believes that a cast of mixed nationality act together to mutual advantage – one kind of emotional temperament offsetting the other. Here Joseph Cotten's direct simplicity of style is offset by the deeper, theatrical style of the Austrian character-actors, and Valli brings a romantic European femininity to the part of Anna which is at variance with the more boyish approach to love represented by Martins. Orson Welles makes his own particular rootless character out of Lime, and introduces a macabre humour into the part, for, in spite of its overwhelming sense of evil, *The Third Man* contains a great deal of humour as well as humanity. This humanity shines through the little scene played between Anna and Martins in her bedroom in the middle of the night among the odd assortment of furniture and luggage and drying stockings which makes up the temporary home of this dispossessed woman. He is a little drunk; she, dressed in Harry Lime's pyjamas, can only weep for the memory of her lover, and smile just once at the spectacle of Martins' immature disillusionment with the world. It is a perfect little scene, beautifully timed and played.

There are many who prefer among Carol Reed's films *The Fallen Idol* or *Odd Man Out* to *The Third Man*. It is true that these other films are more defined in their meaning and structure, particularly *Odd Man Out*, which has a nearly perfect dramatic shape. But *The Third Man* is, I think, the most richly atmospheric of all Carol Reed's films; it probes more deeply into motive; it prefers to create a certain kind of dramatic poetry out of the strange world which it somehow manages to master. It is a film of shadows, of the half-light, and as such it is peculiarly successful and moving.

UMBERTO D, 1952

Production: Rizzoli-de Sica-Amato. Direction: Vittorio de Sica.
Photography: G. R. Aldo. Music: Alessandro Cicognini.
Editing: Eralso da Roma. Script: Cesare Zavattini.
With Carlo Battisti as Umberto D.

Umberto Dominico Ferari (Umberto D.) is a true character in an Italian neo-realist film. His creators are the director Vittorio de Sica and the writer Cesare Zavattini.

Zavattini in an interview published in *Sight and Sound* (Oct., 1953) explains the approach of the neo-realists to their films. They reject the conventional film stories because they superimpose 'dead formulas over living social facts', creating 'metaphorical situations'. Audiences, Zavattini claims, should be saved from the dead end of being moved by unreal people in unreal situations, and learn before it is too late the need to 'reflect (and, if you like, to be moved and indignant too) on what they and others are doing, on the real things, exactly as they are'. Once this attitude to film subjects is adopted he asserts that 'there is no question of a crisis of subjects, only of their interpretation'.

Zavattini, I believe, exaggerates his attack on the 'metaphorical' film; almost every film we have admired, let alone the great dramas of the past 2,000 years, have expressed truth about human nature in 'metaphorical' terms. But his argument is that as soon as metaphor is allowed to drive out truth, as in so many films and plays and novels, we are invited to entertain ourselves by watching dummies go through dummy situations. The neo-realists are determined to serve the truth, psychologically and socially, in their films. *Sciuscia*, *Paisa*, *La Terra Trema*, *Bicycle Thieves*, and *Umberto D*, are the result. Even so, Zavattini is still not satisfied that these films are sufficiently free from the taint of traditional story-telling.

Zavattini is right in claiming that the cinema has a unique capacity for this kind of approach to the human scene. He writes: 'No other medium of expression has the cinema's original and innate capacity for showing things, that we believe worth showing, as they happen day by day – in what we might call their "dailiness", their longest and truest duration. The cinema has everything in front of it, and no other medium has the same possibilities for getting it known quickly to the greatest number of people.'

The essence of a neo-realist film is to put an ordinary person in a simple situation which will make him reveal himself, his associates, and his social environment. The film should analyse, for example, what is implied when a poor woman eventually sets out to buy a pair of shoes; every facet of the situation should be shown, everyone with whom she comes in contact made as real as life itself. 'Thus to analyse "buying a pair of shoes" in such a way opens to us a vast and complex world, rich in importance and values, in its practical, social, economic, psychological motives.

Banality disappears because each moment is really charged with responsibility. Every moment is infinitely rich. Banality never really existed.

'Excavate, and every little fact is revealed as a mine. If the gold-diggers come at last to dig in the illimitable mine of reality, the cinema will become socially important.

'This can also be done, evidently, with invented characters; but if I use living, real characters with which to sound reality, people in whose life I can directly participate, my emotion becomes more effective, morally stronger, more useful. Art must be expressed through a true name and surname, not a false one.' From this it is an easy step to avoid employing actors altogether, and to use only people who belong themselves to the situation on the screen, or understand it by direct contact.

Finally, Zavattini feels this form of film-making is of the greatest social importance. 'I believe that the world goes on getting worse because we are not truly aware of reality. The most authentic position anyone can take up to-day is to engage himself in tracing the roots of this problem. The keenest necessity of our time is "social attention".'

Bicycle Thieves, which has been widely shown and appreciated, and *Umberto D*, are the best examples of true neorealism. Both deal with human beings in a difficult, crucial situation in their lives; both leave them in it. '*Neo-realism*,' writes Zavattini, 'it is said, *does not offer solutions. The end of a neo-realist film is particularly inconclusive*. I cannot accept this at all. With regard to my own work, the characters and situations in films for which I have written the scenario, they remain unresolved from a practical point of view simply because "this is reality". But every moment of the film is, in itself, a continuous answer to some question. It is not the concern of an artist to propound solutions. It is enough and quite a lot, I should say, to make an audience feel the need, the urgency, for them.' At the end of *Bicycle Thieves* the unemployed man with a lost bicycle is still unemployed and without the vehicle essential for getting the only job available to him. At the end of *Umberto D*, the retired civil servant is still so poor that he can live only as a persecuted debtor. But in both cases we have seen the inner light of their human nature – the touching and beautiful relationship of the unemployed man and his small but instinctively understanding son, and the loving companionship shared by the old man and his dog, a trust almost lost, but retrieved at the end of the film like a major triumph.

The faith of neo-realism is a faith in human nature. It is as simple and as difficult as the Christian commandment 'Love thy neighbour as thyself'. Presented with the understanding of artists like Zavattini, Amidei, and de Sica, these films of human nature are profoundly moving.

Umberto D joins in a fruitless strike of pensioners for a living subsistence; he is engaged in a constant war (which he hates because it is beneath his natural dignity) with his vulgar, avaricious landlady. He lives, sick and friendless, in a tenement block, his lonely nights interrupted by the blare of an open-air cinema operating in the courtyard below. His only helper is a pregnant maidservant who tries a little to look after him behind the landlady's back; her slatternly love for soldiers is a constant shock to his sense of middle-class propriety. He is forced eventually to feign illness in order to get a free bed in a hospital, for he owes his rent, and he is unable to borrow more money to pay it. When he returns, it is to find that his landlady has turned him out.

His love for his dog is the light of his life, and the full climax of the film turns on this relationship. For just as, in *Bicycle Thieves*, the father momentarily lets his son down when he desperately and clumsily tries to steal a bicycle, so Umberto D temporarily loses the faith of his dog when he tries to kill them both under a passing train. The end of each film is the re-establishment of understanding and affection, where these had been seriously threatened.

The poverty and the squalor of *Bicycle Thieves* and *Umberto D* sound depressing, but both films concentrate so completely on the warmth of human relationships that neither is depressing in a negative or futile sense. They are profoundly moving. They fill us with a desire to help make things right for these people, to help them personally in some way. Yet they are not propaganda films, agitating for social reform. They are, rather, films of good-will in the fundamental Christian sense. They use the intimacy of motion picture photography, the realism of the camera's unflinching observation of places and people to purge us of human apathy about the state of our fellow men and women. I do not think films of greater significance than these have been made.

3 THE FILM AS AN INDUSTRY

The Pioneers of the Film Industry

IT is impossible to draw any exact line between the participation of the amateur and the professional in the invention
of the moving picture. Its origin was due partly to scientific
calculation, partly to professional invention, and partly to
the 'hunch' of enthusiasts like William Friese-Greene. But
once invented, motion pictures, either projected like the
work of the Lumières or viewed in a peepshow Kinetoscope
like the work of Edison, became a matter of hard business.
Edison wanted to link the new motion pictures to his
beloved phonograph; the Lumières wanted to make quick
money during what they thought would be a brief period of
popular success. But motion pictures had come to stay.

When George Albert Smith, the pioneer film-maker who
began work in Brighton in 1897, showed me his account
books some years ago, the shillings and pence of his first
entries against the cost of raw materials soon blossomed into
three- and even four-figure entries as his business turnover
rapidly increased. Films were still the small man's business
concern in the first years of the century, but this was not to
last long. The enthusiasts, the inventors, and the pioneers
were soon edged out of the industry by the men who
saw there was money to be made out of the exhibition of
films to a public made hungry by the excitement of show
business.

In the early days the man who made the films was the
man who showed them. Cecil Hepworth, later to become
Britain's leading film producer for some twenty years, began
as a travelling showman with some short lengths of film
made by another pioneer, R. W. Paul.

But though my first attempts at the travelling show business consisted of half-a-dozen forty-foot films from Paul's junk basket, plus
a little music and a hundred or so lantern-slides, it required con-

siderable ingenuity to spin that material out to an evening's entertainment. I showed the films forwards in the ordinary way and then showed some of them backwards. I stopped them in the middle and argued with them; called out to the little girl who was standing in the forefront of the picture to stand aside, which she immediately did. That required careful timing but was very effective. But with it all I very soon found I must have more films and better ones. (*Came the Dawn* by Cecil Hepworth, p. 33.)

Here is William Barker reminiscing in 1936, in a lecture for the British Kinematograph Society, on the excitement of making the first newsreels:

All my cinema life I pinned my faith to news. Many in this room – my cameramen of old – know how I stuck to the topical. We have developed the National coming up from Liverpool in the train. We had a luggage van turned into a dark room with water in milk churns. Our legs soaked with developer and hypo right through our trousers – we got swamped every time the train swung over the points – we rushed in a hansom to our drying room to get prints made to show the same night. Not easy when one remembers that the picture has to be cut from about twenty cameras. I used – pre-war – to turn out some twenty-six to thirty copies of the Derby for showing the same night, and no multiple printer in existence. The Boat Race – from start to finish, which was several miles from our dark rooms – has been projected in Tottenham Court Road inside $1\frac{1}{2}$ hours from the time of the winner passing the post, and we had no 50 to 80 m.p.h. motor-bikes in those days. I've seen Jack Smith tearing along Holborn at 8 m.p.h. in a hansom with a portion of film flying in the breeze to get it dry before reaching the Palace Theatre.

These conditions soon changed; the man who showed the films bought his prints from the man who made them, and therefore had no personal pride in what he showed from a creative point of view. The divergence of viewpoint so often apparent in the industry to-day was born early enough.

The Relationship between Art and Industry in the Film To-day

We have to realize first of all that the film is one of those complicated technological forms of communication which have only come into existence during the twentieth century. It is parallel to the linotype machine, which has made possible mass publication during the first half-century, and to broadcasting. Individuals who wish to control these new means of communication must command the capital to do so. To found and launch a daily newspaper in Britain was said pre-war to require £2 million initial capital. The capital outlay of the BBC's broadcasting system represents many millions of pounds. For a film to be successful to-day it should play satisfactorily in some 1,500 to 2,000 cinemas in Britain alone, representing merely as structures an enormous capital outlay. For a film to bring its producer £200,000 it must take approximately six times this sum at the box-office, to allow for the onerous entertainment duty, for exhibitors' overheads and profit, and for the sum required by the distributors for handling the picture.

The provision and manipulation of such large sums of money make it clear that film-making is an industry before it is an art. Though strictly speaking fiction film-making of any kind is creative, since it involves the development of plot, characterization, technical presentation, and acting, the measure of success applied to it by the business interests does not tally with success as this is understood by the artist. For him the measure of success lies in the achievement and stature of his work; for them success lies in the scale of the public's response.

There is still, after fifty years, almost no specialization in the presentation of cinema entertainment, at least as far as the English-speaking film is concerned. If a picture is to be financially successful, whether it be comedy, satire, melodrama, or tragedy, Western or musical, slapstick, or fantasy, it must pass through the same routine of exhibition. This is very different from the conditions which affect the production of printed publications, broadcasting (in Britain), and even the 'live' theatre; in all of these different tastes are deliberately fostered and specialization in kinds and grades of entertainment and information is the very essence of the policy of production. The only specialized form of provision in the cinema occurs in the newsreel theatres and particularly in the few cinemas which screen foreign-language films, in the non-theatrical distribution of films, and in the privately organized film societies.

It must be recognized, however, that among the box-office successes over the years have been many films of great artistic merit, including, for example, since 1946 *The Best Years of our Lives*, *The Overlanders*, *Great Expectations*, *The Naked City*, *Odd Man Out*, *The Third Man*, and, in the specialized market, *La Ronde* and *The Wages of Fear*.

The reward for the care, patience, and feats of concentration required of the film-maker, as well as for the great financial risks run by his sponsors, is the scale upon which success can be achieved, a success not limited to a single country like the success of a stage production, but extended internationally to the limits of the world market open to the distributor. It is the temptations of this mass success which lead to the hard bargaining that goes on between a film-maker of individuality and his producers. Once he has achieved his full stature, a British producer-director working in Britain, such as Sir Carol Reed or David Lean, may reach the position of complete control over both the subject and the presentation of the film he makes, but virtually no one has this power in Hollywood, unless he is able to finance his own productions. Most directors of stature in America have to negotiate very cunningly to make the pictures of their choice, usually by undertaking to make one or more normal box-office films in return for being allowed to make a subject of which the business executives are suspicious. There has been a far greater measure of freedom in this respect in the European industries than in Hollywood, always excepting the Soviet film industry where the political 'screening' of film subjects became so intense during the last years of Stalin's regime that the annual number of Soviet feature productions was reduced to a mere handful.

Nevertheless, highly individual films are being made all the while in Hollywood, films like *A Walk in the Sun*, *Sound of Fury*, *On the Town*, *Intruder in the Dust*, *The Asphalt Jungle*, and

Panic in the Streets. But the kind of argument which goes on behind the scenes in the 'front office' was told in Lillian Ross's book *Picture*, a fascinating record of the production of *The Red Badge of Courage*, made at the invitation of its director, John Huston.

The featured players of Lillian Ross's book are Louis B. Mayer, head of the M.G.M. Studio at the time the picture was made, Gottfried Reinhardt (son of Max Reinhardt, and producer of the film), Dore Schary, then in charge of production for the M.G.M. Studio as a whole, and, of course, John Huston. Behind them glows the power of Nick Schenck, President of Loew's Incorporated of New York, the company in financial control of M.G.M.

Now *The Red Badge of Courage* is the kind of film people concerned with 'appreciation' like to feel is being made. It renews their flagging faith in the over-commercialized art which they adore. It proves that in spite of the overwhelming costs which a feature film of any scale represents (and *The Red Badge of Courage* cost $1,642,000, which was rather more than $200,000 over budget), a commercial company is occasionally prepared to bow to the artist and give him a degree of freedom which is normally withheld.

Every picture is a gamble in public taste, and investment in an artist's ideas is the risk which the company always has to take. Even the formula picture is a risk, because the mere mixture of popular themes and actors may not finally combine into a film which makes the money flow back. Every film is a unique event, a unique voyage into the difficult, shifty seas of popular taste.

This makes the relationship of the artists to their promoters a difficult one. The artists need the money and the production facilities of the promoters; the promoters need the flair, imagination, and showmanship of the artists. Everyone in *Picture* watches the reaction of Louis B. Mayer; he is infallible as regards what will please the public – but that is after the picture is made. Up to that point he, too, must depend on his own hunches and those of his producers, writers, and directors.

Louis B. Mayer was against *The Red Badge of Courage* from the start. His point of view as expressed to Reinhardt is deadly simple. 'You don't want to make money!' he says. 'You want to be an artist! Would you work as an artist for one hundred dollars a week? *You* want to make money. Why don't you want the studio to make money? Are you willing to *starve* for your art? You want to be the artist, but you want *other* people to starve for your art!'

Yet the film was made at over one and a half million dollars. Why? Just because Dore Schary, the new production chief at M.G.M. had set his heart on it? The answer is given by Nick Schenck, and a very human one at that. 'How else was I going to teach Dore?' he said. 'I supported Dore. I let him make the picture. I knew that the best way to help him was to let him make a mistake. Now he will know better. A young man has to learn by making mistakes. I don't think he'll want to make a picture like that again.'

I gather that *Picture* is an accurate book as far as the people and their talk are concerned. It is a brilliant reconstruction of conversation in the carefully contrived casebook style so highly developed in America. This kind of writing is always deceptive because it appears to leave the author out of the work, whereas in fact he is very busy arranging the presentation of the material in such a way as to create what may well be quite artificial characters out of his portraits of real people. But however that may be, the essential truth of *Picture* remains intact. The handling of the film from the first negotiations held in an atmosphere of hectic and conspiratorial enthusiasm ('This is going to be a GREAT picture'), is tempered always by the knowledge that the head of the studio is against the production. The desire to satisfy people whose outlook is completely divergent ('If they're so goddam artistic, why don't they spend their *own* money' – Louis B. Mayer) leads to compromise and counter-compromise until Reinhardt, as producer, is driven years nearer the grave by Huston's individualism on the one hand, and, on the other, the growing antipathy to the film shown by M.G.M. front office. Once the picture was shot, edited, and shown unsuccessfully at a 'sneak' preview in a Hollywood cinema, Huston left America to shoot *The African Queen* and Reinhardt had to take all the raps.

The rest of the book is a lesson to all film-makers, all film critics, all film enthusiasts, addicts, and supporters of art. It is the story of how to keep the roof from falling in once the dry rot is manifest. The picture was cut, re-shaped, given a narrator to explain what is happening, and finally launched with a warning to the public that they had better be willing to go out of their way to respect it, because it was derived from a *great classic* of fiction. Reinhardt's position is pathetic as he tries to meet demands for change which grow ever more drastic, and his memos in which he makes suggestions for radical adaptation of the film while striving to retain its 'integrity' are masterpieces of compromise.

The Red Badge of Courage is an impressive film if those who see it are prepared to match it with their own imagination. It gives a scarifying picture of what warfare does to men. But, cut down to a bare eighty minutes, it is satisfactory neither as film art nor film commerce, for no one had really faced the issue whether Stephen Crane's wholly *introspective* story of a young man's conquest of his cowardice could ever be satisfactorily made manifest through the action and dialogue of a film. John Huston, Gottfried Reinhardt, and Dore Schary all had a hunch that the *subject* was a good one for the screen. But what of the actual story as conceived by Stephen Crane? Only after a million and a half dollars had been spent was Louis B. Mayer virtually proved to be right over this particular film.

Graham Greene is quoted by the British publishers of Lillian Ross's book as saying that it presents a terrifying picture of how a great film can be slashed into incoherence through the timidities and the illiteracy of studio heads. I think this is far too simple an interpretation of what actually happened. It is not a picture of illiteracy or of timidity. It is an analysis of the kinds of technical and artistic compromise which become necessary when large sums of money are invested in entertaining large masses of people. Nothing can be left to chance with such audiences. The frightening moment in the book is when men of the capacity and intelligence of John Huston and Gottfried Reinhardt stand nervously watching the adolescents in a Pasadena theatre filling out reaction cards after a 'sneak' preview. They realize that the slangy gibes of these children will mean more to the front office with its million-and-a-half dollar investment than the odd cards handed in by people of mature judgement who found real value in the production. But that is picture-show business. The undefined taste of the mass customer becomes more right as the budget for a picture mounts, and the people who suffer most are those who have spent anxious months in the studio getting their work by those who for one reason or another are opposed to it. The only person with a defined taste in Lillian Ross's book is Louis B. Mayer: ' "Art. *The Red Badge of Courage*? All that violence? No story? Dore Schary wanted it. Is it good entertainment? I didn't think so. Maybe I'm wrong. But I don't think I'm wrong. I know what the audience wants. Andy Hardy. Sentimentality! What's wrong with it? Love! Good, old-fashioned romance!" He put his hand on his chest and looked at the ceiling. "Is it bad? It entertains. It brings the audience to the box office. No! These critics. They're too tony for you and I. They don't like it." ' And on another occasion he says, 'I saw *Show Boat* and the tears were in my eyes. I'm not ashamed of tears. I cried. I'll see it thirteen times. Thirteen times! Tears! Emotion!'

The conditions which obtained during the making of *The Red Badge of Courage* are the result of the development of the present state of the industry from the days of raw gambling which built it up. The age of the accountant has succeeded that of the gambler, and the old instinct of the showman (who was often extravagant and wasteful, but still a spirited and attractive character who was the heart and soul of show-business) is being carefully tempered by the man with his eye trained to scan the showman's budget. The accountant learns to adjust to the instinct of the entertainer and the entertainer learns how to get the results he needs by more disciplined expenditure and by the use of technical ingenuity.

The Production Budget

Here are the budgets for two typical British first feature films of rather differing kinds, based on figures given in the P.E.P. Report, *The British Film Industry*.

A film costing approximately £150,000

Producer's and director's fees	8.2% of the budget
Story	10.1%
Two stars	8.2%
Supporting artists	8.1%
Unit salaries	13.3%
Manual labour	7.0%
Set materials, props, etc.	4.2%
Location costs, costumes, music	6.3%
Film and laboratory costs	5.5%
Studio rent and equipment	14.4%
Finance, insurances, and legal costs	14.7%

A film costing approximately £360,000

Producer's and director's fees	6.8% of the budget
Story	0.7%
Two stars	3.9%
Supporting artists	7.3%
Unit salaries	11.4%
Manual labour	9.5%
Set materials, props, etc.	5.7%
Location costs, costumes, music	21.8%
Film and laboratory costs	4.7%
Studio rent and equipment	21.3%
Finance, insurance, and legal costs	6.9%

The direct labour costs on a film average between 40 and 50% of the total expenditure.

The Position of the Film Producer

A standard question is always being put, what is the position exactly of a film producer? The trouble is there is no standard answer, because so many film producers assume different functions for themselves between the two extremes of being the financier who puts up the money while leaving every aspect of production to partners or subordinates, and the producer-director who assumes financial responsibility for those films which he chooses to make personally.

Between these two extremes are producers of many kinds. The most famous kind of Hollywood producer is a man like Sam Goldwyn, who has achieved outstanding personal success with a long line of films all of which he has supervised in every detail, treating his writers, directors, and editors as artists subordinate to himself. The final decision on every point of presentation in the picture rests with him, as the experienced showman with a hunch as to what the public wants. I have heard him say that the quality most needed in a producer is the ability to cut his own films, to which he added the ability to cast his writers, directors, and other technicians as he casts his actors. This kind of producer is a true father to his films; they bear the stamp of his personality like children, though they may share characteristics brought to them by the senior technicians.

In the big Hollywood studios, however, there is usually a producer-in-chief, who is in charge of all production, though his policy may be guided from a head office in Hollywood or New York. (We have seen this to be the case for *The Red Badge of Courage*.) In these studios a staff producer will be assigned to each production, and his responsibility is to watch the studio's interests, both financial and artistic, at all stages in the making of the picture. He will discuss and supervise scripting, casting, and all studio and location problems, keeping his team of film-makers and artists as happy as possible, and seeing that they work to schedule and produce the picture within budget. He is the buffer between the team making the film and the head office which employs both them and him. He had better be successful, for if head office lose confidence in him because his pictures tend to run over schedule or exceed their budgets or prove 'box-office poison', he can be fired like anyone else when his contract expires!

In Britain the range of responsibilities varies just as greatly as in Hollywood. Again, one might say, producers are of two kinds, those directly associated with the detailed work of making films, or those who, however much they may be personally interested in films, are concerned solely in the financial aspect of their production.

Sir Michael Balcon, who has been in charge of production at Ealing Studios for many years, described his view of the work of a film producer in a paper on *Film Production and Management* written for the British Institute of Management; it is based, of course, on his own unique position at Ealing Studios:

His duties are an extraordinary blend of administration and creative work; and, secondly, they are to a high degree involved and interlocked with those of a number of other technicians. Very occasionally, an outstanding genius appears (Charles Chaplin is one) with the necessary personality and versatility to superimpose himself completely on the actors and technicians associated with him. But he is certainly the exception. No other art or craft or form of entertainment demands such absolute co-operation to ensure good quality, and that co-operation can only be achieved in a selfless manner. A film is made by a producer (with, in some studios, an associate producer), a director, writers, designers, sound engineers, cameramen, cutters, actors, and members of many other trades and professions. More than fifty different professions, trades, and arts are represented, and the work of each is inextricably interlocked and the producer is confronted with this strange co-operative society.

The producer himself is the pivot of the whole of his unit or studio and his work must be considered under the two headings of administrative organization of a studio and supervision of production. In some cases, a producer will be relieved of the former task and his responsibilities will be devoted to the actual production of a film, but to give a complete picture I am assuming that the producer is responsible for studio administration as well.

He has immediately next to him a man known as the production supervisor or studio production manager who, under the producer, is responsible for the co-ordination of production requirements. Everything of an administrative or practical nature passes through his office and all individuals and departments look to that office for their production directive. Parallel with that office, though not necessarily under its directive, are departments such as accounts, legal and casting, each carrying out their particular function in advising the producer of the progress of expenditure, the clearance of the copyright, legal aspects of the stories under consideration, contracts for writers, artistes, advisers, etc., contracts with major artistes.

A studio must be kept going whether or not a film is actually in production, and a medium-sized studio such as Ealing has a permanent staff of over four hundred. The producer has his responsibilities to the workers of his studio, as well as they to him. Carpenters, plasterers, painters, electricians, property men, etc., are those who make up the main bulk of the unit personnel, in addition to the creative and clerical staffs.

The producer is therefore dependent on departmental heads to carry out the details and on his choice of the key personnel around him greatly depends the smooth running of the studios. The situation is particularly delicate when it comes to the creative side of his work, when he becomes more involved with technicians to whom he delegates their particular jobs. As they co-operate in bringing to the screen the producer's film they must be chosen not only for their technical efficiency but for their sympathy with the producer's point of view and ideas, and he must choose people with whose work he himself is in sympathy.

It is usual for a studio to have a number of key creative personnel on contract – associate producers, directors, and writers. To obtain a balance of subjects it is obviously advisable that these men shall each have his own particular type of subject. Thus the producer may have at his disposal one director who specializes more than anything else in comedy, another in domestic drama, another in outdoor subjects, and so on. While his production schedules must be worked out with one eye on the box-office requirements, he must also bear in mind an equal distribution of subjects to contract personnel. Bearing this in mind has a certain influence in the origin of subjects.

This choice of subjects is, of course, the most important consideration in the running of a studio. The producer must not only bear in mind the merit of the story, but its relation to, and effect upon, his proposed production programme, which must be carefully balanced to ensure that one particular type or style does not predominate. He must also consider the selling organization through which his films pass to the exhibitors. The subject must be one which can be produced within the budget the studio and the selling organization can best work. And above all, it must be one which coincides with his forecast of public taste at the time of its release to the cinemas.

Film Production

With many individual variations, the processes through which a film passes from conception to public exhibition are the same everywhere. It is the complicated business of translating a story originally conceived in some form of writing into an acted drama which will be seen through a long sequence of motion pictures. Or, in the case of the film of fact (the documentary, the instructional film or some other form of specialized production), it is usually the translation of a line of argument or a demonstration of some process from a script which is often no more than a general description of how the film should develop. This is called a treatment, though it may be, of course, a shot-by-shot description of how the film should be built up. A highly-individual filmmaker like the late Robert Flaherty may avoid the use of a script altogether if he is left free to do so.

The first stage of film-making, then, is the choice of a subject and the development of it into some form of working script. The form of this working script will vary with the individual studio and the individual film-maker.

The selection of a story subject may be made originally by a film-maker, perhaps either a writer or a director, who offers a story he likes to his producer, or it may be made by the producer himself, who then invites a writer and a director to elaborate it for him. Screen-writers in Great Britain normally work free-lance; directors, on the other hand, may either be free-lance, or attached to individual studios (this is the case at Ealing) or may, in a few cases, head their own individual producing companies, like Sir Carol Reed, David Lean, or Frank Launder and Sidney Gilliat. In Hollywood there is a much closer system of contracting writers and directors for the staffs of the larger studios. It is necessary for both writers and directors to have outstanding success and strong personality to gain control of their subjects. The studio tends to cast them as it casts the actors, expecting a writer to script a subject assigned to him, and a director to shoot a script which is not of his own choice. Both writer and director are treated as executive technicians working for the producer who has entire charge of the subject and who can, where he wishes, entirely alter their treatment and overrule their judgement. This is not entirely the case in Hollywood, but it is still usual; in the European industries, where most production is based on smaller teams of film-makers, many of them working independently, greater individuality of work is possible.

America, Britain, France, and Italy, the leading industries distributing films on a world basis, together produce some 600 to 700 feature story films a year. The greater number of these are derived from novels, non-fictional books, and plays which have already been published or put on the stage. Large sums are paid for the screen rights to novels and plays which have achieved a high degree of success with the public. These rights become 'properties' which are frequently sold at profit or loss between companies or individual producers. Many screen-plays, however, are 'originals', which producers commission as the result of their interest in treatments, more or less brief, which established screenwriters submit to them. Plays written for television have more recently become another source for films.

There are no rules about the stages through which a script must pass before it is ready for the studio floor. Some screenwriters feel the need to reach a dialogue stage as early as possible, in order to get a proper sense of characterization. Usually the first stage is a description of the story told in a few pages, followed by a treatment showing how the film will be shaped into its main sequences, or phases of action, from the point of view of its development and structure as a screenplay. Dialogue follows this, and, where the director himself is the screenwriter, or is working closely with the screenwriter, a shot-by-shot breakdown of the action may then be prepared. Some directors, most notably Alfred Hitchcock and also Walt Disney for his live-action films, prepare a shot-by-shot picture script – a series of sketches which show visually the camera set-ups and the order of screen compositions which will reveal the action, the dialogue together with the point of action being neatly typed under the drawings. Each director, however, prefers his own methods of work – Sir Carol Reed, for example, a freely flowing script showing the action and dialogue only; David Lean a script more tightly controlled on paper as to specific shots.

Here, for a first example, is a section of the advance shooting-script for *Odd Man Out*;* it is the scene when Johnny, mortally wounded, leaves Rosie's house where he has found temporary shelter.

112. *Hall. They crowd into the hall and see Johnny. He draws himself erect and regards them all with a look of firm resolve. They stand aside in awe as he moves slowly and with a curious steadiness towards them.*

JOHNNY: I'm going now. The thing is settled for you, and you won't need to worry.

Rosie goes past him and lifts his overcoat from where it has dropped from his right hand, and drapes it about his shoulders, and does up the top button.

ROSIE: There, now!

JOHNNY: Let me go now. Open the door and I will go out and never trouble you again. Close the door when I am gone, and forget me.

Johnny moves with a stiff motion towards the door. They make way for him.

Alfie is moved by a generous, kindly impulse, which springs from a feeling that he has been inhuman in his attitude to Johnny.

*The extracts from *Odd Man Out* and *Brief Encounter* are taken from the scripts edited by the author for publication by Methuen in *Three British Screen-plays*.

ALFIE: Here! Hold on a wee moment!

Alfie takes a bowl from the mantelpiece and lifts a tiny bottle of whiskey from it and unscrews the stopper.

ALFIE: I was keepin' this for when my boy comes home from the east. It'll do you a power of good!

Johnny clenches his teeth on the neck of the bottle and tips some of it into his mouth. His right hand extends, and gropes for the door, and as he finds the handle and opens the door a blast of boisterous wind whips into the house and buffets him. The black night gapes before him and he falters. He summons his strength in its remnants, and turns to Rosie for an instant and then lurches out. The door swings back against the wall in the wind. Alfie closes it. Maudie passes Alfie and is seen to be holding the revolver. Alfie stops her.

ALFIE: Drop that thing in the drain at the gutter!

Maudie snatches a cap from a hook and hurriedly goes out.

113. *Street. Maudie drops the revolver into the drain at the gutter, and runs after Johnny who has gone only a short distance in the darkness. The whiskey has given him a momentary strength. He leans back and faces her, and she claps on his bare head the big cap.*

MAUDIE: Here! Put this on you! Quick. There y'are now!

Maudie sees his slow smile of gratitude, and then scampers back out of sight towards the house, leaving him in the darkness and wild wind. He huddles down and shuffles off.

114. *Parlour. Maudie enters. Rosie and Alfie are standing there.*

ALFIE (*feeling ashamed*): We acted charitable.

Rosie and Maudie turn away.

ALFIE: He took and went, and that's the best thing.

The women make no reply.

ALFIE: My tea ready, Rosie?

It is interesting in this connexion to study the difference between the advance shooting script and the post-production record script of *Brighton Rock*, illustrated by an extract in Karel Reisz's book *The Technique of Film Editing*. This extract shows clearly how editing is anticipated to a certain extent in the shooting script, but how in its final form the presentation of the film depends considerably on the modifications introduced during the final process of cutting.

Here again, is a section of the script prepared for *Brief Encounter*, clearly giving camera set-ups:

293. *Medium shot of the door on to the platform from Laura's eye-line. The sound of Alec's train is heard as it starts to move out of the station. Cut to*

294. *Close-up of Laura.*

LAURA'S VOICE: I said to myself – ' He didn't go – at the last minute his courage failed him – he couldn't have gone – at any moment now he'll come into the refreshment room again pretending that he'd forgotten something.' I prayed for him to do that – just so that I could see him once more – for an instant – but the minutes went by. . . .

There is the sound of the station bell. Cut to

295. *Close shot of Laura and Dolly.*

DOLLY: Is that the train.

She addresses Myrtle.

DOLLY: Can you tell me, is that the Ketchworth train?

MYRTLE (*off*) : No, that's the express.

LAURA: The boat-train.

DOLLY: Oh, yes – that doesn't stop, does it?

She gets up and moves out of picture towards the counter. Cut to

296. *Laura jumps to her feet and the camera pans with her as she rushes blindly out of the door, leading to Number 2 platform. (As the camera pans to the door it goes off level, giving the effect of Laura running uphill.) Cut to*

297. *Medium shot of Laura as she runs out of the refreshment room towards the camera and the railway lines. Cut to*

298. *Medium shot of the railway lines from above. The express hurtles through the picture (camera tilted). Cut to*

299. *Close-up of Laura from a low angle (camera tilted).*

She is swaying on the edge of the platform. The lights from the express streak past her face. The noise is deafening. She stands quite still. The lights stop flashing across her face and the sound of the train dies away rapidly. Slowly the camera returns to a normal angle.

LAURA'S VOICE: I meant to do it, Fred, I really meant to do it.

Lastly, in the illustrated section to this book a series of sketches prepared by John Bryan for the opening sequence of *Oliver Twist* is reproduced. This was the very stylized sequence of Oliver's mother dragging herself in agony through a night of storm to reach the poor-house in time to be delivered of her son. The sketches correspond to shots 15–26 in the extract which follows.

FADE IN:

1. *Ext. Country Road. Night.*

   Long Shot. Ominous dark clouds.
   They are piling up angrily in the sky. A distant rumble of thunder.

2. *Close Shot. Tree.*
   The wintry branches, silhouetted against the gathering clouds, are quite still. A shrivelled leaf falls gently from a branch and flutters towards the ground.

3. *Close Shot. Pond.*
   The stillness is emphasized by the motionless reeds in the foreground of the picture. The mirrored surface of the water reflects the clouds above. The first puff of wind ripples across the water towards camera and wipes the reflection away. The reeds in the foreground quiver.

4. *Close Shot. Tree.*
   The smaller branches begin to crack and rattle.

5. *Medium Shot. Road.*
   Tufts of moving grass form the foreground of the picture. A gust of wind sweeps up the road collecting on its way a heap of leaves. It chases them forward. The camera *pans* with them into a *long shot* of the road. The road, not much more than a track, rises to the crest of a hill. The lonely figure of a *woman* appears over the brow.

6. *Close Shot. Woman.*
   She stops suddenly. She puts her hands to her side, and clutches her body with pain. A flash of lighting stabs across her figure. The wind buffets against her. Leaves swirl past her. The pain leaves her. She looks up.

7. *Long Shot. Deserted Roadway Ahead.*
   A peal of distant thunder.

8. *Close-up. Woman.*
   She collects herself, and hurries on.

9. *Close-tracking Shot. Woman.*
   The camera tracks behind her as she hastens on down the hill.

10. *Close-up. Woman. Tracking.*
    She looks anxiously ahead.

11. *Long Shot. Sky.*
    A dark band of angry cloud is racing towards the moon.

12. *Long Shot. Road.*
A great shadow sweeps along the road towards the WOMAN. As it is about to envelop her, she slackens her pace.

13. *Close-up. Woman.*
She stops. The shadow passes over her. She is seized with another pain. A flash of distant lightning silhouettes her against the sky.

14. *Close-up.*
The branch of a sharp prickly briar against the clouds. The wind shrieks out.

15. *Close-up. Woman.*
The shadow passes her. She lifts her head, looks forward, and sees something.

16. *Long Shot. Road.*
On a hill beyond there is a single light.

17. *Close Shot. Woman.*
Encouraged she continues on her way.

18. *Long Shot. Sky.*
Clouds are heavier and blacker. A terrific clap of thunder.

19. *Close-tracking Shot. Woman.*
Heavy rain lashes against her.

20. *Close Shot. Trees.*
Branches heaving in the wind and rain.

21. *Close-up. Woman. Tracking.*
She struggles on.

22. *Close Shot. Pond.*
Heavy raindrops bespatter the surface of the water. A flash of lightning pin-points the downpour.

23. *Close Shot. Woman.*
She is standing quite still clutching a post on the side of the road. The wind and the rain beat against her. The lightning flickers across her face. The wind momentarily subsides. She looks up.

24. *Long Shot. Road.*
The light is from a large building. It is much nearer.

25. *Close Shot. Woman.*
She steels herself for one last effort, and pushes on.

DISSOLVE:

Ext. Workhouse Gates. Night.

26. *Medium Shot.*
    The light is in the foreground of the picture. It hangs above a large iron gateway. Through the torrential rain, the WOMAN makes her way towards camera.

It is during the early stages in the preparation of a film that other senior members of the production team must meet under the producer's supervision. These will include the production designer and art director (these may be one and the same person; where they are separate, the designer is responsible for the overall design of the sets, costumes, and properties, while the art director is responsible for their realization on the studio floor), representatives of studio management (who must work out to what extent and when the studio stages and staff will be required for shooting each scene in the film), the director of photography (who will have to interpret pictorially what the director wants to get out of the art director's sets, and the artists' performances), and possibly the editor (who will start cutting the film as soon as the best results of the first day's shooting are selected, and who must, therefore, study the script beforehand and understand his director's intentions). If there are particular problems affecting sound, then the Head of the Sound Recording Department will have to be consulted. It depends on the degree of importance that music will play in the production whether or not the composer comes to the picture early or late. Normally he does not begin work until the picture is virtually completed and assembled by the editor in the form known as a rough-cut. He is then shown by the director those sections of the film which require the support of music, and this, once it is composed, is recorded separately and later dubbed, or re-recorded, on to the final sound track, which combines the recordings of speech, sound effects, and music.

The degree of advance planning before a director is ready to go on the studio floor varies greatly as between individuals. Some (like Alfred Hitchcock) plan on paper the shape, movement, and mood of every shot and fix each camera set-up which will be necessary to achieve these shots. They could, in effect, leave the shooting to a competent assistant, if they so wished, apart from the direction of the acting itself. Others, like Sir Carol Reed, while knowing in advance what they want, prefer to work as freely as possible to achieve it on the studio floor or on location. Others, again, like Charles Frend, work out their camera positions and order of shooting a day or so in advance of the actual work, preparing, perhaps, overnight the following day's set-ups. The trim of the budget, however, demands that the production be as carefully pre-planned as possible, so that sets can be built in the most economical order, the supporting players and crowd artists engaged by the week or the day only, and the studio staff be shared out to the best advantage over the various films in current production. The building and furnishing of sets is in itself a vast and expensive undertaking, and conditions the whole planning of the production and the order of shooting. It is a considerable administrative as well as constructional undertaking, for once a production is 'on the floor' the money begins to flow like Niagara. Hence a strict day-to-day control of the work is essential, when each morning or afternoon on the floor can cost a thousand or more pounds.

The work of shooting a film is, first of all, the lighting of the set in relation to the position and movements of the actors and the position and movement of the camera, which, in addition to recording the actions from a static position, can be moved silently backwards or forwards on wheels (often using a track laid down on the floor), or mounted on a crane and swung into, out of, or over the action. On location the camera can obviously be mounted on any kind of moving object, car, train, plane, or helicopter. One of the most magnificent shots in the history of the film was the one taken by D. W. Griffith from a captive balloon pulled slowly down over the vast crowds with which he peopled his great Babylonian sets for *Intolerance*. But the greater the complexity of the camera-movement in relation to the action, the greater the time it will take to set, light, and rehearse the scene, and this is where the costs begin to rise. The cheapest kind of film to make is the one which uses the closest approximation to a primitive television technique – scenes depending on close-shots of dialogue between as few people as possible with as little movement as possible. That is why half-hour films for television can be shot in a couple of days. But these same films produced for the big screens of the cinemas require a much higher degree of visual interest to command the attention of the film-goer. This requires taste, skill, and time to create. It requires much greater variety of shot, which means that the editor must have a good range of material at his disposal to bring together into the final assembly of the film. In a television play produced by the BBC I counted 121 changes of shot (that is, change-over backwards and forwards from one camera to another during the continuity of the performance), whereas in *The Third Man* there were 1,250 cuts made by the editor to give visual variety and detailed interest as well as pace to the action. This point is not being made to the detriment of television production, but to prove that drastic cuts in the budget of a film may well lead to less variety of shot, greater emphasis on close shots, and, above all, to dialogue at the expense of action. There is every case to be made for the elaboration of film structure now that television is here to give its audiences the screen dialogue drama both cheaply and efficiently. Television is beginning to evolve its own forms of visual variety (for it, too, has pressing problems both of budget and of rehearsal time with the cameras) but it cannot as yet cope with much visual detail. Dialogue is still the mainspring of television drama, and a full-length play can be mounted for as little as £1,500 to £2,000 (excluding overheads for studio maintenance and the full-time staff). A film production assuming the same prominence as the main part of an evening's entertainment in the cinema can cost anything between, say, £100,000 and £400,000. But whereas the 'live' television production dies with each performance (though it can technically be recorded on film with some loss of definition, and then repeated when Union agreements allow), the film lives on as a permanent record for endless performances, as long as the negative and the positive prints are kept in existence.

The television play is rehearsed normally for two or three weeks in rehearsal rooms without cameras and then for two days with the cameras and sets in the studio itself. The full-length first feature film is normally anything from ten to twenty weeks on the studio floor or on location, completing, perhaps, between two and three minutes of the action each day. With elaborate set-ups and intricate action only one shot may be achieved in a day. Several simpler shots, however, may be satisfactorily taken in a single day's work. Most shots are taken a number of times to give the director and editor a margin of selection (Take 1, Take 2, etc.). Those takes which seem to the director likely to prove useful are processed, and viewed the following day; those that pass this test are then handed to the editor with the director's comments to be made up into a first assembly, until gradually the whole film is pieced together. Virtually all the sound track, except the dialogue spoken by the actors in the studio, is added synthetically, after shooting, by the sound recordists, working in association with the editor, and even the dialogue itself, where sound recording conditions are bad on the set, is post-synchronized, that is to say, the actors record the dialogue on a later occasion, following closely their own picture on the screen, so that the words they are recording at this later stage synchronize with the movements of their lips when they were photographed. This requires a special professional skill if the scene being post-synchronized is one of atmosphere, mood, or emotion. Dialogue for scenes shot on location is almost always post-synchronized.

An extra time-allowance must be made when lighting the set for colour, and this, together with the additional requirements in the total design of a colour production in contrast to one in black and white, leads to considerable extra cost. Colour can add a minimum of 15% to the costs of a film, and the cost of making prints for exhibition is considerably higher.

Gradually the work is done, against time in the studio, against weather conditions on location, against the delays of temperament and the human factor, against contingencies of illness and accident and unavoidable delays. Five per cent is added to the production budget for insurance against the worst of these calamities. A great sigh of relief goes up as the last shots are completed, the last rushes viewed; the worst is over, and the comparatively quiet work of the final stages of editing starts. This is the stage that many film-makers enjoy most, the shaping of their raw material to achieve the greatest dramatic effect – the rearranging of shots, the exact placing of sound effects, the decision for or against the touch of music here, or the development of a full musical theme there, the rhythm, the timing, the paring, the polishing; what weeks of labour, what need of concentration, of living only for the work in hand! For the men who enjoy the command of artists and technicians in the studio and have it all in their mind's eye, or drawn or described in their scripts, editing may only seem a necessary nuisance; but for the men who find the final fulfilment of their creative work in this process of shaping and calculation of effect, editing is the climax of film-making.

When the film is finished it has to be press shown, given a premiere, and trade shown. The first brings it to the notice of the press and secures reviews (which need not be favourable to be useful as additional publicity); the second gives it the prestige of a first night before as distinguished an audience as possible (more publicity and more photographs); the third brings it to the notice of the exhibitor, for trade shows are held regionally as well as in London.

The Problems of British Producers

A British film has to earn at the British box-office about six or seven times its cost to secure its producer against loss. This is how the box-office takings are divided, very approximately:

Entertainments Tax	35.4%
Exhibitor's share	41.6%
Distribution	7.1%
Newsreels hire	2.1%
Producers' share	13.8%*

British exhibitors observe at present a 30% quota, that is a legal obligation to show in their theatres this percentage of films registered as British quota films of feature length. They must also show 25% of British short films. Applications can be made by cinemas for a reduction in their quota obligation or for entire exemption under certain conditions, but this tends to apply only to very small or specialized cinemas. A film can be registered as quota if a fixed percentage of its labour costs went to British technicians. This admits to British quota films sponsored in this country by American companies using American directors, writers, or stars; it admits films made entirely in any of the Dominions where the film technicians are of British nationality.

An abnormal amount of publicity is given to the British film production industry because it is show business. The capital invested in the seventy-six films of first feature length made in the years 1950–51 was about £11 million, which is in point of fact a very small amount of capital compared with that invested in most of the important productive industries of Britain.

The number of film technicians in Britain has stood as high as about 8,000, but in January 1953 the Association of Cine and Allied Technicians reported that its membership was now only 5,566, including laboratory workers, many members having left to take up employment outside the film industry. 2,500 left the Association during 1951 and 1952. Since the artificial boom period of production lasting for a short period towards the end of, and just after, the War,

*The breakdown figures for 1953 published by the Rank Organization express rather similar divisions in fractions of each pound paid into the box-office. The pound divides as follows: Entertainments Tax – 6/11; Eady Levy (British Film Production Fund contribution) – 6d; Exhibitors' Share – 8/2; Distributors' Share – 1/7; Producers' Share – 2/10.

the industry has been the subject of recurrent financial crises, which are all part of the same crisis – to make ends meet at the studios.

The Board of Trade is not unaware of the national importance of this small industry. British films save dollars at home and earn money overseas. It is recognized that good films are of the greatest help in keeping the name of Britain alive abroad, not only from the cultural but also from the commercial point of view. And no one would wish British theatres to show virtually nothing but the products of Hollywood, however good the best American films may be. There are, therefore, many sound reasons for fostering the development of British production.

The interest of the Labour Government in the welfare of the film industry was considerable, though it can scarcely be argued that the best was done for it. The industry as a whole is difficult to help, and only those who take the pains to study its intricacies, rivalries, and tensions can understand the disunity it frequently shows. The three branches of the industry – production, distribution, and exhibition – may seem to be part of a whole (especially where, in the cases of the Rank Organization and the Associated British Picture Corporation, production, distribution, and exhibition are interlinked), but in fact their interests are not always held in common. They all want to make money, but they have to make money through each other. The producer must persuade the renter that his product is what the public wants – which normally means following traditional lines of box-office success and incorporating stars of proven box-office quality. The renter must get the best deal he can out of the exhibitor, and publicize a picture in which he has no creative interest. And the exhibitor must take what he can get from the renters with whom he operates, good films and not-so-good alike.

The pressure from the producers' end should tend to be for innovation, for the discovery of elements which are new and fresh in entertainment both as regards stories and stars. The pressure from the renters and exhibitors, on the other hand, tends to be for material following past lines of success. No artist is happy chained to the past; few financiers are happy risking big money on products which they do not believe will attract the public. The dilemma of art versus commerce, of show business on sale by the week, is seen most acutely in the case of the cinema. Exhibitors and renters prefer to play for safety in all but exceptional circumstances; producers who are true showmen want to test public taste against what is exciting in a new way. The compromise reached, as we have seen already, is that the artist must normally be prepared to produce half-a-dozen formula films to one more original work, and that the unimaginative though often competent craftsman holds most of the cards in production. There are, and always have been, exceptions to this – Chaplin, for example. But they are rare, and even directors of considerable reputation frequently turn out formula films when the economic pressures of the industry are applied to them. This is more true of Hollywood, the most commercialized production centre in the world, than it is of the leading European industries, where, as we have seen, greater individuality is allowed owing, in part, to the smaller scale of production and the comparative absence of highly pressurized production organizations.

British production, faced with the almost overwhelming competition of Hollywood which still has a home market in the States capable of covering the greater part of the production costs, has passed through a series of crises ever since the first World War. The major problem of British production is to maintain a regular flow of films of high quality, and to develop an increasing number of brilliant filmmakers, especially writers and directors, who can be relied upon to maintain a steady output of films which must never be less than good entertainment, and which must as often as possible be better than a good average. Britain undoubtedly has fine technicians; the lack of numbers tends to be on the purely creative side in writing, direction, and acting. Hollywood has always been able to produce a reliable quantity of outstanding pictures each year backed (and this is most important) by a comparatively large number of the standard, competent formula films with well-known players universally attractive to audiences. This is what appeals to the exhibitor. It is now generally agreed that the best policy for British producers is to concentrate on sheer quality of production, especially in the face of the competition now offered by television.

The recurrent crises from which British film production has suffered have always been due in part to the fact that only the best films have in certain periods been successful either as art, entertainment, or as box-office. This was especially true before the War. Since the War, other mainly economic factors have made a smooth continuity of production very difficult to maintain. The producer, who gambles highest in public taste, gets the lowest reward. The State and the Exhibitor share nearly four-fifths of the takings, and leave the renter to take a further cut before giving the producer a sixth or a seventh of the box-office takings which his film has earned from the public.

The Government has given the film producers two main forms of help. The first was the foundation of a film bank administered by the National Film Finance Corporation, from which producers could, against certain guarantees of distribution, borrow varying proportions of the money they would need to complete their films. The Corporation was set up in July 1948 with capital of £5 million supplied by the Treasury; by 1952 this sum had been increased by stages to £8 million. The Corporation was originally established for five years, but this period was increased by a further three years in 1953.

The second form of governmental assistance was one of even greater importance. This was the creation in 1950 of the British Film Production Fund, the so-called Eady Fund, named after Sir Wilfred Eady, who devised it while he was Second Secretary at the Treasury. The source of money for this fund is a levy on the middle and higher priced seats in the cinemas, and under current arrangements should reach £3 million in a full year; from it all producers of British quota films (including those American companies which make films qualifying for British quota) can draw grants in proportion to the distributors' receipts for their productions; these grants naturally vary according to the number of British productions in process of distribution, but feature films normally receive a grant amounting to between 30% and 35% of the total of the distributors' gross receipts. This grant makes all the difference between showing a small profit or incurring a considerable loss to the average British producer. Short films in commercial distribution also receive a grant calculated on the basis of $2\frac{1}{2}$ times their gross earnings; the earnings of short films are so small that any grant below this level would be quite ineffective. A small section of the fund, originally specified as about 5% of the total, was set aside for 'special purposes'; in practice this has been interpreted by the Committee of the Four Trade Associations (representing exhibitors, distributors, and the producers of feature and short films) which administers the fund, as the source for special annual grants to the non-profit-making company, Children's Film Foundation Ltd, which was set up in 1951 to make entertainment films for children under the supervision of Mary Field. This company is administered by representatives of the Four Trade Associations, and so is promoted by the industry as a whole.

The key to production is distribution; a film must pass the hurdle of Wardour Street if its production costs are to be retrieved. Nothing is better known in the industry than the axiom that without circuit distribution no British-made feature can regain its costs.

British cinema theatres are divided up roughly as follows:

The Odeon Circuit, owned by the J. Arthur Rank Organization.

The Gaumont-British Circuit, also owned by the J. Arthur Rank Organization.

The Associated British Cinemas Circuit (in which Warner Brothers have a $37\frac{1}{2}$% interest).

The 'independent' cinemas (either grouped in circuits, like the Essoldo circuit of over ninety theatres, or operating as single independent theatres).

The three main circuits total some 950 theatres representing one-third of the total seating capacity of the country, and 44% of the total annual box-office; they also control about two-thirds of the 'first-run' theatres in the key London area. The main theatres operating in the West End of London act normally as the advance 'shop window' for all the chief films before they are generally released (including the foreign language films on which the smaller specialized cinemas concentrate). The Warner Theatre (Warner Brothers), the Empire and Ritz (M.G.M.), the Carlton (Twentieth Century-Fox since 1954), the Plaza (Paramount) and the London Pavilion (United Artists) are controlled by the American distributors. The Rank Organization owns others, such as the Odeon, Leicester Square.

In order to provide their audiences with a constant change of programme, all these cinemas must draw on the products of American and British studios. Most cinemas (excluding those in the West End) show two feature films, and change their programmes weekly. They need from America and Britain every first feature film on which they can lay their hands, whatever its quality. The quota insists that most cinemas play films registered as British for 30% of their programmes. The rest of the time the product of Hollywood will be shown, though a very thin sprinkling of foreign-language films (either dubbed into English, or, more rarely, shown with sub-titles) has begun to find its way into provincial theatres. *The Wages of Fear* was the first foreign-language film to achieve a circuit release in Britain in its original tongue.

This, then, is the state of the industry in Britain to-day. I do not believe that the challenge of television is too great for the cinema to answer. In 1954, with the BBC's Television Service almost universally available in the country and with some four million receiving sets in action by the end of the year, cinema attendances showed an increase, not a decline. The need for good film entertainment will never cease; the theatres, with the attraction they offer of a night out as a member of a large audience, will always prevail over entertainment received in isolation at home. But cinemas consistently offering mediocre entertainment in dull surroundings will certainly suffer, and it is difficult to care much if they do. The future of cinemas in the age of television lies in high level entertainment which exploits the full resources of the film, and in more intelligent and attractive publicity. A good film well publicized will always find its public.

THE CINEMA AND OTHER FORMS OF ENTERTAINMENT

A GREAT deal of hot air has been blown over the cinema by the social reformers and other amateur censors who enjoy a good puff at a sitting target. The fact that they are now turning away to direct their distended cheeks at television brings a momentary relief to the movies.

The cinema is one, and only one, element in the world around us which brings some measure of influence to bear on our attitude to life. On many people it has no influence whatsoever – they never see a film in a cinema. Formerly this section tended to be the professional and administrative class, the busy people leading preoccupied lives who left such tomfoolery as films to the lower orders and to silly adolescents. Nowadays cinema-going permeates all classes of society, and the habit of seeing films with some regularity has been established in youth for people who are now in middle life. Constant patronage by older people is beginning to have its effect, and make it more possible for films with a maturer kind of story and treatment to gain wider audiences.

The cinema should be judged in perspective, alongside the other forms of entertainment which the twentieth century has to offer. Commercialized entertainment exists now on a scale for which there is no comparison in the past. This, and not the cinema alone, forms the revolution in human communications which is surely one of the most challenging developments of our time. The linotype machine pours out printed matter at a rate which destroys many square miles of forests each day. Some four thousand bound novels are published each year. The radio provides in this country alone some forty hours of entertainment and information every day. In New York there are about one hundred hours of televised entertainment every day. Theatres and music halls flourish, but on a scale which is dwarfed by the cinema, whose audiences in Britain are as great in one week as a whole year's attendance in all 'live' theatres in the country added together. The outpouring of entertainment and information never seems to stop; but what is probably the most influential element in this constant supply of enjoyment, broadcasting in sound and later in vision, has only been possible for a quarter of a century.

The distinction to be made between entertainment provided at home and in public is discussed in the chapter on television. But even if the dramatic impact of broadcasting at home is much less than that in the 'live' theatre or the cinema (that is, entertainment in public), it is far more pervasive; it is there virtually all one's waking hours and accessible on such easy terms that it is as familiar as the furniture. It is so much a part of ordinary life that no amount of cinema-going is likely to take its place as a constant factor which colours people's lives, knowledge, and sense of values. Virtually every home in the country has a radio set; in 1954 nearly 14 million licences were issued for sound radio, or nearly one licence to every three persons alive in Britain, adult and child alike. A licence may represent a number of receivers operating in one home, and there are always the pirates who cannot be bothered to take out a licence at all.

Here are the main statistics of cinema attendance in Great Britain.

1. *Average Weekly Admissions.*

    1946: 31.4 millions. 1949: 27.5 millions. 1951: 26 millions. 1954 : 25 millions.

2. *Spread of Adult Attendance (1950).*

    38% regular cinema-goers (14.7% going twice a week or more; 23.3% going once a week).

    42.5% occasional cinema-goers (27.9% going less than once a month; 8.5% going once a month; 6.1% going once a fortnight).

    19.5% those who never go to a cinema.

Of the 14.7% who go twice a week or more, 36.4% are under twenty-five years of age. (*Hulton Readership Survey*, 1953.)

3. *Spread of Cinema-going by Children* (1949).

22% twice a week or more.
31.5% once a week.
38.5% occasional.
8% never.

About 38% of the cinemas in this country run cinema clubs on Saturdays, and play to about one million children each week. (*The British Film Industry*: P.E.P.)

Working-class children attend the cinema more frequently than middle-class children. (*Social Survey: The Cinema and the Public*.)

In a survey conducted by the late Dr Maurice Woodhouse at a school in a slum area in Leeds he found 13% of the children aged between 10 and 15 went to the cinema 4 times a week or more, and that 83% went twice a week or more.

4. *Sex, Age, and Class Differentiation in Adult Film-going.*

There is an almost equal balance between the number of women and men in film audiences. (*Hulton Readership Survey*, 1953; also *Social Survey: Cinema and the Public*.)

Young people patronize the cinema far more than older people:

Social Survey: The Cinema and the Public reports:

'69% of those aged 16 to 19 years and 57% of those in the twenties go once a week or more often, and these age groups form 37% of the total adult cinema audience as compared with 24% of the total adult population.'

Hulton Readership Survey, 1953, reports:

'Of those aged between 16 and 24, 69.2% go to the cinema regularly, more than half twice a week or more.'

Among the various occupation groups, factory, clerical, and distributive workers attend the cinema most frequently. (*Social Survey*.)

5. *Exercise of Choice in Film-going.*

Social Survey: The Cinema and the Public:

'It is clear that more of the younger than of the older people go to the cinema regularly choosing which of the cinemas available they will go to according to the films that are showing. Older people more frequently stick to the same cinema and more of them do not go regularly but only go when they want to see the films that are on. In other words younger people tend to make sure of getting some entertainment regularly, exercising choice within a limited field, and older people tend to forgo entertainment unless it is of the type they require. There is however also a substantial proportion in all groups, ranging from 19% of frequent cinema-goers in the youngest group up to 31% in the oldest, that go to the same cinema regularly, exercising no choice whatsoever.'

What the Audience Wants

From all these facts and figures it is obvious that, though the younger people in the audience still predominate, the average age of audiences is tending to rise. This encourages the more responsible film-makers to take some risks in the choice of unusual subjects. Among the more successful films from British studios in the past few years have been *The Overlanders*, *Great Expectations*, *Odd Man Out*, *Oliver Twist*, *The Fallen Idol*, *The Third Man*, *The Blue Lamp*, *Mandy*, *Genevieve*, and *Doctor in the House*, as well as the more conventional 'box-office' type of film. The fact, too, that an increasing number of the younger people appear to be selecting their films, rather than taking whatever the local cinema has to offer them, is encouraging, even though the selection is usually based on the choice between stars and not between subjects.

It has always been important for the cinema to take the measure of its public, and estimate whether the general standard of films which are made and shown is likely to attract the maximum number of people to the box-office. This has only been done to a very limited extent in the past. Films are tested at 'sneak' previews, like those for *The Red Badge of Courage* which are described by Lillian Ross in *Picture;* at these screenings audiences are sometimes asked to give their opinion about the film on cards posing simple questions about it. More rarely audiences have been asked to give their opinions on programme policy – in Britain the best known of these tests were those made for the Granada circuit by Sidney Bernstein. Writing before the war in *Footnotes to the Film*, he makes a distinction in his audiences between the gaga and the film-fan, a distinction which is still relevant. The gaga's

> ... approach to the film is one of identification. For him the hero is the answer to his own day-dreams and the picture a world which causes the realities around him to dissolve for a while. The films are his release from the frustrations of a dull day.

The number of film-fans of the kind described by Sidney Bernstein is small in proportion to the gagas.

> His critical faculty is developing, he can distinguish between good and bad photography and knows something of the technique of film-making. Sometimes he can even differentiate between the good and bad acting of his favourite stars. He is acquiring some degree of articulateness in the correspondence columns of his fan magazines and is eager for pertinent information.

The industry seems on the whole to be shy of testing public opinion other than through the medium of the box-office. Very occasionally conferences are held under the auspices of national bodies of various sorts, but these conferences are almost always inspired from outside the industry, by the British Film Institute, for example, or organizations within the youth movement. It is true that in the United States the Motion Picture Association of America tests public opinion. The M.P.A.A. has a Community Relations Department, and it has formed a panel of representatives of America's numerous women's organizations – such as the National Society of the Daughters of the American Revolution, the Protestant Motion Picture Council, Parents' and Teachers' Associations, and the National Federation of Women's Clubs, as well as representatives of various professional bodies – to meet and express their opinions on current films, opinions which are published in what has come to be known as the 'green sheet'.

Does the Industry Aim at too Narrow an Audience?

The industry's main interest has always tended to concentrate on a single section of its potential audiences – the teen-age-minded public of comparatively limited education.

This, in my view, has become too narrow an assessment of the present potential film-going public. It tends to neglect the many millions who seldom or never go to the cinema. It is quite true that film audiences are still dominated in numbers by young people with restricted tastes, but they can seldom afford to buy the medium- or higher-priced seats in the larger cinemas. Nevertheless, it is still their patronage which is most courted by the greater part of the publicity put up on the hoardings and in the press; the appeal is nearly always made to people who have little education and who respond only to sensation. In spite of this, we have seen that films with an appeal which is wider in interest can be highly successful at the box-office, since they invite the patronage of people who tend to avoid the cinema unless a special appeal is made to them which acknowledges and even flatters their intelligence.

It appears that there are three main kinds of public patronage of films — first, the general kind of patronage based on star appeal and the more obvious forms of sensationalism and glamour; second, the patronage based on the appeal made by film artists appearing in the finer kind of film which reaches the screen only a relatively few times each year; third, the specialized form of patronage which supports foreign-language films and revivals of good but old films mainly in the limited number of theatres in London and the provinces devoted to this kind of programme.

The neglect of the important 'adult' section of the public by the film industry is the main complaint in Gilbert Seldes' excellent study of mass entertainment in the United States which was called *The Great Audience*, and was published in New York in 1950. The cinema caters, he believes, for a special youthful minority of its own creating, and seems quite prepared to sacrifice the patronage of this youthful audience when they enter middle age. It is, he admits, true that adolescence is prolonged in American society, and that a teen-age outlook is extended into middle life, especially in the attitude to sex. This is reflected in almost every film – the exceptions are so rare that they are heralded by the critics as if they were landmarks. Gilbert Seldes joins with those who argue for the specialized promotion of exceptional films as the best means of establishing maturity in both subject and presentation.

The Film Addict and Delinquency

It would be absurd, however, to overlook the addiction of some young people to the cinema. This is emphasized in the books of J. P. Mayer (*Sociology of the Film* and *British Cinemas and their Audiences,* published in 1946 and 1949, and written during the period when film-going was at its height in this country). Exception has been taken to the limited field of research which Mayer's surveys represented, but the statements he obtained from schoolchildren and adolescents are often very revealing. His second book is based on essays written by readers of *Picturegoer,* the best of Britain's film-fan magazines. The important part that films can play in the experience of many working girls living in the poorer districts of our cities is shown in Pearl Jephcott's notable book, *Rising Twenty.* Pearl Jephcott writes:

The trouble with intensive picture going lies not in the sinfulness or inanity of so many films, but in the simple fact that the girl has only a limited amount of time in which to learn to become a fully developed adult, and that a routine of several nights every week at the pictures eats into this time with a regularity and persistence that is the more alarming as one watches it taking place from childhood till the girl has become adult in body, even if she is still immature in mind and emotions. It is really heart-breaking, to take an actual example, to give an intelligent girl an entirely routine job from 8 a.m. to 5.30 p.m. and for recreation to provide her with a film of the *Czarina* calibre as the high-spot of her life two or three nights each week; and moreover to realize that this has been happening for the last four years; and that she is still only 18.

Arthur Collin and Vera Poole, in their disturbing account of the life led by children in an English industrial slum area, have their realistic comment on the cinema in *These Our Children*:

There is no point in entering at this stage into the controversy about the influence of the cinema on children and its relation to the problem of juvenile delinquency. Whatever the direct effect of the films shown at our cinemas to-day – there are people who argue that many of the films are an obvious inducement to impressionable youngsters to commit crime, whilst others claim there is no evidence to prove this – there can be little doubt that films which continually stress the seamy side of life with the accent on wealth, dress, and sexual matters must inevitably have an unsettling effect on the child's social adjustment.

Examples of the self-revelation of the statements quoted in J. P. Mayer's books are these:

Girl aged 17: 'No, films have never influenced me in the big moments of my life, only in the small things such as clothes. They do influence my manners and behaviour to a certain extent. I shall never look like Vivien Leigh but that is no reason why I shouldn't copy her walk and the way she sways her hips. I shall never act like Greer Garson, but I still try to laugh as she does. There is a right way and a wrong way of holding a cigarette; they do it the right way on the pictures and when I begin to smoke I shall do it like Katherine Hepburn in *Philadelphia Story*.'

Another older girl: 'The pictures I saw became the chief source of subject matter for day-dreams. I would lie awake for hours after going to bed day-dreaming. After seeing an especially good show I have gone off to bed especially early to get those dreams started.'

Girl aged 18: 'After every film I see I find myself consciously or unconsciously copying the voice, walk, dress or mannerisms of some star, male or female, but this usually doesn't last, unless in such a small degree that I am unaware of it.

'I just stated that I "copied" the dresses of the stars, but this is not quite true. I merely "noted" the styles and formed my ideas on dress from the good (and bad) points of the stars' dresses.'

Girl aged 21: 'Music, films, and writing are the only things in life which really transfer me to a brighter and happier world. Reading makes me more serious and thoughtful but also helps me to get away from the toils and worries of the world to-day. Life is so dull and ordinary that I intend getting all I can out of films that they have to offer. I don't envy folks who don't like films, they must find life too dull for *words*.'

Girl aged 19½: 'I don't think films have made me more receptive to love-making – maybe "soft lights and sweet music", but not films – but they certainly have taught me how to handle men – how to adapt my own personality to please different men, and how to hold their interest, once gained.'

Man aged 21: 'I freely admit that I have learned a lot on the technique of love-making from the films. Probably all I know, in fact. So you see from my point of view, films are a good thing.'

These statements all go to prove that there is a certain minority of young film-goers who are addicts – in other words, they depend on the day-dreams that films can inspire rather than enjoy them quite simply as a passing amusement. This minority of young people cannot imagine how to live without the stimulation of films. Some of them are mentally underdeveloped and emotionally unstable; many, though not all, come from poor homes. They are easily touched off by the immediate appeal which most films aim at providing. Often they seem to be the merest children – the youngest adolescents just discovering the new freedom of working for a pay packet instead of for a school-master or schoolmistress. Sexual attraction is a new, wonder-ful, and uncharted experience, for which films provide an endless example based on flesh and fantasy. The constant love-talk, fatuous or sentimental, provides for the in-articulate, struggling young lovers the oil of courtship, eas-ing sexual embarrassments and providing a conventional bridge of emotion between girl and boy.

The evidence is all against the cinema being regarded as a training centre for the juvenile delinquent. On this point the Report of the Departmental Committee on Children and the Cinema is unequivocal. Speaking of its enquiries, the Committee says:

The results do not, in our judgement, fasten on the cinema any primary share in the responsibility for the delinquency or moral laxity of children under 16.

The heads of approved schools were almost unanimous, this being the point of view generally agreed between them:

During the last two years I have carried out a systematic investigation of the causes of delinquency in some 130 youths aged 15–18. . . . In nearly every case the delinquency can be traced to a grossly defective home situation, to a lack of parental affection, to severe anxieties centring round the parents or to a hypertrophy of the fear reactions due to a succession of accidents. I have found no cases of delinquency being caused by a casual influence, whether of the cinema or otherwise. The most that can be said of the influence of the cinema is that it may determine the pattern of the delinquent's breakdown.

A report from a group of probation officers offered this opinion on the effect of the cinema on delinquent girls:

It appeared likely, in respect of adolescent girls under the age of 16, that emotional disturbances might be over-stimulated by the romantic types of films, but the fundamental difficulties with such girls were probably operative factors before cinema going became a habit, and although films are regularly discussed with probationers no evidence has been forthcoming that the films themselves were having a direct bearing on delinquency or moral laxity.

The Magistrates' Association in their Annual Report published in 1948 stated:

There is general agreement among psychologists that the cinema is seldom, if ever, a cause of juvenile delinquency. The young are not more wicked than they were before cinemas came, but cinemas are a convenient scapegoat. The cinema keeps boys out of mischief, men out of public houses, and girls off the streets. Investigations have never found any correlation between delinquency and attending the cinema. There is no evidence from any other country that there is any relationship between the cinema and juvenile delinquency.

Speaking in Parliament as Home Secretary, Sir Samuel Hoare (now Lord Templewood) said:

My very expert and experienced advisers in the Home Office are of the opinion that the cinema conduces more to the prevention of crime than to its commission. It keeps boys out of mischief –

it gives them something to think about. The Home Office opinion is that if cinemas had never existed there would probably be more crime than there is, rather than less.

Finally, Sir Cyril Burt, the eminent psychologist, spoke on behalf of the cinema in *The Young Delinquent*:

The cinema has been freely censured and abused for stimulating the young adventurer to mischief, folly, and even crime. Perhaps no one is so eager to advocate this view as the young culprit himself, who frequently sees in such a derivation of his deeds a chance to deflect blame from his own moral laxity to that of the producer of the film. For the others . . . the steady and healthy-minded, the cinema supplies an alternative, and not a provocative, to mischievous crime.

False Values in Some Films

Like literature and the 'live' theatre, film drama is fond of lifting the lid off human nature through stories of crime and passion. Human beings behaving outside the social conventions is the stuff of all forms of drama from classical Greek tragedy to the modern Hollywood thriller. Without this excess there would be no development of conflict, and the essence of drama is the development and final resolution of some form of human struggle. Though the practice of film censorship, particularly in this country and America, insists on the observation of certain moral formulas in the resolution of human conflict at the end of a film, no blue pencils or moral scissors can alter the effect of watching human passion and violence developed on the screen, however much the moral point that crime and lust do not pay is rubbed in – often quite arbitrarily and artificially. We cannot escape from the eternal dilemma that children will always learn about life and its evils far too young, whether there is any cinema in the neighbourhood to illustrate this for them or not.

In my earlier book, *Film*, I launched an attack on the less-than-good films which I still strongly maintain. It was written in the cause of entertainment, the true purpose of the cinema, and it was meant to describe the kind of film which in the end bores its audience by its repetitive stupidities. There are still too many of these films – American and European alike – and the cinema can no longer afford them, for they are the main cause of the empty seats for which television is blamed. I wrote in *Film* of these innumerable bad pictures that they are hectic rather than recreative, and try to entertain through presenting more or less stupid adventures derived from an equal mixture of so-called original screen-plays and scripts based on novels (some of them best-sellers) and short stories acted by the sexier sort of stars and starlets.

The influence of this cynical attitude to the pleasures of life as far as young people are concerned is debatable. Those with stable backgrounds and sound education will realize that a great deal of what these films show is spurious living and will either reject it with adolescent prudery or just laugh because they have seen through it. But others without these advantages of background and upbringing will feel themselves slipping into the attitudes and codes which these films represent, in spite of the morality clauses of the censorship code. It is common enough to see very young girls dolled up like starlets and young men with stove-pipe trousers and an ape-like gait. These points of appearance and public behaviour reveal lives which are being developed without any decent social standards behind them. The dry rot of irresponsibility has set in. How far constant attendance at the cinema is the *root* cause of this attitude in both boys and girls is debatable, as we have seen, but that it must exercise some influence upon them seems to me to be irrefutable.

The business of the cinema is to provide recreation through entertainment. This recreation should re-create. It should have human appeal, enlivening emotion, stirring the heart; it should invigorate one's attitude to life and enlarge one's humanity. At the least it should be a good pastime; at the best a fine and lasting experience. It should enable people to leave the cinema for home feeling exhilarated and emotionally moved. To be absorbed into a good story, however light or farcical, thrilling or comic, melodramatic or tragic, should be an experience which to a varying extent re-makes the soil of the individual and allows new life to generate. It must be admitted that some kinds of entertainment offered by the cinemas are degrading rather than exhilarating, flaccid rather than invigorating, emotionally debilitated rather than strong and exciting. Passion is ill-served, and the mind atrophied to a few nervous platitudes acceptable to the meanest intelligence in the audience. This will no longer do for the cinema to-day or in the future.

The Star System

The fiction film is one of the dramatic arts because it is normally performed by actors before an audience. It is a highly specialized dramatic art, because its pictorial presentation can offer the audience much more than acting alone could achieve. But many, in fact most films, are vehicles for stars, and nothing about the cinema has been so calculated in its influence on world audiences as the Hollywood star-system.

The worship of the stars begins with the publicity put out about them. Publicity is a fertilizer, building up a fine crop of audiences. But in films nothing succeeds better than success itself. Publicity can lay the foundation of success; after that only the actor and the picture together can turn the bubble of advance reputation into genuine audience appeal.

The hold that individual players could have on the public was discovered almost by accident during the famous 'war' between the early American film companies. Carl Laemmle saw that the dark beauty of the anonymous Biograph girl, Florence Lawrence, was attracting attention; audiences were following her from picture to picture and sending her employers letters asking who she was. So he offered her more money than Biograph were giving her, revealed her name to the press, and announced that she was dead. Then he cashed in on the sensation he had caused by the statement; he claimed that after all she was alive and that the rumour had been created by his rivals to injure him. Florence Lawrence's name was made by this publicity device; she was a star. She made a triumphant 'personal appearance' before a riotous crowd of enthusiasts.

Since then the era of the stars has been largely the public exploitation of various kinds of human glamour, a curious tale of varying tastes in what constitutes fascination in men and women. The Victorian 'little woman' idea of femininity associated with Mary Pickford and Lillian Gish, though always liable to reappear when male stars are in the ascendant, was soon replaced in Hollywood by bolder ideas of what women could really become if encouraged along the right lines.

A girl called Theodosia Goodman of Cincinnati was turned by skilful publicity into the most astonishing sensation of the American screen during the first World War. By spelling Death and Arab backwards Hollywood created a professional name for her; Theda Bara. She represented the vamp who became a vampire; she was said to be the daughter of a French artist and his Arab mistress, and to have been born in the Sahara. She was the 'fascinating and the unfathomable, whose passion is touched with death'. She made film after film in which she dragged respected citizens from their wives and families and finally left them, destitute, exhausted, and suffering from delirium tremens, clawing the air in some last melodramatic finale. Her publicity photographs showed her with the skeletons of men stretched at her feet. But her films, in spite of such exotic titles as *The Tiger Woman*, *Purgatory's Ivory Angel*, *Salomé*, and *Gold and the Woman*, were really as moral as a tract, although their mass popularity only thirty-five years ago set the scene for a more realistic form of female glamour.

During the twenties a more daring kind of film was introduced to the public by that great showman Cecil B. de Mille, beginning with *Male and Female* in 1919. This was the true defeat of Mary Pickford's innocent little Pollyanna girls, as this kind of heroine was called. *Male and Female* (adapted in a 'raw' way from Barrie's *The Admirable Crichton*) featured Gloria Swanson, who appeared in many of de Mille's so-called problem films about the vices of wealthy society – *Don't Change Your Husband*, *Why Change Your Wife?*, and *Forbidden Fruit*. Gloria Swanson, unlike Theda Bara, portrayed the realistic siren – the woman in active pursuit of her man. She was, needless to say, voluptuous, and the title of her film *Manhandled* added a new descriptive term to the social jargon of the time.

Official censorship had not yet been established in America, though it was, of course, constantly threatened in one shape or another. The twenties became a wild period in film-making, and themes of marital infidelity and licence of all kinds were again carried to the heights of a new absurdity in titles like *Temptation*, *Passion Flame*, *Flaming Youth*, and *La, La, Lucille*. The glamour star was in real demand, and names like Pola Negri, Norma Shearer, and Greta Garbo began to be well-known. This was also the period when Elinor Glyn's novels occupied the same place in public demand as *Forever Amber* did recently. 'It' became the sex-phrase of the period, and Clara Bow was the screen's 'it' girl. The parts she played were of the frivolous, irresponsible girl of the jazz-mad age, the sample of frenzied post-war youth having its fling. She was quite different from the sirens of the problem films. They exploited the female mysteries: she did not. They fascinated men by their elusive differences from them, while she rushed around with the boys, being modern and free, on the love 'em and leave 'em principle. All this activity filled the cinemas without much difficulty twenty-five years ago.

Joan Crawford portrayed an intermediate kind of woman. The mysterious draperies were laid aside, but the melodramatically provocative attitude of the vamp remained. This attitude was to continue successful with audiences until well into the thirties, when eventually neurosis was to become the fashionable attribute to glamorous woman.

Before Mae West arrived to throw the old-fashioned

draperies and artificial feminine mysteries to the winds, the real star of this fashion in women was Greta Garbo. The way was prepared for her by that fascinating and almost forgotten star, Alla Nazimova, a Russian vaudeville actress who had begun to work for the films during the War.

Nazimova had that kind of personality which creates an audience of people from every section of the public, whether they are normal film-goers or not. Thirty years ago she exercised a power which extended beyond the attractions of publicity. While other women 'acted' the mysterious qualities of womanhood, she possessed them. Her films were as bad as she was good – *An Eye for an Eye*, *The Red Lantern*, *Camille*, and *Salomé*. She was not provocatively pretty like the usual successful screen star: she created her own beauty out of a face which was as plain as it was unusual. She was a dancer whose movements created a poetry that the cinema did not realize it needed till she embodied it, and as she moved her impenetrable face left the mystery of what she was feeling unsolved. This curious yet passionate 'remoteness' is the greatest gift a woman star can have, because it leaves her audience possessed with the desire to discover what they cannot understand about her.

This great gift of mystery was inherited by Greta Garbo, whose publicity was often unfortunate. One famous photograph superimposed her face on to that of the Sphinx itself. She, too, possessed that rare 'withheld' quality, which it is useless for any actress to try to assume if she is not endowed with it by nature. When she stood at the prow of the ship at the end of *Queen Christina*, there was no member of any cinema audience who quite knew what she was thinking, and so the shot remained indelibly fixed as a challenge to the imagination. Here again was a star personality, a great actress who did not have to assume the full attributes of womanhood: she embodied them whether she played a vamp, a courtesan, or a woman possessed by a love the strength of which was never in doubt. She transformed hokum into art.

Then into the arena of glamour strode the show-woman

231

Mae West, whose vigorous sex plays had been denounced by the moralists. But she knew her strength and exercised it in films like *She Done Him Wrong* until the forces of censorship, which had originally kept her away from the screen, once more forced her off it. Although she played the man-eater she scorned the devices of the vamp; she had an unconquerable bluntness which by-passed the humour always underlying sex in the sheer resplendent showmanship of her opulent personal appearances. Mae West was a cave-woman who had no use for the trickeries of glamour.

Since her brief time in films twenty years ago, just after the great economic depression of the early thirties, the vamp, the siren, and even the shimmering courtesan portrayed by Marlene Dietrich have seemed dated, if not a little absurd. No great star has risen to take the place of Garbo, and inherit her indisputable and hypnotic hold upon her world audiences.

The screen players of to-day do not even try to be the legendary figures of which great stars are made: their aim is to be representative of their audiences rather than to seem exceptional and remote. They become as a result familiar and favourite actors instead of irresistible sources of audience fascination, except perhaps for the more impressionable adolescent.

If the hold of the stars on cinema audiences is on the wane, then I think this is the reason for it. It can only survive as a major force in the cinema if performers of the calibre of true stars emerge once more to symbolize and so maintain the star-system as it once was.

There is a good and bad side to the star-system. First of all it is not in itself the invention of the film industry; the theatre established it in the performances of Greek and Roman drama and in Elizabethan times it was established afresh in this country. Ordinary human beings will always gape at the extraordinary ones who succeed in public life, and success in acting is one of the most obvious ways of exciting public attention. For what is it but the stirring of varied emotions in an audience through individual skill in impersonation? Actresses become for their fans the beautiful symbols of emotional self-expression, actors the noble embodiment of manly prowess – or so we would have them be on stage and screen. Critical audiences require subtleties of human interpretation of a kind adolescents cannot appreciate, and the greater artists of the screen in fulfilling this need may have to forfeit popularity with the largest sections of their public. Therefore Hollywood sees to it that the majority of film stars appeal only at a level likely to excite the adulation of very young people. As far as these adolescents are concerned, they need young adults whom they may idealize as projections of what they themselves would like to be.

Margaret Thorp writes in *America at the Movies*:

Fortunately for those who make the films not many of the weekly attendants at the movies can get to Hollywood and try actually to touch their dreams. Most of the eighty-five million must feed their reveries with newsprint. The fan magazines are very good to them; they supply just those bits of information which the screen has no time to give; they make it possible for the worshipper to identify herself with the glamorous star as she can do with no other character in fiction. When you read a book you know only what the author tells you about the heroine, even though you follow her through sequel after sequel. On the stage you may not see the same actress once in five years but on the screen you can watch her over and over again, in different poses against scores of different backgrounds, and then you can follow her into the fan magazines. They will fill in for you all the little intimate details that make a personality real, that make identification close and exciting.

I do not think that the star-system will ever lose its power in the cinema as a whole; it would be inhuman to expect that film-goers, whether they are young or old, will lose their fundamental interest in the attraction of actors and actresses who are successful in their expression and interpretation of human experience or are merely amusing as personalities. After all, why should they? What will happen, indeed what has been happening gradually as both the cinema and its audiences slowly mature, is that the number of films which can be made to appeal widely without resort to the star personality is increasing. The relative importance as between the players and the drama in the cinema is gradually achieving the same kind of balance which exists in the live theatre.

Children and the Cinema

The special attraction which films have for children is always the subject of comment. It is only to be expected that a moving picture will tend to appeal to a child more than a story told in words alone, for words will always present a measure of difficulty to a child, especially if the standard of his literacy is low.

It is generally agreed that just as there are books specially written and published for children, so there should be films specially produced for children. It is also well known that Britain and Soviet Russia are the only countries which have consistently produced films for children over a number of years. In this country production was sponsored by the Rank Organization from 1944 to 1950, and, since 1951, by the Children's Film Foundation working with a special annual grant from the British Film Production Fund. Miss Mary Field, who has had charge of this work for both organizations, has given her views on the subject in her book *Good Company*.

Mary Field has made a special study of the way children react to films, and has used the results of her observations to guide her in the choice of subject and technique for her productions. She writes in *Good Company*:

Gradually, after viewing some hundreds of audiences, we learnt to interpret for our own information the movements and sounds of the children. Most interesting were the sounds. We learned to distinguish seven: the bad noise when the children were bored by adult pictures and were playing among themselves and getting fractious; the equally bad scream of sheer excitement that greeted adult coloured cartoons and scenes of unreasoned violence in serials and Westerns; the good healthy shout of intelligent excitement when the story they were following intellectually reached its climax – a useful emotional cathartic; the equally useful cathartic, the healthy laughter at simple comic situations that appealed to the children's sense of humour and not to their latent streak of cruelty; the good noise of interest with members of the audience happily talking to each other, to themselves, or to the characters on the screen, the kind of sound one hears in a classroom where the best kind of free activity is prevailing; the 'coo' of pleasure at a baby or a small animal or a softly coloured scene that appealed to them emotionally, with the kindred breath-take when camera movement proved aesthetically satisfying; finally, the complete silence when the audience was spellbound by the unfolding of the story on the screen.

Children of seven to twelve years of age, she found, want to identify themselves with the children on the screen – like some adults and many adolescents, only rather more so. They do not want too much dialogue, and they dislike action developed too quickly for them to follow with care. (Many of Walt Disney's cartoons are far too quick as well as too sophisticated for children.) They do not want to see their favourite characters in danger or expressing real fright. They like the continuity of characters to be found in serials, but they can easily become over-stimulated by situations which seem desperate at the point when the so-called adult serials are designed to break off.

Miss Field has gradually built up a team of film-makers who have a special aptitude for this type of work, which includes the creation of original stories for films, since few of the children's classics in literature translate well to the screen. Children have their own special attitudes to the adult characters in the films intended solely for them, and to the balance of power between good and bad in the world.

Children see adults in their way, not in ours. For them there are young adults, fifteen or sixteen years old, and worthy objects of respect, grown-ups who are really old – over twenty at least, but who may well be attractive, and then the very, very old to whom children can feel protective. There is no place for the middle-aged in this age-range. In real life children see in their mind's eye their parents, their teachers, all adults whom they love and respect as they wish them to be, not as they are. So, in children's films, all fathers should be tall, slim, and handsome in a thin-featured way. Mothers should be young, slender, pretty, and well-dressed, but not too glamorous or fashionable, while teachers, policemen, and all other adult characters that are on the side of right should be cast in the same mould. Only bad men in this dream-world may be fat, middle-aged or bald.

To achieve that sense of security for which they crave, young children like to think of a world divided into the good, who in the long run win, and the bad, who eventually lose. It is a sign of adolescence when a child begins to complain that 'the goodies always win', and he can safely move on, with his parents, to 'A' films.

Ethics in children's films present their own problems. On the whole small children need a black-and-white world so that they may clearly identify themselves with the 'good' side. On the other hand, the first children's entertainment films made for the Rank Organization were obviously too conventionally moral, amounting almost to preaching about matters of behaviour. Children expect the characters offered for their identification to be vigorously good, not goody-goody; it is always a matter of their actively adopting the action which is the result of right-mindedness, and never talking about it!

The films made for the children include magazines of children's doings all over the world, documentary, nature and travel films, serials, cartoons, short-story films and short feature-length productions lasting about an hour. Great emphasis is put on international subjects. Films made abroad are acquired for the children's entertainment, and many films have been specially produced abroad under British sponsorship, like *Bush Christmas*, which was made in Australia, and *The Boy Who Stopped Niagara*, which was made in Canada. The films are shown mainly at the children's club shows on Saturday mornings. The problem behind produc-tion remains a financial one, for at the prices children can afford to pay it takes about twenty years to make a children's

feature film cover its costs! Some form of subsidy is therefore essential, and, after the Rank Organization's generous
sponsorship had to come to an end, assistance was eventually
forthcoming from the British Film Production Fund.

The Report of the Departmental Committee on Children
and the Cinema states the case against children seeing films
designed to entertain adults in a more or less dubious way:

> A large number of films are exposing children regularly to the
> suggestion that the highest values in life are riches, power, luxury,
> and public adulation, and that it does not matter very much how
> these are attained or used. According to these films, you can eat
> your cake and have it too. You can be happy without much effort
> or hard work, so long as you have a lucky star, or an influential
> patron, or some brand of personal glamour which you are prepared
> to capitalize without much restraint of conscience. This general
> kind of easy and selfish philosophy is fringed with other supporting
> illusions, involving the distortion of history and biography, and of
> people of other nations and their national heroes. We are prepared
> to believe there is much force in these criticisms, and we are con-
> vinced that the regular portrayal of false values is more pervasive
> and dangerous than the depiction of crime or impropriety. Films
> suitable for children which lay emphasis on spiritual values are too
> few and far between, and we regret the lack of films depicting
> happy marriage and contentment in family life.

The remedy in some countries is to prohibit children
under sixteen years of age from going to the cinema at all.
In this country the cinema club and children's matinees
scarcely begin to meet the demand of children for film
entertainment, and our film censorship arrangements are
chiefly concerned to assess the suitability or otherwise for
children under sixteen years of age of all films released for
public showing. And so we come to the problem of censorship, on which everyone must have some point of view.

Puritanism and the Cinema

Whether or not we attend places of worship or adhere to
the various Christian orthodoxies, we remain members of a
Puritan nation. It is in some ways a great source of strength

237

to us. When we speak of our British integrity, of our revolt at any obvious sign of corruption in our public life, of our personal standards of loyalty and honesty, we speak of qualities which are quite real to the greater number of British people, however much it is true to add that love of graft and lack of scruples may influence the actions of a considerable minority.

On the other hand, Puritanism has its weaknesses. It is scandalized by the cynical Continental who lifts his shoulders and smiles at the intrigue of local officials and the wanton activities of human flesh. The Puritan British always want to put these things right, to force their national standards of truth-telling and official integrity upon people to whom this kind of behaviour seems impossibly idealistic and romantic.

The Puritan leads a double life. He inherits a body which has the simple functions and cravings of an animal, desires which are accepted by the non-Puritan as natural or inevitable and to be allowed for in the general code of living with your neighbours in the ordinary kindliness and rivalries of social life. But the Puritan always carries the dream of Heaven in his pocket. When the wrath takes him he will beat goodness into his children and discipline his wife by starving her of natural affection. He will build up organizations to resist the exercise of boisterous humour or public amusement on a Sunday, although Christ himself was among the most humane and liberal of all the religious teachers. He will above everything else suppress humanity in a strait-jacket of ideal moral behaviour, advocating a cold rectitude of conduct which may at best have a stern kindliness about it, but is seldom attractive or warm or vital. He would rather see a Sunday with adolescents on the streets than an open cinema, or no alcohol at all than the risk of a few people getting drunk. The Puritan regards the arts as a profession suitable only for casually paid eccentrics, for a work of art is often the result of emotional expression of a kind no Puritan wishes to experience in his own heart.

However liberal we may think ourselves to be individually,

few British people remain unaffected by our national Puritan climate which has been created by our forebears since the time of Shakespeare, and has also in various other national forms affected the Protestant countries of Europe and some sections of American society. Censorship of the arts on moral as distinct from political grounds (which raise other issues which I am not discussing here) is characteristic of Britain, America, and some European countries, though it must always be remembered that cinema attendance in Britain and America is a more widespread habit, involving all age-groups from childhood to old age, than it is, for example, in France, where audiences are only a third those of Britain. Many European countries exclude children from normal cinema performances; if such a suggestion were made here, apart from attendance at the comparatively rare film given an 'X' certificate, it would scandalize most exhibitors, who look on their 'family' audiences as providing a staple part of their box-office returns.

The double life led by the Puritan, whether he is harsh or comparatively liberal, results in a strange romanticism of outlook. In the world of fiction he believes that all people who do wrong according to his code must automatically be punished as a warning to those who may be tempted to commit similar sins. It does not matter that in so many cases the sinner patently triumphs in actual life and appears, to judge by his complexion and his complacence, not to suffer the appalling tortures of conscience allotted to him by his poorer and more honest Puritan brother. However, what cannot be applied to life itself can certainly be applied to films, however artificial the retribution imposed. The criminal is invariably brought to justice or some equally sobering or tragic end.

Too artificial a morality has its own peculiar dangers. It is obviously necessary for all of us, adolescent or adult, to evolve a code of social and personal behaviour in which we instinctively come to believe and according to which we act. It will no doubt be a somewhat elastic code, graded by many people according to what they feel they can in the current circumstances get away with while retaining a reasonable measure of private and public esteem. Yet how rare is it for us to see this common human attitude portrayed honestly on the screen. The bogey of moral retribution haunts our conception of screen censorship. The result for our children and adolescents when they have to face life as it is on entering employment is the shock of realization that dishonesty and corruption often pay, and that bad social behaviour as often as not results in increased power. The spectacle of the obvious unpleasantness of selfish, cruel, or otherwise bad people should in itself be sufficient warning to those whose personalities are still malleable, without having almost always to drag in artificial forms of last-minute retribution to show that evil does not pay in purely physical and material terms, when it so often does so in real life.

In no branch of human life does Puritanism bear so hardly as upon our attitude to sexual behaviour. Few Puritans are free of desire, but all of them fear what seems to them to be the personal disintegration which its indulgence brings about. In no theme is the contrast so sharp between Anglo-American productions and French and Italian or Swedish films. The French cinema treats the love relationship both inside and outside marriage quite realistically: it is an important part of life, a symbol of its completeness, a source of bitterness and suffering as well as of happiness. Sex in Anglo-American films is too often a matter for coy and salacious embarrassments, or that kind of airy romanticism which has no body, root, or savour, while ineffectual dialogue is given a false significance by lush musical accompaniments. By bowdlerizing the novels and plays from which our films are often made, the Puritan conscience sows false seeds in the adolescent heart. Nurtured on happy endings and totally ignorant of the problems the institution of marriage really raises for human beings, the romantic adolescent jumps into matrimony without any of the wise scepticism with which a balanced portrayal of life should arm him.

It is said that the Romance races are realistic and the

Saxon races romantics. There is a great deal of truth in this. There is little attempt to bowdlerize marriage and sexual relationships in French, Italian, or Swedish films. The happy ending, though frequent, is not the inevitable part of Continental box-office policy. The Italians like gay, earthy films, the French like sceptical comedies. Neither really suits the greater British public. They do not worship the stars as amusing entertainers or great histrionic artists, but as their own sublimated selves living an ideal life of luxury, ease, and unreality. This is the lowest ebb of Puritan romanticism, the escape from realities into a kind of simple Heaven from which the vitality of the older Christian tradition has long since vanished. The active Puritans now are mostly content just to close things down and see that life is kept as grey as possible on Sundays.

I do not think the Puritan conscience will easily relinquish its hold on the soul of Britain: it is too firmly ingrained and has become now as much a national as it was once a purely religious characteristic. It has also, as we have seen, a certain importance in strengthening the fibre of our private and public life. But it always has been and will continue to be the bane of the artist, who is the eternal opposite of the Puritan, warm, volatile, often undisciplined, and unstable, free in his expression and rich in his zest for new experiences of every kind. The British public as a whole find such people difficult either to understand or to tolerate, and a steady persecution of them and their works soon follows in the form of public censorship. Meanwhile, the Puritan British are left to seek their imaginative outlet in dreams of success in material terms (the luxury flat and the rich, handsome husband), and in the continuous reaffirmation that it pays to be good. Of one thing there is no doubt, it certainly pays to represent life this way.

The Public and Film Censorship

Are you the sort of person who wants to decide absolutely for himself whether he should attend a play or see a film or read a book or visit an exhibition *whatever it may be about?* This question is the first test of your own attitude to censorship. If you answer 'yes' to the whole of it without any reservation whatsoever, then I would say that you are against any form of censorship in the arts, that is as far as you yourself are concerned.

Only a minority of people would have the courage to answer 'yes' if they were really pressed. When you consider that without some form of censorship, whether administered by an official or a policeman is for the moment beside the point, it would be possible for the arts to portray to the public, quite indiscriminately, lewdness and blasphemy, unrestrained vice and perversion, sadism and the cruelties of the jungle, you will begin to see where censorship quite naturally begins. The real problem lies in deciding at what point it should end.

Now this bold minority of people who are prepared to face anything rather than seek the protection of the police or hide behind a censor, may well draw the line when the same freedom is permitted to other people who they think are weaker-minded than themselves! What is all right for you may not, in your opinion, be all right for your maiden aunt or your fourteen-year-old daughter or your brother-in-law who is a country parson. So you guide them away, or perhaps tell them bluntly they are not to look. And so you will have become a censor yourself.

All this goes to show that there is no easy answer to the censorship problem. Abolish it altogether, and you will soon get an exploitation of public curiosity which will invite some kind of police intervention. Public behaviour over street accidents and murder trials shows there are always plenty of people about who are keen to get a low sort of thrill at any price. It was because of this that censorship began here, and, for that matter, in America.

It is a curious story. Most people think the film censor is a Government official like the Lord Chamberlain, who has been the official Censor of Plays since an Act of 1737 and is a member of the Royal Household. The plays are actually read by one or other of a number of official Readers of Plays appointed by the Lord Chamberlain. But the film Censor is not a Government official: he is an official of the film industry itself. The films of forty or fifty years ago, especially the comedies and farces, were gradually getting so low in tone that the British film producers felt it was time to put their own house in order before someone else from outside came and did it for them; there are always plenty of people only too ready to clean up the activities of others in the name of virtue.

So the Kinematograph Manufacturers' Association, as the main film producers' organization was then called, set up the British Board of Film Censors in 1912. G. A. Redford, who had been the Lord Chamberlain's official Reader of Plays for nearly twenty years, was appointed the first President, and he was succeeded by T. P. O'Connor in 1916. O'Connor's name became famous on the smudgy censorship certificate which preceded the tens of thousands of films shown to the public during his Presidency. F. Brook Wilkinson, who died in 1948, was the Secretary of the Board from its commencement. The President now is Sir Sydney Harris, and the Secretary is A. T. L. Watkins, who was Brook Wilkinson's chief assistant. It is perhaps typically British that the Kinematograph Manufacturers' Association, which has long been superseded as a representative organization of the British film producers, still survives as the body which appoints the President of the British Board of Film Censors. The President is then left free to choose his own small staff of censors, who are responsible for viewing every film, long or short, shown on our public screens, except the newsreels which are not required to be censored.

Yet if you were to ask the Censor what is really the protective or prohibitive power in the cinema, he would tell you it is the Local Authority. Although the certificate which precedes the film looks as official as a dog licence, it is really only an advisory certificate warning all comers that in the view of the Censor the film is in a special class (X) entirely unsuitable for showing to children under sixteen years of age, or Adult (A) and therefore only to be seen by children if the adult with them will take on the responsibility of introducing them, or Universal (U) which means that anyone of any age can go into the cinema if he has got the money. But the individual certificates given are advisory only. Any Local Authority can alter them for its own locality; for exexample, a good many authorities changed the certificate A given to Walt Disney's *Snow White and the Seven Dwarfs* to a U.

The main distinction between the British and American systems of self-censorship, built up in each case by the film industries themselves in order to avoid intervention by the state, is that the American Hays Office committed itself to a written code while the British Censor has so far left matters to direct argument with the film-maker. In Britain, therefore, the general rules concerning what is forbidden remain open to discussion. This, at any rate, allows for a certain elasticity, and British film censorship since A. T. L. Watkins became Secretary has achieved a reputation for liberality which is not entirely shared by the American Censors.

All censorship is a dead weight on the more progressive artist. The idealist in these matters has always said that the artist alone should take responsibility for what he says, and that the public itself is the best judge of whether its baser instincts are being exploited. The greatest freedom of expression undoubtedly belongs to the writer, provided he can find a publisher for his work.

The dramatist has to be more circumspect, for his work is performed in public. But the least freedom of all belongs to the film-maker; because his audience is so extensive his work has come to be hedged in by restraints unknown to any other art in Britain. The more accessible a work of art becomes to an assembled audience representing all ages, child and adult, the more it has to observe the restrictions of codes or unwritten rules.

Nevertheless, if the Censor suddenly decided to abolish himself, it would almost certainly be necessary to re-create him again in one form or another. The conditions of film-going in this country make it a very mixed affair; audiences are dominated by the permanent presence of young adolescents and family parties, whereas in some Continental countries children under sixteen years are excluded from the cinemas altogether.

But the Censor claims he does not exist to administer or reform the industry, but to deal with it as it is. He must take into account the youthful element in virtually all the cinema audiences in Britain. Therefore he gives *Snow White and the Seven Dwarfs* an A and not a U certificate on account of the frightening scenes of witchcraft, and *Oliver Twist* and *Great Expectations* similarly became A pictures on account of certain scenes which appear in them. The only certificate which excludes children is that for the X category. This was introduced in January 1951, partly to enable the censor to pass with as little interference as possible foreign language films made in countries where censorship restrictions do not operate in so narrow a way as in Hollywood, and partly to enable him to deal more strictly with films containing horrific, violent, or 'difficult' themes totally unsuitable for children. The X certificate is unpopular with exhibitors when it is applied to American or British films intended for wide distribution, because it keeps the family audience away from the cinema, and the family audience is an important part of the regular patronage. Typical of the better films gaining an X Certificate have been the American productions *A Streetcar named Desire*, *The Well*, *Death of a Salesman*, *War of the Worlds*, and *Sound of Fury*, and the foreign-language films, *Rashomon*, *Los Olvidados*, *Casque d'or*, *Les Jeux interdits*, and *La Ronde*.

The attitude of the British censorship is expressed in an article written by A. T. L. Watkins, Secretary to the Board of Film Censors, for *Penguin Film Review* (9):

The Board has no written Code, no neatly docketed list of things which are allowed and things which are not. It has been suggested that such a Code would help producers. The Board thinks it would have the reverse effect. The absence of a Code enables it to treat each picture, each incident, each line of dialogue on its merits. No two pictures are alike, everything depends on the treatment and the context. If the Board worked to a Code, it would have to stick to the Code. Films would be dealt with on the basis of hard-and-fast rules, no discretion would be exercised – and producers and public alike would be the losers.

But if the Board has no Code, there are certain broad principles on which it works. In judging a film there are three main questions to be considered: Is it likely to impair the moral standards of the audience by extenuating vice or crime or by depreciating social value? . . . Secondly, is the story, incident, or dialogue likely to give offence to any reasonably minded section of the public? Repeat 'reasonably minded'. . . . Thirdly, what will be the effect of the story, incident, or dialogue on children – that is to say, children of all ages under sixteen?

In America the chief form of censorship is once again that of the industry itself, administered by the Motion Picture Association of America. The famous Code, the full and fascinating text of which can be found in the annual publication *The Motion Picture Almanac*, was first drafted in 1929 by Father Daniel A. Lord, S.J., in association with Martin Quigley and Father F. J. Dineen, S.J. This Code was finally accepted by the M.P.A.A. (the Hays Office) in March 1930, and after a trial period the M.P.A.A. set up the Production Code Administration under Joseph J. Breen, a Roman Catholic, who has administered it ever since. The Code occupies eight closely printed pages, and lists every kind of offence conceivable which could be committed in a film against the moral susceptibilities of society.

An introduction to the Production Code (published in 1944) explains that, though it is not obligatory for producers to conform to the Code, producers in fact do observe it; this is meant to underline the producers' own sense of responsibility which self-regulation implies. It ends by claiming that the freedom of the artist is not curbed by the Code, and that it reflects responsible public opinion as to what is 'clean and artistic' in film entertainment. Few writers would agree with this claim that the Code leaves them free.

The main implications to be derived from the regulations which follow in the Code are examined very fully by Ruth

Inglis in her book *Freedom of the Movies* (1947). Here only a brief reference can be made to the main clauses. Crime comes first; the details of technique of murder and methods of theft must never be shown in detail, the illegal drug traffic and the use of drugs must be kept in the background so that curiosity may not be stimulated, and 'the use of liquor in American life, when not required by the plot or for proper characterization, will not be shown'. Sex follows: 'The sanctity of the institution of marriage and the home shall be upheld.' 'Adultery and illicit sex, sometimes necessary plot material, must not be explicitly treated, or justified, or presented attractively.' Scenes of lust and passion must be restrained; seduction and rape should never 'be more than suggested'. Among the direct prohibitions are references to or representations of sex perversion, white slavery, and miscegenation. Obscenity and profanity are forbidden, and a list of indecent words is appended which must not be used; these include 'damn' and 'hell' used as expletives. Nudity (except where it is natural in natives), indecent exposure, and indecent dances are prohibited, and 'undressing scenes should be avoided, and never used save where essential to the plot'; 'the treatment of bedrooms must be governed by good taste and decency'. Religious ceremonies, ministers of religion, the national feelings of other countries and the appearance of the American flag must all be treated with respect. Finally certain 'repellent subjects' must be 'treated within the limits of good taste'; these are actual hangings, electrocutions, third degree methods, brutality, branding of people and animals, apparent cruelty to children or animals, the sale of women, women selling their virtue, and surgical operations.

Further special regulations modify the representation of crime; they affect the slaughter of police and law-enforcement officers by criminals, the use of murder and suicide in films, the use of illegal firearms, or the flaunting of weapons by gangsters, the use of kidnapping, the inclusion of minors as criminals, or scenes using animals which may have been made to suffer in the process of film-making.

Another form of censorship, this time political rather than moral, is that imposed by the Government of the U.S.S.R. on Soviet film-making. The film industry was nationalized in August 1919, and, after supervision by a series of different authorities reflecting the changes of policy of the regime, came under the Ministry of Cinematography in 1946, replacing the former Committee on Cinematography founded in 1938. Each constituent Republic of the U.S.S.R. has a corresponding though subsidiary Ministry of its own.

It has always proved difficult to supervise the work of the Soviet film-makers effectively. At its worst the controls may be so irksome that the repressed artist loses his creative energy or declines into a conformist technician providing what is needed and no more. Soviet film production has never been adequate to the needs of the vast potential audiences which still remain relatively cut off from the cinema.* The Communist Party watches most carefully every stage in a film's scripting, production, and exhibition. The Ministry of Cinematography must obtain the approval of the Council of Ministers, one of the hierarchies of Government, for its annual programme of film production, and the Council usually makes annual pronouncements on the industry and its shortcomings. Directives for individual film subjects may be given from the highest level. An Art Council was established in 1944 by order of the Party within the Committee of Cinematography and later within the Ministry, to supervise the progress of each film during production and to ensure its ideological correctness. Many films have been withdrawn after production on ideological grounds – famous examples were the second part of Eisenstein's trilogy *Ivan the Terrible*, and the film of the post-war reconstruction

*The population of the Soviet Union was about 200 million in 1950. The annual audience for films in 1939 was only 1,200 million, and in 1945 573 million. In 1950 it had not reached the 1939 figure, in spite of the efforts made to replace equipment damaged during the war. In 1951 the audience figure for Great Britain was 1,350 million.

of the mines and industries of the Donets Basin, *A Great Life*. This latter was condemned because it concentrated on the so-called 'primitive' description of the private lives of certain miners and narrowed its scope to only one example of reconstruction in an area where so much had been done. The very title was considered to be ironic, and therefore anti-social!

Socialist realism is the basis of the policy behind Soviet film production. The words of Lenin and Stalin about the powers of the film are famous. Lenin declared as early as 1907: 'When the masses take possession of the film and it comes into the hands of the true supporters of socialist culture, it will become one of the most powerful means of educating the masses.' Stalin said that 'the film is a great means of mass agitation', and that it is 'a great and invaluable force . . . aiding the working class and its Party to educate the toilers in the spirit of socialism, to organize the masses . . . and to raise their cultural and political battle-fitness'.

Socialist realism did away with what was regarded as the bourgeois and reactionary stylization of such film-makers as Eisenstein and Pudovkin during the famous period of the Russian silent film. These self-conscious techniques did not speak directly to the mass audience; they were the product of the intellectual. They were supposedly swept away twenty years ago when, in 1934, the slogan for all workers in the arts became 'socialist realism'.

The basis of socialist realism in the arts was very clearly summarized in an article by G. Nedoshivin called *On the Relation of Art to Reality*, published by Voks in 1951. The following quotations give the essence of his arguments, and they are of great importance, for they explain the philosophy of all Communist film-making since the War.

The basic problem of aesthetics as a science may be defined as the relation of art to reality. . . . Thus art is one of the forms through which all human mind reflects social being.

Art loses all meaning as soon as it divorces itself from reality. Modern formalism clearly bears this out. Abstract cubistic or suprematistic combinations of forms do not contain a grain of the real content of objective reality; this makes them absolutely empty, meaningless, devoid of the least objective value.

In other words, reality existing outside of us is primary and its artistic reflection is secondary. 'The existence of matter does not depend on sensation. Matter is primary. Sensation, thought, consciousness are the supreme product of matter organized in a particular way.' (Lenin.)

Art generalizes about these matters through carefully selected characters in action. The essence of this generalization in art derives from the ideas these characters and their actions represent.

The great Lenin was the author of the principle that art must be partisan; this was one of the elements of his theory of the partisanship of ideology generally in antagonistic class societies. Mercilessly exposing reactionaries of all hues and shades, Lenin showed that their assertion that art is independent of life screened their defence of the interests of the exploiting classes. Lenin developed this brilliant principle of the partisanship of art in struggle against the theory of 'art for art's sake', against all spokesmen of reaction. Counterposing the false 'freedom' of bourgeois art to the tasks of the art which links its destinies with the emancipation movement of the working class, he said in this article:

'In contrast to bourgeois customs, in contrast to the bourgeois privately-owned and commercialized press, in contrast to bourgeois literary careerism and individualism, "aristocratic anarchism" and rapacity – the Socialist proletariat must advance the principle of *Party literature*, must develop this principle and put it into effect as fully and completely as possible.' . . .

Social consciousness has always served human society as a weapon of struggle with nature, as a weapon of social struggle, forming the basis of practice and acting as its conscious expression. And art has been just such a weapon from the very first days of its existence, remaining such to the present. In the hands of the progressive classes it has been a powerful means of revolutionizing consciousness; reactionary classes have exploited and are still exploiting it as a brake on the development of society. In the latter case, art loses its true content and significance, and generally ceases to be art, as we see with modern reactionary imperialistic 'artistic creation'. Art has reached its true heights only when it has performed its function as a force revolutionizing society. . . . Stalin's brilliant definition of the artist as an engineer of the human soul reveals the innermost kernel of this aspect of the problem. . . . The life-giving power of the idea is the basis of the florescence of the art of socialist realism, which is advancing on the foundation of growing ties between art and the struggle the Soviet people are waging under the guidance of the Bolshevik Party, led in its creative work by the genius of Lenin and the genius of Stalin, to build Communism.

The sharp contrast between the communist and democratic attitude to the artist is fully explained by these quotations. In democratic society the burden of social judgement rests with the artist himself; short of offending society utterly he may seek his own values and speak his mind about society as he finds it. In this way the rich, complex evolution of human consciousness is developed like a great river with a hundred twists and turns, or a thousand exploratory rivulets. Experiments and mistakes are part of the larger process of learning; art can learn just as much by being wild, absurd, extravagant as by being wise and far-seeing. In communist society the artist must conform to the Party view in all the facets of its policy, expressing in literature, drama, film, poetry, sculpture, and even music the current ideology, changing his viewpoint only when policy dictates that this change is necessary.

Soviet culture does not recognize the right of the artist to comment *as an individual* on the life of the society in which he lives. The responsibility of criticism rests with the Party and with those placed in authority by it; the artist's responsibility is a technical one, to translate the directions he receives about Soviet society into the most effective form of propaganda through the medium in which he specializes. When the artist is a man of the calibre of the late Sergei Eisenstein the result is a tragic frustration even when he is a sincere Communist. For there are in any generation a few men and women endowed with a superlative understanding of their fellow-beings and with an overwhelming desire to express what they observe and know through the arts. Their work is often regarded as anti-social because of the universal unpopularity of the truth when it is expressed with an undisguised vitality. As a result they are persecuted as Eisenstein was persecuted both by the Soviets and by the West when he visited the United States, where he was felt to be a troublesome and difficult man. The artist is almost always difficult and troublesome; he is meant to be so both by nature and temperament, otherwise he would conform and become as other men are. But there is no place for this kind of individualism in Soviet society; such behaviour is the symbol of decadence and bourgeois selfishness.

The tragic result is seen in the waste of the great talents represented by Sergei Eisenstein, whose unhappy life is told by his friend Marie Seton in her biography of him. Between 1929 and 1948, the year of his death from *angina pectoris*, he completed only three films, one of which, the second part of *Ivan the Terrible*, was forbidden public screening. He was forced to make a humiliating public recantation of his work. Here are passages from it:

Like a bad sentry we gaped at the unessential and secondary things, forgetting the main things, and so abandoning our post. We forgot that the main thing in art is its ideological content and historical truth. Like a bad foundryman, we light-mindedly allow the precious stream of creation to be poured out over sand and become dispersed in private unessential side-lines. This brought us vices and mistakes in our creations.

A stern and timely warning of the Central Committee stopped us Soviet artists from further movement along this dangerous and fatal way, which leads towards empty and non-ideological art for art's sake and towards creative degradation.

The resolution of the Central Committee reminds us with new force that Soviet art has been given one of the most honourable places in the decisive struggle of ideology of our country against the seductive ideology of the bourgeois world. Everything we do must be subordinated to tasks of this struggle.

In the second part of *Ivan the Terrible* we committed a misrepresentation of historical facts which made the film worthless and vicious in the ideological sense. . . . The centre of our attention is and must be *Ivan the builder, Ivan the creator of a new, powerful, united Russian power*, Ivan the inexorable destroyer of everything that resisted *his* progressive undertakings. . . . The play of doubts crept out to the front line and the wilful character of the Tsar and his historically progressive rôle slipped out of the field of attention. The result was that a false and mistaken impression was created about the image of Ivan. The resolution of the Central Committee accusing me of a wrong presentation which disfigures historical truth says that in the film Ivan is presented as 'weak and indecisive, somewhat like Hamlet'. This is solidly grounded and just.

Eisenstein, through lack of practical expression as the great film-maker he undoubtedly was, became a theorist whose restless mind and sick body did not permit him to complete the books on film aesthetics he so often planned to write. He was, however, most successful as a teacher in the Moscow Institute of Cinematography. But his life stands as a warning of what can happen to men of unusual talents who cannot be made to fit into the mould of Communist artistic policy.

Freedom of Expression and the Pressure Groups

In America the forces repressing the artist have become closely associated with the violent anti-communist campaign. This has reached its climax in the investigations of the various Committees for Un-American Activities when they have turned their attention to Hollywood. The atmosphere of the campaign as it affects the entertainment industries has been brilliantly and sympathetically described by Irwin Shaw in his novel *The Troubled Air*, which shows what happens to an undistinguished, decent, and liberal-minded director of a weekly radio programme when he becomes involved in defending five members of his regular team of actors who are initially threatened with an attack in a muck-raking political journal. Dismissal of these players is recommended by the sponsor of the programme, a Philadelphia industrialist, and also by the manager of the radio station responsible for the programme. The novel is all the more effective because the director of the programme is essentially a man uninterested in politics but generous in his relationship to human beings.

The Troubled Air becomes the record of the workings of a social poison emanating from all sides of the struggle – from the bigoted, Fascist-minded anti-communists who become foul-minded and foul-mouthed when they suspect left-wing sympathies, from the bigoted communists who are willing to betray any personal relationships in the service of their cause, and from the tragic fears of ordinary folk who find, through some slip in their past or present life, that they have become associated with the political left, and are vulnerable. Some, because they are Jews or Negroes, are fair game to those who have deep-seated racial antipathies. The whole atmosphere is that of a whirlpool, the centre of which is a terrifying social neurosis into which innocent people are being drawn. Careers are ruined and the informer becomes all-powerful. The timing of public confessions of former left-wing associations becomes a matter of the greatest concern. It affects the hack script-writer and the famous director equally. Some have come to Europe to work, finding life in the States intolerable; some have timed their confessions accurately enough to escape the worst censure and the horrors of unemployment and degradation; and some have 'peached' to save themselves.

Another brilliant novel which at one stage in its development shows these political problems operating in the film industry is Richard Brooks's *The Producer* (1952). This tells the story of Matthew Gibbons, an established producer of high-class Hollywood films who is beset with worry over a production which he believes to be crucial to his career. He engages a well-known writer called John Shea to help re-work the script, but when the film is finished and the New York premiere is set, Shea is subpoenaed to appear before the Un-American Activities Committee. The manoeuvring which follows over John Shea's screen credit as screenwriter offers a good measure of the fears which result from the pressures of right versus left in Hollywood.

When I was in America in the spring of 1952, I opened the *New York Times* to find a statement, published as an advertisement, and made by one of the most famous

American film and stage directors, a name which would be well known to every reader of this book. The essential paragraphs of this statement were:

> In the past weeks intolerable rumors about my political position have been circulating in New York and Hollywood. I want to make my stand clear:
>
> I believe that Communist activities confront the people of this country with an unprecedented and exceptionally tough problem. That is, how to protect ourselves from a dangerous and alien conspiracy and still keep the free, open, healthy way of life that gives us self-respect. . . .
>
> Whatever hysteria exists – and there is some, particularly in Hollywood – is inflamed by mystery, suspicion, and secrecy. Hard and exact facts will cool it. . . .
>
> I joined the Communist Party late in the summer of 1934. I got out a year and a half later. . . .
>
> To be a member of the Communist Party is to have a taste of the police state. It is a diluted taste but it is bitter and unforgettable. It is diluted because you can walk out.
>
> I got out in the Spring of 1936.
>
> The question will be asked why I did not tell this story sooner. I was held back, primarily, by concern for the reputations and employment of people who may, like myself, have left the party many years ago.
>
> I was also held back by a piece of specious reasoning which has silenced many liberals. It goes like this: 'You may hate the Communists, but you must not attack them or expose them, because if you do you are attacking the right to hold unpopular opinions and you are joining the people who attack civil liberties.'
>
> I have thought soberly about this. It is, simply, a lie.
>
> Secrecy serves the Communists. At the other pole, it serves those who are interested in silencing liberal voices. The employment of a lot of good liberals is threatened because they have allowed themselves to become associated with or silenced by the Communists.
>
> Liberals must speak out.
>
> I think it is useful that certain of us had this kind of experience with the Communists, for if we had not we should not know them so well. To-day, when all the world fears war and they scream peace, we know how much their professions are worth. We know to-morrow they will have a new slogan.
>
> First-hand experience of dictatorship and thought control left

me with an abiding hatred of these. It left me with an abiding hatred of Communist philosophy and methods and the conviction that these must be resisted always.

It also left me with the passionate conviction that we must never let the Communists get away with the pretence that they stand for the very things which they kill in their own countries.

I am talking about free speech, a free press, the rights of property, the rights of labor, racial equality and, above all, individual rights. I value these things. I take them seriously. I value peace, too, when it is not bought at the price of fundamental decencies.

I believe these things must be fought for wherever they are not fully honored and protected whenever they are threatened.

The motion pictures I have made and the plays I have chosen to direct represent my convictions.

I expect to continue to make the same kinds of pictures and to direct the same kinds of plays.

It is just as intolerable that writers and other artists whose work is a contribution to our entertainment and to our understanding should be subjected to the kind of persecution suggested in the first sentence of this statement. It is just as intolerable that this should happen in the so-called free world as it is intolerable that the writers and artists should suffer the controls imposed on them in the Communist countries. There is only one judge of the responsibility or irresponsibility of what the artist presents to the public – and that is the members of the public themselves. If he produces pornography or if he creates a riot which endangers life and limb, and threatens the national security, then he can be dealt with by the proper method of public investigation in which he should have the right to defend himself against the charges brought against him. The methods of conducting the investigations in many of the public enquiries by the Un-American Activities Committees are unjust because the men and women accused have been denied the elementary rights of self-defence. Nor have those whose association with proscribed left-wing organizations is wholly of the past, or was casual or inadvertent, been distinguished from those whose political activities could be described fairly as dangerous to the community.

No one denies the suitability of the film as a medium for public information and instruction, and, when it is in the public interest, for propaganda. The British documentary movement has always tried to make clear the distinctions between these various uses of the film.

As everyone knows, the intellectual protagonist of British documentary during the nineteen-thirties was John Grierson. In 1929, the year he made his first and only personal film, *Drifters*, he was a young man who had taken a degree in Philosophy at Glasgow University after spending most of the 1914 War on auxiliary patrol and mine-sweeping in the Navy. He returned to England in 1927 after studying Public Relations for three years in America on a Rockefeller Research Fellowship in Social Science. He joined the staff of the Empire Marketing Board, whose Secretary was Stephen Tallents (now Sir Stephen Tallents), himself one of the most brilliant students of the practice of public relations of that period.

Grierson wrote the main theory of British documentary and practised the principles he advocated as its chief producer. In *Cinema Quarterly* (edited in Edinburgh by Forsyth Hardy and Norman Wilson 1932–35), he described the basis of his attitude to the use of the film for social education:

First principles. (1) We believe that the cinema's capacity for getting around, for observing and selecting from life itself, can be exploited in a new and vital art form. The studio films largely ignore this possibility of opening up the screen on the real world. They photograph acted stories against artificial backgrounds. Documentary would photograph the living scene and the living actor. (2) We believe that the original (or native) actor, and the original (or native) scene, are better guides to a screen interpretation of the modern world. They give cinema a greater fund of material. They give it power over a million and one movements, and power over a million and one images. They give it power of interpretation over more complex and astonishing happenings in the real world than the studio mind can conjure up or the studio mechanician re-create. (3) We believe that the materials and the stories thus taken from the raw can be finer (more real in the philosophic sense) than the acted article. Spontaneous gesture has a special value on the screen. Cinema has a sensational capacity for enhancing the movement which tradition has formed or time worn smooth. Its arbitrary rectangle specially reveals movement; it gives maximum pattern in space and time. Add to this that documentary can achieve an intimacy of knowledge and effect impossible to the shimsham mechanics of the studio and the lily-fingered interpretations of the metropolitan actor. (Winter, 1932, p. 69.)

Later he wrote in the same journal (Spring 1933) of the documentary film-maker:

They believe that beauty will come in good time to inhabit the statement which is honest and lucid and deeply felt and which fulfils the best ends of citizenship. They are sensible enough to conceive of art as the by-product (the over-tone) of a job of work done. The opposite attempt to capture the by-product first (the self-conscious pursuit of beauty, the pursuit of art for art's sake to the exclusion of jobs of work and other pedestrian beginnings), was always a reflection of selfish wealth, selfish leisure, and aesthetic decadence.

Two years later he underlined in *Cinema Quarterly* (Summer 1935) the analytical approach to their subjects made by the young directors associated with him:

Many of us, brought up in the post-impressionist revolt, have made structure our god. 'Observe and analyse', 'Know and build', 'Out of research poetry comes', were the slogans we set before us. They suited the academic and the radical in our minds. They brought us more readily to the new material of our times.

I have watched with some closeness the working of these influences in the films of Wright, Elton, and Legg. All are painstakingly and rather proudly academic. When they shoot a factory, say, they learn how to ask the right questions. Elton, for example, knows more than a little about railways and mechanics; Wright has mastered the history of every subject he has touched; and I will swear that Legg knows more about the organization of the BBC than any outsider decently should.

The only point at which art is concerned with information is the point at which 'the flame shoots up and the light kindles and it enters into the soul and feeds itself there'. Flash-point there must be. Information indeed can be a dangerous business if the kindly process is not there. Most professors are a dreary warning of what happens when the informationist fails to become a poet.

Paul Rotha was equally vigorous in the appeal he made, in the first edition of his book *Documentary Film* (1935), that motion pictures should contribute to public enlightenment in social education:

The big films of cinema, few as they are, have all served a special purpose and have not come into being primarily as the result of mere artistic endeavour or the desire to make profit. They are significant because of the sincerity of their creators in the part they were intended to play in social and political enlightenment. *Kameradschaft* and *Potemkin* are the two favourite examples. They were both propagandist.

Without this aim of special service, I cannot see that cinema has any real significance beyond that of providing a temporary emotional refuge for the community, making profit or loss for its moneyed speculators and preserving a record for future historical reference which will give a partly erroneous picture of our age.

. . . Real and creative thought must be about real things. Let cinema explore outside the limits of what we are told constitutes entertainment. Let cinema attempt the dramatization of the living scene and the living theme, springing from the living present instead of from the synthetic fabrication of the studio. Let cinema attempt film interpretations of modern problems and events, of things as they really are to-day, and by so doing perform a definite function. Let cinema recognize the existence of real men and women, real things and real issues, and by so doing offer to State, Industry, Commerce, to public and private organizations of all kinds, a method of communications and propaganda to project not just personal opinions but arguments for a world of common interests.

The story of British documentary before, during, and since the War has been told often enough, and most notably in the P.E.P. Report *The Factual Film* (1946) and in Paul Rotha's *Documentary Film* (1936, revised 1939 and 1952). There is a further summary of its scope in my previous book in this series, *Film* (revised edition 1950), while Grierson's main essays on this important subject have been collected by Forsyth Hardy in the book *Grierson on Documentary*.

Films concerned with information, fact, or opinion can be of many kinds according to the uses to which they are to be put. First of all there is the film of record for research purposes, part now of the equipment of science in the collection of its data. Then there is the film of record for public use – the newsreel, the 'interest' film which records a public event, or the purely descriptive documentary. Next, there is the instructional film, demonstrating, for example, a mechanical process or some aspect of geography or science, to be used as part of the usual equipment for teaching children or adults or as a part of their general or specialized training. There is also the advertising film intended to sell products. Further, there is the propaganda film designed to awake the interest or stir the emotions of people so that they will be induced to act in some way desired by the Government or the promoters of the film. Lastly, there is the kind of documentary which John Grierson described as 'the creative treatment of actuality'. Here we are in the hands of the artist; his manner of presentation, his interpretation of his subject as he observes it, become the important factors – making his film rhetorical or poetic or intellectual according to the way in which it is conceived by its maker.

The Specialized Use of the Film

The specialized use of the film as a branch of scientific research is not a new development. X-ray motion picture photography was used for medical diagnosis by Dr R. G. Canti during the nineteen-twenties, for example, and the astonishing and beautiful films in slow motion which show the growth of plants and flowers were first developed by Percy Smith in London as early as 1909.

It is the fantastic speeds of modern motion picture cameras which open up new fields of research. One of the most beautiful record films I have ever seen showed in slow motion the movements of the wings of the humming bird, which were invisible to the human eye. If a camera can photograph 3,000 images each second it is possible, when the result is projected on to the screen, to expand an action of one second's duration to three minutes! Films taken at these fantastic speeds are now being used, for example, to discover what causes the breakdown of complex machines, which no observation of the machine working at its normal speed could reveal. Studies in the behaviour of fluids when they are sprayed or of the penetration of armature by bullets are made by means of these slow-motion films. Another example of the application of films to industrial research has been in the development of time-and-motion study, which is the analysis of the most efficient co-ordination of a worker's movements in relation to different kinds of routine job where speed is essential to the level of output as well as to the comfort and welfare of the worker.

Sometimes the movie camera has been used for very spectacular purposes – when it was placed in a pilotless aircraft to observe at close range the explosion of the atomic bombs at Bikini, or when it has been put into high-altitude rockets to record their flight at heights where the curvature of the earth becomes visible.

Some of the most astonishing films ever made, however, have come from Dr Comandon's cine-laboratory at Garches, near Paris. They are photomicrographic – that is, they are made as a result of combining the motion picture camera with the microscope so that the processes of life may be observed. Dr Comandon began this work in 1910. He and his assistants have minute instruments of dissection made of glass and platinum that can only be used under great magnification, and are controlled by a system of tiny pneumatic pumps which scale down some hundreds of times the movements of the human hand that guides them.

Probably it is in this biological and medical field that the motion picture camera has been most useful. There is a long record of this kind of film-making in Britain, for surgery in particular, though the first film records of surgical operations were made by Dr Doyen in 1909. In Canada, among other countries, a great deal has been done to make the film useful to psychologists and psychiatrists; for example, films which record the behaviour of the insane in uncompromising terms are used for study by specialists in mental health.

It is not possible in the space available in this book to discuss fully what is called the non-theatrical exhibition of films. Non-theatrical exhibition implies the screening of films outside the theatres, or places which are being used temporarily as theatres, such as village halls to which a travelling showman comes once in a while. It may mean the exhibition of films as part of a commercial cooking demonstration, the screening of medical films to an audience of students, the use of films in the classroom or other centres of instruction, and exhibitions to illustrate a lecture, or the special performances for film societies.

The non-theatrical use of films is of the greatest importance in the public service. It reached its height in Britain during the War, when the Ministry of Information maintained a staff of projectionists and a fleet of travelling cinema vans for showing programmes of officially-sponsored films. These vans were used in every part of the country and gave during 1943–44 over 64,000 shows to over 11 million people. A similar system was developed by John Grierson in Canada, and flourishes to this day both in the form of travelling cinema vans and the maintenance of libraries of films in each of the Provinces. In Britain this wonderful work in public education, for which no charge was made, was discontinued by the Conservative Government at the end of March, 1952, at the same time as the Crown Film Unit was closed down after nearly a quarter of a century of public service, first as the Empire Marketing Board Film Unit, and later as the G.P.O. Film Unit, before its name was changed finally to the Crown Film Unit in 1940.

Within the field of commercial theatrical exhibition there is a small section of the industry concerned with specialized exhibition. Whether the average cinema is controlled by one of the great production companies or by independent exhibitors, it exists solely to make money, and this is done most effectively by maintaining a continuous policy of showing films of the widest possible appeal.

The development of specialized exhibition and its link with the Film Society movement is an interesting story. Specialized cinemas began to grow up in the middle nineteen-twenties in cities like Berlin and Paris and London. parallel with the formation of the film clubs and societies which were founded partly to meet the needs of the *avant-garde* film-maker and his audience, and partly to enable those who wished to do so to see foreign films of a kind never likely to be exhibited in the normal commercial theatres. In London, Elsie Cohen started showing Continental films at the Academy in 1929; the Everyman at Hampstead was opened by J. S. Fairfax-Jones in 1933, and the Curzon followed in 1934. A most important addition to the specialized public exhibition of films was the National Film Theatre in London, founded by the British Film Institute in 1952; previously it had been the Telecinema designed by Wells Coates for the 1951 Festival of Britain.

The London Film Society, the pioneer of the film society movement in Britain, was formed in 1925 by a Committee which included both film-makers and people not professionally connected with the industry. The film society movement stands for the right of the audience to select the films they want to see from as wide a range of the past and present work of the cinema as can be made available to them. The fact that the selection is to a considerable extent governed by what the industry is prepared to make available does not alter this fundamental principle. The growing number of enthusiastic pioneer film societies in the provinces of Britain during the nineteen-thirties proved that there was an audience for films made in languages other than English and employing techniques and styles outside the normal pattern of film-making shown in the cinemas. A few specialized theatres opened outside London in the years before the War, but it was not until after the 1939–45 War that the distribution of foreign-language films began to be a commercial proposition through the normal channels of exhibition. That it became so was due to the hard work put in by the film societies and the few established specialized theatres like the Academy in London or the Cosmo in Glasgow. Among the most enterprising of the larger film societies was the Merseyside Film Institute and the Edinburgh Film Guild. The latter, inspired by Norman Wilson and Forsyth Hardy (who edited the memorable *Cinema Quarterly* 1932–35), founded after the War the Edinburgh Film Festival, which is still entirely the responsibility of the Guild, and has now become one of the most successful annual international film festivals to be held in Europe.

The Federation of English and Welsh Film Societies and the Federation of Scottish Film Societies together represented in 1953 over 200 organizations. Their link with the British Film Institute is dealt with in an appendix to this book, which describes the Institute's work as a whole. The Institute itself was founded some twenty years ago as an official body to further the study of the film and to preserve in its archive, the National Film Library, those films which it is thought at the moment will have importance to the future as historical records or as contributions to the general understanding of the film's development, both as an art and as popular entertainment.

It was a sign of the coming of age of the cinema that an official body should have been created, with public money, devoted to the study of the cinema and to the permanent preservation of films of significance. The film then took its proper place alongside the other arts. It is now no longer neglected by people responsible for education, as, for example, the founding of the Society of Film Teachers shows. The society had by 1954 some hundreds of enthusiastic members, who are trying in various ways to encourage the discussion of the film in schools and youth clubs. Though I hope the film will never follow literature and music into the strait-jacket of becoming a set subject for school examinations, it obviously should take its place in the livelier branches of formal education. In this sense film appreciation is very necessary, if it is in the hands of teachers who love films, know something about them, and can recognize the best that has been and can be done in good film-making. For in this art at least both teacher and pupil are on common ground; they are discussing something in which both of them have a lively and active interest.

The Ownership, Copyright, and the Wilful Destruction of Films

Very few films are legally protected on behalf of their true creators. It is very rare for a film-maker to control completely the manner in which his work will be shown, or to possess the power to withdraw it or revise it for re-issue. The film-maker has few, if any, of the powers of protective copyright possessed by the author or the dramatist, and he seldom has even the right of appeal if his work is re-shaped or otherwise materially altered by the production company which is the legal owner of his film.

The tragic results of this position are only too apparent to all lovers of the cinema. Negatives of films which are part of the history and development of the cinema have been ruthlessly junked by ignorant and indifferent owners and distributors; many a film-maker has found it impossible to preserve the only record of his work (in positive or negative form) because he has no legal right to possession of a copy. In addition, the film rights to a particular story can be re-sold after a period so that a new film version may be made, and part of the conditions of this re-sale may well be the total destruction of all the prints of the original version, or their withdrawal from any form of public exhibition for an indefinite number of years. Many fine films have been lost to the cinema and to the film societies through this process, while unworthy substitutes take their place on the screen, or badly cut and re-edited versions are put out commercially and supplant the original work made by true artists of the film.

It is for these main reasons that certain prominent film-makers have begun to agitate for the legal deposit and preservation of films. One of the pioneers in this matter has been René Clair in France, and the British Film Institute has for a long time urged that one of the requirements of the British laws of copyright should be that producers or distributors of films shown in this country must by law deposit a print of any film they make or distribute in the National Film Library Archive, if requested to do so. The National Film Library should become the recognized *legal* depository for films, just as the Library of the British Museum has become for books. At present used copies of films are preserved only by courtesy of owners and distributors, who have a perfect right to refuse to place prints of important films in the National Film Library, or to withdraw them from the Library once they are there.

It is necessary to be uncompromising about this. The dignity and the status of the film as a form of art and a medium of record demand that the wilful destruction of films should be prohibited, in the interests of both the film-maker and of the public. Each country must create its own legislation to effect the preservation of its films. There is no time to lose, for the life of a film is far less than that of a human being.

5   TELEVISION AND THE FILM

Television versus the Cinema

It was not until after the War that the cinema industry realized that a great competitor had arrived in the field of entertainment, which it had so successfully dominated for half a century.

The public for television before the War had been limited to a handful of enthusiasts; there were 20,000 licences for receiving sets in Britain in September 1939, when the outbreak of war led to the closure of the BBC's television service. Britain had played a prominent part in pioneering television, as she had formerly done in the development of the film. The name of John Logie Baird, who had given his first public demonstration of a televised picture in Selfridge's London store in April 1925, is to British television what the names of William Friese-Greene, George Albert Smith, R. W. Paul, and Cecil Hepworth are to the British cinema. Britain was the first country to offer a section of the public a regular television service when the BBC's transmissions began in November 1946. Television licence holders in Britain have since the War risen to 4 million (1954). In America the development of television has been far more striking; in 1954 there were estimated to be some 30 million sets in operation. The number of other countries with television services already functioning is over twenty. The U.S.S.R. first developed television in 1938 in Moscow and Leningrad; since the War services have been extended to several of the great cities in the Soviet Union.

The ever-extending television services seemed like a vast cuckoo in the snug nest of the cinema industry in the U.S.A. Hollywood has turned over to substantial wide-screen film-making in an attempt to hold back the receding tide of fortune by offering audiences large-scale sensations which contrast as markedly as possible with the millions of insidious little images peeping out of the home viewers. And a number of producers have deserted the cinema altogether as a means of film exhibition and are mass-producing hundreds of half-hour 'quickies' shot cheaply in a day or two for showing over the television networks.

In other words, television has radically altered the position of the cinema within a very few years after the War. It has robbed it of its unique position as a mass-entertainer through motion pictures. The general public cannot be expected to bother themselves about the finer points of distinction between film entertainment in the cinemas and the broadcast image on the screen at home. One is the kind of motion pictures which it costs money to see and which involves leaving your home. The other is motion pictures which are free or nearly free, once you have paid for your receiver, and which you can switch on at home whenever you feel like it. That might almost seem to be the end of the argument. You save your money. You stay at home.

But the argument does not in fact end here. There are at least two main points of attack on the thrifty husband who stumps in at night ready for his supper, his slippers, and his television. First, his wife has been in most of the day, and she wants to go out. More than that, she wants to be taken out; she wants to have money spent on her in public by her husband. She wants to be seen out with him. Television is very nice some nights of the week, especially when the children are small, but she will not let her husband get away with it for ever. The young people, too, want to slip out and meet each other away from the presence of their elders. And secondly, you cannot see on television the same kind of entertainment you can see in the cinemas. The big stars in the big melodramas and the big dramas, the big spectacles, the big colour and the big display, all of which have been the stock in trade of the cinema for nearly fifty years, are, broadly speaking, missing from television. Its kind of entertainment, restricted by many technical and economic limitations, differs very greatly from what is showing at the pictures. Take any month's entertainment at your local cinema and contrast it with what you could see on television. The scope of the big screen film, its expensive production values, the exciting American and European settings and subjects, and the performances by world-famous stars are all virtually excluded from television (except in the form of some very old films), though a number of film-stars have their own regular shows on American television.

The strength of the cinema lies, first of all, in the money represented by its box-office takings. This money, or the proportion of it returned to the producer, should be invested in the care and skill and artistry of the film-maker, because this is the second strength of the cinema. For no production made solely for television can cost the money which gives a good artist the time he requires to make a first-rate film, unless a widespread optional system of subscription television is established. Nor does the small television screen give him a canvas on which his talent can be displayed. For the great film normally shows either or both of two qualities – on the one hand, range of movement and background and, on the other, a most careful development of detail. The film with the two-day schedule can cope with neither of these virtues; it must talk its way through its action, and talk fast with a minimum of rehearsal and a minimum of camera change or cutting. It must forgo the main powers of the mature film and revert to the elementary simplicities of the old-fashioned screen talkie. Television with its small screen, poor picture (compared, that is, with the photographic potentialities of the film), and high quality sound, favours the screen talkie in a way the cinema could never do. But this brings us to some consideration of the differences between film and television technique; these depend partly on the attitude of the audience and partly on the differences inherent in production for these two very different forms of pictorial entertainment.

The Television Audience

The owners of television sets in America and Britain represent a normal cross-section of the population; the lower income groups are not left behind by the higher income groups in their purchase of viewers. Adolescents and adults in Britain appear to view between 7 and 8 hours a week; children of between 12 and 14 years of age seem to view for up to 11 hours a week.

The television audience is substantially the same as the cinema audience. But though their desire for entertainment must therefore be the same, they soon become habituated to expect something quite different from television compared with what they expect from the cinema. Both the creation and the satisfaction of audience-anticipation is the job of the showman in whatever form of entertainment he is working. The public has a stolid and highly conventional attitude to entertainment. Although the publicity for a new show may proclaim its novelty, the public normally resists anything that cannot be easily recognized as stock entertainment, both in comedy and sentimental drama. Hence the success of formula films and the hearty laughter at the set-piece gags and jokes of the music-hall comics. To share a laugh or a cry with their neighbours, the members of an audience must be able collectively to recognize what is coming and give it the right response. Novelty may mean exercising one's wits rather more than usual and so failing to get the point of the entertainment.

The BBC took over television in Great Britain because it is, speaking technically, a form of broadcasting. The BBC has spent a quarter of a century evolving its own particular pattern of entertainment in sound and radio, and the public have grown accustomed to this pattern and are, in general, well content with what they get, as, indeed, they should be at the price they pay. They have been more critical of the BBC's television service because of the inevitable comparisons a pictorial form of entertainment invites with the cinema, whose conventions and patterns of entertainment, so largely created by Hollywood, are quite different from those of the BBC. In building up a new series of conventions in television entertainment, the BBC has had to stick doggedly to its own policy of what it believes to be right for the

British public, in spite of the accusations of amateurism so constantly hurled at it. On the whole the BBC has won, as it must inevitably do since until 1955 it has had no rival in its own particular field to compete with it and inspire new kinds of public anticipation as to what television should offer. The BBC had to prove to the public that a television service of thirty hours or so each week was not a cheap substitute for the movies, but was, in fact, something almost entirely different from the cinema. The BBC had to prove that television was a new kind of medium which could only fulfil its duties to the public by developing its own conventions, and not by attempting to oust the cinema from public favour. The BBC has, I think, been successful in doing this. The comparatively high figures for appreciation of television programmes published by the BBC's audience research department prove, at least, that the public tends to enjoy rather than otherwise the greater part of what the BBC has to offer on its screen. There is ample room in the public patronage for both television and the cinema, each providing in their different ways the forms of entertainment and information for which they are best suited.

Broadly speaking, the BBC has set up a convention for the intimate, homely kind of presentation suitable for audiences sitting in their living-rooms in family groups. A great deal of American television (though, of course, not all) seems to be addressed to a mass meeting – the raised, hectic tones which enthusiastically proclaim the virtues of a sponsor's product or the state of a sporting event could be poured alike over the ears of a thousand people gathered in a cinema or two sitting half asleep at home. But it would surely be more appropriate if such a commentary were done differently for the living-room audience. The best television presentation in both America and Britain is more informal and quieter in tone, and often slower in tempo. For the television audience is normally a relaxed audience, seeking entertainment within the familiar domestic surroundings of a home. Tension and excitement can be developed in this audience made up of small units, but it is generated in conditions which differ greatly from the mass excitement of the public theatre and public cinema. The BBC's policy has been to provide as wide a range as possible of programme coverage within the limits of a single channel. The main forms of programme (with the proportion of the total programme time they occupied in 1952–3) are:

1. Outside broadcasts, including sport   20.3%
2. Children's programmes   12.7%
3. Films   12.1%
4. Plays   12.1%
5. Light entertainment, including variety and comedy shows featuring established comedians 10.9%
6. Talks   9.2%
7. TV newsreels   8.4%
8. Documentary and magazine programmes   3.7%
9. Music and ballet   2.3%

In the multitudinous hours of American television, either sponsored or sustained by the stations, a similar variety of entertainment can be found, but it is buried under an enormous heap of light entertainment, sport, and films. Sponsors take note of popularity polls, and in 1952, of the eight programmes which led in public favour, six were forms of variety, one was a husband-and-wife comedy half hour, and one was a half-hour drama series called the Fireside Theatre.

Public Service versus Commercial Television

Since BBC television has broadly satisfied its public in the absence of any competition, over a post-war period little short of ten years, there was a general feeling in Britain that the monopoly should be left undisturbed. The horrible fate of American television was held up as a bogey when the flood gates of argument were finally opened and the Conservative Government announced its support of commercial television in addition to the BBC's own service. The matter became a party issue in the House of Commons. Without doubt the instrument of television, potentially so much more powerful than sound radio in its future influence within the community, burst open the protective covering which Lord Reith had managed to weave round the BBC's monopoly of public broadcasting in Britain, a covering which did not suffer any damage whatsoever during the quarter-century when sound radio was the only form of broadcasting which counted.

The monopoly was in many ways a good thing in the pioneer days when radio had to establish itself and discover its powers at the same time as it served the public with entertainment and information. It established, in particular, responsibility in the handling of news and in the discussion of public affairs, and a high level in the presentation of drama, documentary programmes, and music. A public was gradually built up until symphony concerts could command an average audience of two million, a programme like *The Critics* a million listeners, and the Third Programme over $1\frac{1}{2}$ million who listen at least once a week. Such large audiences could never have been forecast before the BBC created them. Provision was nine-tenths of the law. The so-called cultural programmes were shown to be habit-forming.

A similar policy of audience-building (which is the same thing as audience education) was pursued by the BBC television service. But vision provided new economic problems, because production costs were for the most part out of all proportion to the precedent established by sound broadcasting. Provided the BBC kept to the limited hours of a single-channel service and did not indulge in too many shows which cost high sums to produce, it could just get by on the proportion of the licence fees allocated to it.* But it

*During 1953–54 the BBC received, after the Government tax deduction of 15% and the Post Office's levy of $7\frac{1}{2}$%, under £13 million out of which to run the home radio and television services. The BBC also spends about £4.5 million on its overseas services, paid for out of a grant-in-aid from the Treasury. From 1 June 1954, the annual combined radio and television licence was increased to £3, giving an estimated revenue to the BBC, after allowing for the tax and levy deductions, of £17 million in 1954–55 and £20 million by 1957. (The BBC receives £2 9s 3d out of each £3 paid for a receiving licence.) By 1956 some £10 million will be being spent on the television service, instead of, for example, £3.4 million in the year 1952–53. TV will be self-supporting when it reaches the 5 million licence mark, which it is estimated it will do by 1956. It is hoped to provide an alternative BBC programme (in addition to that of the new Corporation operating commercial TV) not later than 1959.

soon became plain as the vogue for television grew that the service must expand, and that public demand for more ambitious forms of television entertainment would soon outstrip what the BBC's financial resources could supply. Nor did the Senior Service of Sound Broadcasting seem to look with any more favour on the rising tide of television than the cinema proprietors themselves, although the policy of the BBC was, and is, gradually to integrate the two forms of broadcasting into a combined service. In any case, the BBC points out that even by 1963 it is unlikely that there will be as many television receivers operating in this country as there are sound receivers operating at present.

The solution to the economic as well as the monopolistic problem is the introduction of commercial television. Commercial television differs markedly from sponsored television. In commercial television all programmes are originated and controlled by a licensed station, and it is claimed that the advertiser would have no *positive* control over the contents and nature of the programmes broadcast. He would merely buy advertising time in association with the programme he thought likely to appeal to the greatest number of viewers who might be persuaded to buy his product. In the case of sponsored television the advertiser buys programme time and originates the programme himself. Both commercial and sponsored television operate in the United States, but normally it is sponsored television which is criticized in this country. The critics of commercial television usually claim, with some cynicism, that the advertiser exercises a *negative* control over the programme even though the station actually originates it. The defence then claims that commercial television operates like a newspaper, and that the editorial columns of the press are free from any pressure from the advertisers. Precisely, reply the cynics, no pressure whatsoever provided they say nothing likely to offend the advertisers' interests. The advertisers' interests, on the other hand, represented by the Incorporated Society of British Advertisers and the Institute of Incorporated Practitioners in Advertising, have issued a statement to the Postmaster

General in which they state categorically that they do not want to sponsor their own programmes; they want commercial television and commercial television only in Great Britain. In any case, cry out a further body of critics, who is to say the commercial stations themselves will originate programmes which do anything else but pander to the lowest level of taste! And so the argument goes on.

Of at least equal importance is the evidence from the United States that, once the public vote is taken, all that audiences seem to want is variety followed by yet more variety, followed by sport and light entertainment! So the sponsor puts on variety, sport, and light entertainment until all the leading shows duplicate and reduplicate each other – variety following soap operas, following quiz programmes, following audience-participation programmes, following sporting events, following comedy half-hours, following women wrestlers, following the more sensational news at the peak hours every night! The BBC claims, however, that once the rot sets in they could not compete against the drive by commercial television for the big popular audiences at peak hours; audiences would inevitably switch over to the lowbrow programmes and leave the BBC high and dry with *Ballet for Beginners*, *The Doll's House*, and *The Cure for Cancer*. Gresham's law would operate, they say; the bad would drive out the good, and force the BBC to lower its own standards in order to retain any audience at all.

I do not believe that this would be so. I think that there will always be majority audiences for good variety shows and for sport (as the BBC has proved on sound radio), but that, provided the documentary, and drama, and discussion programmes were excellent of their kind, they would at least hold their own with substantial audience figures. The BBC claimed in 1953, and claimed rightly, that it must increase its licence fees to £3 a year or even more if it were to initiate an alternative programme, and introduce those regional and specialized interests which are proper for a fully developed television service, invest capital on the construction of television studios in London and the Regions, and build transmitters which will bring television to every remote part of the Kingdom. A £3 licence was introduced in 1954. I believe the only solution to this dilemma lies in the development of popular commercial television, letting the advertiser pay for the more expensive forms of light entertainment and leaving the BBC free to devote its licence money to the provision of first-class programmes of all kinds which the policy of public service television requires.

In 1954 the Independent Television Authority was established, with Sir Robert Fraser as its first Director-General. Like the BBC, the ITA is an independent organization responsible to the Government for the correct administration of its affairs through the Post-Master General. Its revenue comes partly from a grant deducted from the annual television licence fees paid by the public, and partly from the fees paid to it by the various Programme Contractors whom it appoints to entertain the public in the various Regions into which the country has been divided for the purposes of commercial television. The ITA is responsible for transmitting the programmes and for general supervision of the new television service. The Contractors are responsible for originating and producing the programmes for the Regions allocated to them. After paying the fee due to the ITA and covering the production costs of their programmes, the Contractors hope in the end to make a profit out of the over-all fees paid to them by the advertisers for the right to show 'commercials' before and after the programme of their choice. The advertising agents are in turn responsible for originating their clients' commercials; these will occupy three minutes out of every half-hour of programme-time. It is the duty of the ITA to see that advertising plays no part in the programmes themselves. This, put very briefly, represents the complex system of commercial, as distinct from sponsored, television devised by the Government after endless debate and pressure from all sides. It may well be that the restrictions imposed on it will prove too onerous. Ultimately it will depend on the confidence of the advertisers whether British commercial television is successful or whether it will have to be bolstered up by subsidies to keep it solvent.

In the United States another solution to television's economic problems, subscription television, has been put forward by certain companies. Subscription television provides a box-office for particular programmes similar to that of the cinema. The programmes are put out on fixed channels which are not made clearly available to the receiver until the subscriber makes his choice known and is prepared to pay to see the programme. This he may do by various systems, by telephone, by buying a ticket giving him the code for the programme, or by paying on a slot-machine principle. Subscription television provides direct revenue on a mass scale to meet production costs; once it is accepted on a national scale, the advocates claim, an expensive programme could pay for itself overnight. Several million receivers would produce several million dollars for a single programme. Against such returns as these the television film-maker could begin to produce on normal extensive schedules, as against the two-day shooting schedule which is about all that can be spent on the present TV 'quickie'. Subscription television may be one way out of the financial dilemma of the TV services. Another way out is to recognize frankly the nature of television and cease to confuse it with the kind of entertainment which belongs properly to the cinema.

The Film and Television

A film camera records its image on celluloid; it stores the picture up for future use. A television camera receives its image for immediate transmission; the picture is then lost for ever unless it is independently recorded by a film camera which reproduces the image as it appears on the television screen. A television image has no more permanence than the image reflected by a mirror. The virtue of the motion-picture camera lies in its power to reproduce photographically the movements presented before it; from the audience's point of view it deals with what is past. The virtue of the television camera lies in its power to transmit to its audience the image of the living present.

The broadest distinction between film and television lies in these extremes. We share the actual moment of Coronation with the Queen herself; the immediate emotion of the event extends over millions of people as far as the direct image can be spread. Later we may recapture this emotion at the cinema when we see the colour films of the ceremony with their infinitely superior picture which has been permanently recorded by the motion picture cameras. But it is the past with which we are dealing, and the quality of the emotion is therefore quite different. It is no longer a great experience simultaneous with the event itself. It is only a record, capable of infinite repetition.

A lively audience always expects the best performance which the circumstances of a production permit. From a film it expects the carefully selected image and the finesse of technical presentation which the editing process involves. From a television outside broadcast or even a 'live' studio performance the audience is prepared to take a certain degree of informality and improvisation, because it knows that the technicians, like themselves, can only prepare their presentation up to a certain point – the rest is not under their control, since the event is only happening as we watch it. This happy tolerance recedes as the nature of the production itself becomes more capable of control – as, for example, in the case of a studio drama production. Here too much improvisation and the errors of chance irritate the audience and destroy the illusion. It is for this reason that in the future plays and variety shows will probably be the first main branches of television normally to be presented by means of film. Already specially produced films have become a staple part of the dramatic shows on American television.

For television can transmit films more readily than the cinemas can exhibit big-screen television. In the future there will obviously be some overlapping between the kind of entertainment offered by the cinema and television. The present untidy relationship between sound radio, television, and the cinema will have to be sorted out, and the current rivalries settled by agreement. But however these current problems may be resolved, the cinema will remain a centre for public entertainment using a big screen, and the home will be the centre for private entertainment using a relatively small screen.

I think it would be unfortunate if we were to create too many hampering theoretical rules out of these broad distinctions – such rules as are really necessary arise in actual practice. The smaller screen diminishes the content in a picture which can be conveniently absorbed by an audience; the subtleties of the cinema – details of setting and dramatic lighting, the finer points of composition and cutting rhythm suitable for the big screen cannot be appreciated on the small one, and are often, in fact, difficult for the eye to tolerate. As the home screen increases in size and the definition and quality of the televised picture improves, it will be possible to convey more within the picture itself, but this will inevitably lead to the extinction of the present 'live' productions of drama. At the present level of picture size and quality the audience is conscious of very little except the faces of the actors. The director of a television play works largely in terms of small groups of actors; he uses group shots and close-ups, cutting from camera to camera according to a carefully rehearsed series of 'set-ups' for which the actors have been prepared in rehearsal. As far as the actor is concerned, the television 'live' production provides an ideal medium. He has all the advantage of the theatre in being able to go straight through the play as a single creative whole, and all the advantages of the cinema in being able to interpret his character intimately through close-up. The director is therefore very much more the servant of the actor in the television 'live' production than he is in the cinema-film. Although his personal style may emerge in the way he plans his production and directs his actors, in the end he will depend almost wholly on them to sustain the atmosphere of the final performance. The cinema-film director, on the other hand, can impose his own style more noticeably in his handling of backgrounds, locations, and the many physical details he incorporates into the production, as well as in the finer points of tempo and in the use of sound effects and music during the final assembly of the picture, when the actor's performance is so much raw material on the editing bench to be handled and arranged at leisure. On the small screen tempo must be reduced, and dialogue comes to the fore in the place of photographed action. Shots which would seem intolerably long and pictorially dull on the large screen are acceptable without any strain on the small screen. The late Fred O'Donovan became highly skilled in handling complete acts of stage plays with a single camera, amounting to twenty-minute or even half-hour 'takes'. Alfred Hitchcock's experiments with ten-minute 'takes' in his film version of the play *Rope* seemed in contrast tedious and unimaginative in the cinema, largely because they involved the rejection of editing, which is the main principle behind film-making for the cinema. In a television 'live' production the rate of 'cutting' may well average about one-fifth or one-sixth that of the cinema-film.

When films are being made for small screen television, they follow the same principles as the live production, partly for economic reasons, and partly because of the conditions imposed by small-screen reception. Live production direct from the studio is the cheapest form of production; one's costs are multiplied by, say, six times to perform the same action under conditions suitable for filming. Recording a live-action production on a kinescope or telefilm is cheaper, but produces a picture generally inferior to the original small-screen picture.

A new method of film-making derived from telefilm recording has been developed at Highbury Studios by a company known as High Definition Films. With proper rehearsal beforehand and careful pre-planning, it is claimed that up to one hour's finished production (edited as you go by selecting the shots from the various cameras covering the action, after the manner of live television production) can be achieved in a day's work at the Studios. The cameras used on the set are electronic; the director pre-plans in rehearsal the shots and camera changes he wants, and the apparatus putting image and sound on to film records only those shots he chooses as the drama develops before the various cameras. As in live television production, the sound is mixed as the show proceeds; the dialogue is taken direct as the actors speak, while additional sound and music (performed live or pre-recorded) is mixed in as desired by the director at the same time. While it is clear that many subtleties of normal studio production must be forgone in this vastly quickened form of film-making, and the finer values of lighting and photography diminished, High Definition Films is well equipped to make inexpensive productions of good quality for television using screen-plays which are mainly dependent on dialogue and on close shots taken in the comparatively modest studio sets which are all that the small screen requires at this stage in television.

The economic arguments for making films for television seem therefore to be these:

1. The live production is the cheapest immediate method of producing any kind of show, but, once the show has been performed, one's work in rehearsal and production organization and one's investment in sets are of no further value, unless one repeats the performance live while the cast and the studio facilities are still available.

2. The live production may be recorded by kinescope at reasonable cost, provided there is an agreement to do this with the performers' unions and the owners of the copyright of the work concerned. The kinescope can then be televised by the station which originated the production, or, with suitable arrangements for payment of fees, exported for use by foreign television stations. In America many live productions put out over the networks have to be kinescoped for repeat performances owing to the necessity for staggering the timing of transmissions over the four time-belts into which the United States is

divided. A kinescope is not normally of sufficiently good picture quality to be suitable for big-screen projection, though this is no doubt a temporary phase.

3. The most expensive form of production for television is to work entirely on film, either on location or in a film studio. For this reason the films at present being produced, for example, in America or in Britain, work to a very tight schedule in order to keep costs as low as possible; two days' shooting is normal for a film of roughly half-an-hour's duration. This is working at approximately ten times the speed of normal film production. Of necessity, dialogue predominates over action, since dialogue is the quickest to shoot; change in camera set-ups is strictly limited, and subtleties of lighting and photographic quality are almost entirely eliminated. This roughness of production is temporary and will last only so long as audiences remain satisfied with the very small screen in the home viewer. As screen size increases and picture quality improves, the production of films for television will require more care, and costs will rise in proportion. The market for these films is at present largely in the United States.

The BBC has established its own Television Film Unit which is responsible for assembling and shooting the daily news-shots, for producing a certain number of documentary subjects each year, and for shooting inserts required for other programmes which need odd sequences of location material or shots it would be impossible to obtain satisfactorily during a live studio production. For television lacks the mobility of the film; it is normally either studio-bound or limited to the cameras linked to the specially equipped Outside Broadcast units. The American 'creepie-peepie' and the British 'roving eye', by means of which a single independent television cameraman can chase a picture within a limited field, is a further step forward towards television mobility. So is the ever-increasing range of direct transmission of Outside Broadcasts from foreign countries. But to gain complete freedom in time and space, television must use film. The insertion of pre-filmed sequences or shots into a live production must be subtly done if it is to seem in keeping with the rest of the show; audiences are apt to wonder how it is possible for an actor who they know is giving a live performance from the studio suddenly to be seen walking down the Old Kent Road. It is in documentary and discussion programmes that the filmed insert comes into its own, or, to take another less obvious example, in visual 'gags' for comedy programmes, such as Kenneth Horne and Richard Murdoch introduced in a brilliant show they devised in 1953.

Documentary can exploit the so-called 'immediacy' of television to its fullest extent, apart, that is, from the Outside Broadcast itself. It can take the viewer from the studio talk or discussion to selected points in the world outside – the factory, the hospital, the laboratory, the conference room, the election platform, the foreign scene. The speakers can make use of film inserts, still pictures, and animated maps, charts, or diagrams. The whole programme can be so imaginatively bound together that it produces an entirely new form of presentation, born directly out of the television medium. What is actually happening in or away from the studio can be combined with what has already been filmed.

The root of television's power as a medium of information lies in this direct and immediate visual contact with the viewer in his home. Illustrated news and illustrated comment on every aspect of current affairs is at the disposal of increasing millions of people. Television is a revolution in human communication greater than the film itself, though it will take an appreciable time for it to reach audiences on the same geographical and social scale as the cinema does at present. But those countries which already have it are becoming aware of its political powers. It played a substantial part for the first time in history in America's Presidential elections during 1952, as anyone will realize who read Alistair Cooke's brilliant accounts of the Party conventions in Chicago published in the *Manchester Guardian*.

The BBC and the British political parties are proceeding very cautiously in the use of television for party political broadcasting in this country. But television will bring party politics into the homes of millions of people in terms of the most persuasive television personalities who can be found among the politicians. The effect of this party political intrusion into the home will ultimately be far greater than that made through sound broadcasting, and this has in itself been very considerable, more especially in the United States.

Television has also introduced a new patron for the writer. The tendency among producers in both sound radio and television is that of all people who have to work in a hurry, the tendency to use the established people who are known to be reliable. But television can and should be the means of discovering new dramatists and writers of actuality programmes. Over a hundred plays are televised by the BBC alone each year, and among these there is a slowly growing number of new works, some of which have been subsequently bought for production on the stage or as films.

But television will have to solve its economic problems; the issue of standards as between public service, commercial, and sponsored television will have to be resolved. The nature of its use on the big screen inside the cinemas will have to be decided and put into practice, just as the relative merits of using pre-filmed material in the normal television services must be more fully understood. Television is already becoming a major exhibitor of those films which have never found adequate exhibition in the commercial cinemas – the public service documentaries, the films of fact of every kind, the experimental *avant-garde* films. British television not only makes and shows its own documentary films, it shows many documentaries produced in the normal way both in Britain and abroad.

Television, too, will take on new forms; colour has now arrived in America and television 3-D is even being discussed! Telephones may become televisual, and receiving sets become so portable that we can carry them in our pockets or even on our wrists!

284

Of more immediate importance, however, is the experimental development in the United States of magnetic tape for recording moving pictures either in colour or in black-and-white, together with accompanying sound. This remarkable innovation, first demonstrated by the Radio Corporation of America in 1953, avoids altogether the lengthy business of the chemical processing of film, and enables the motion picture or the television director to see the results of his work in the studio in the form of an immediate play-back. It is claimed that electronic film-making, once the new equipment is introduced, will reduce production costs in a number of ways. The significance of this invention is that film and television production of the future may well be 'shot' by magnetic-tape cameras and reproduced electronically on tape for distribution, and that news pictures may be 'telephoned' from one centre to another to speed up their showing to the public either on television or in the cinemas.

But, to return to the present, although the monopoly of the cinema in visual entertainment is at an end, television will never supersede it. Television will, in fact, offer the cinema healthy competition, encouraging the production of films which have sufficient merit to make people want to pay good money to see them. If television increases the number of good films in our cinemas, no one should grumble, not even the exhibitor!

CONCLUSION

WITH A WORD OF WARNING TO THE PEOPLE
WHO SAY THEY HATE FILMS AND TELEVISION

MANY critics of the older, fully-established arts tend to regard the criticism of films as unnecessary or impossible or as an easy way to earn money without the exercise of intelligence! The circumstances of film exhibition are perhaps too blatantly popular for them. The film seems to them to be the symbol of a public decadence, destroying any vestige of taste which might be developed through education, and leaving respect for the highest levels of artistic achievement to the so-called 'cultivated' minority.

Such critics choose to disregard three facts: first, the demands made by great art on those who are capable of absorbing it have always limited its full appreciation to a comparatively few people; second, great art has this in common with life itself, namely, it has something to offer to everyone according to his capacities to take what he can from it; and, third, the use of the evil word 'highbrow' disguises the fact that much art of the past has been made to be enjoyed by large numbers of people, whether they were 'cultured' or not. A rich vein of vulgarity runs through a great deal of the work created by men like Chaucer, Shakespeare, Rembrandt, and Beethoven.

It is easy to sympathize with the specialist who is quite frank about having no time for the cinema or radio or television or newspapers. His work absorbs the whole of his attention, and the price of his specialization is that he cuts himself off from the forms of expression which most greatly affect the largest number of his fellow creatures. He lives in a modern extension to the ivory tower, which only a few people can in the end afford to do. For the sober truth is that these new-fangled, popular forms of expression, these twentieth-century commercialized developments of the inventive genius of the nineteenth century, are things which affect the life of the whole population of the world. They affect our total outlook, our desires, our social morality, and our politics. They help substantially to make modern civilization possible. They are alike part of our educational system and our lack of education. They are instruments at the disposal of those people ambitious enough to get control of them, whether they are politicians, entertainers, artists, or business men.

It is fatal for people who wish to play any influential part in contemporary life, however restricted it may be, to disregard the forms of communication and expression most favoured by the general public. Through them the best as well as the worst kinds of entertainment and information can reach audiences far greater and more widespread than is possible by any other means. That is obvious enough, but it represents the essential revolution in communications for which the twentieth century stands. It is a situation which has no parallel in the past, and it is one which too few qualified people have begun to examine with any seriousness. The time and the evidence are both too short.

The cinema is twice as old as broadcasting. Its range as far as its audience is concerned is much more limited. It is a very considerable extension of the theatre on the one hand (it still requires the public to assemble themselves in fixed places and pay to see its entertainment), and of the lecture meeting and classroom on the other (when people use the documentary and specialized film outside the cinemas). It does not, therefore, represent the complete revolution in human communications which broadcasting in sound and vision represent, reaching into people's homes whether they be near or far away. But the film as an art will always be a more impressive and a more exact form than visual broadcasting. During its first half century it has grown into a medium of great technical complexity, subtlety, and beauty. It is for this reason that growing numbers of people are delighting in the best work of the more imaginative film-makers, actors, and technicians. No television transmission can fulfil this demand – the meticulous technique of the large screen, and the excitement of audiences grouped in public theatres. The essential values of television lie elsewhere, for it is a homely form of entertainment and information service. The higher art of the film remains in the cinema, and will never leave it.

THE WORK OF THE BRITISH FILM INSTITUTE

By Denis Forman, Director of the Institute, 1948–55

THE 'Fine' Arts, as we call them to-day, presumably had their upward struggle before they earned the adjective. Since the days of Athens, however, they have enjoyed a distinguished career, adorning the market places of rich states and illuminating the salons of great men. During the more violent moments of history they survived the storm by sheltering in some cloister or by passing a century or two within an academy of scholars, always emerging punctually to be welcomed by a new aristocracy and to be reshaped to the taste of the age. To-day we accept them as the aristocrats of pleasure, they have an hereditary antiquity of twenty centuries and more, they have distinction, they have the *haut ton*. But as the Edwardian élite replenished their blue blood from the depths of the ladies' chorus, so from time to time have the great and ancient arts admitted to their circle some more vulgar form of amusement, giving to it grace and distinction, and at the same time gaining from its freshness and vigour.

To those of us whose lives are bound up with the development of cinema, this process has a peculiar fascination. For the newly born medium of film is in the main a type of folk art, brash and vigorous. This is due not so much to its kind, for it is capable of infinite imaginative expression, but to its employment. Be so absurd for a moment as to imagine the response of an Aristophanes or a Sophocles to the film, conceive an Aeneid scripted and directed by Virgil, shorts produced by Horace under the sponsorship of Maecenas, or consider the superb Technicolor savagery that Akbar would have had his men produce. Yet owing to the accident of its mechanical nature the film was not born until the industrial age, it had no decent cultural descent, it did not even emerge from the people; it was thrust in front of the people by the showman.

The people have never really recovered the initiative. They accepted the cinema readily but passively; soon it was to become their favourite indoor entertainment, as the showman developed it sturdily along his traditional lines, borrowing largely from the cruder forms of story-telling, drama, and mime to exploit its appeal. It was not, however, through any older art that the film found itself. It became a serious medium only when the experimental artist found in it new dimensions of time and place, new rhythms and new sensibilities, and when, in the late flowering of the silent period, he forged these elements into an idiom susceptible of high artistic expression – an idiom soon to be given yet another dimension in the form of the sound-track.

It was in the dual recognition of the film as an art and as a mass influence that the British Film Institute was founded in 1934. In form it was a non-profit-making limited liability company governed by a Board whose members were appointed by the Lord President of the Council. In function it was to fulfil a wide range of purposes. The older arts had their academies, libraries, and museums, each with its traditional field of responsibility. The new Institute, in that it was to collect films for preservation, was something of an archive; in that it was to promote the study of the art of film it was something of an academy, in setting out to raise the standard of public appreciation something of an Arts Council, in concerning itself with the social effects of the film something of a public welfare body, in promoting the use of film in schools something of the formal educationist, in lending and displaying films it was a public library, and in forming its own membership, a club.

From small beginnings the Institute, financed from the Sunday Cinematograph Fund (a fund endowed from a percentage of Sunday box-office takings), gradually grew; and as would be expected, it found a centre of balance in those functions which proved to be most practicable. Thus the establishment of the National Film Library in 1935 and the development of the film society movement in the late thirties were significant landmarks in the course it was destined to take.

During the war there were two notable developments in the field of British films: first the emergence of a strong indigenous feature production industry, and secondly a rapid expansion in the documentary and educational uses of the film. These developments resulted in the formation in 1947 of the British Film Academy as a meeting ground for artists and technicians; in the peace-time continuance of an informational film service through the Central Office of Information; and in the institution in 1946 of the National Committee for Visual Aids in Education. The house was setting itself in order, and the Institute, lightened of several borderline responsibilities, could see before it a clearer task, defined by the Radcliffe Committee which considered its affairs in 1948 as 'To encourage the development of the art of the film, to promote its use as a record of contemporary life and manners and to foster public appreciation and study of it from these points of view'.

To-day the Institute receives, in addition to some £20,000 from the Sunday Cinematograph Fund, a Treasury grant which, together with its own trading turnover, makes up an annual revenue of £125,000. From this total the largest net amount is devoted to the National Film Library.

In the field of literature it is possible for the British Museum to preserve a copy of every published work. Films, however, are more bulky than books, their expectancy of life is shorter, their storage and maintenance is an expensive and highly technical affair. Hence, since its establishment, the National Film Library has selected for preservation only the more significant films from the spate of current production. The method of selection has been aimed at fulfilling three principal objects: to provide a record of contemporary life and manners for the social historian of the future; to survey the development of science and technology; and to preserve for posterity an anthology of films which reflect the development of the art.

The first of these objects entails a wide and judicious selection of material based not so much upon the journalistic value of 'news' as upon the value of events as an interpretation of the age. This intention can be clarified by asking the question: 'If you could recall to life the Britain of the eighteenth century, which scenes would most vividly reconstruct the life of the period?' The gardens at Vauxhall, the new manufactories at Birmingham, the interior of a coffee house, or a sustained view of Charing Cross would all be candidates at least as strong as the funeral of Queen Anne or the opening of George III's parliament. So to-day the backgrounds of fashion, sport, and social life are given their due weight in relation to the events which make headline news. Thus the History Selection Committee includes a sports journalist and an expert on dress as well as more orthodox historians.

The selection of films important to the development of the art of the cinema is a simpler affair. Great films are an automatic choice, as are any films made by artists of the top rank (actors, directors, and others are allotted gradings which reflect the selector's view of their importance). This, however, is not all; any film which uses a novel technique such as *The Lady in the Lake* or *Rope* would be certain of inclusion. This selection committee is composed mainly of film critics; it includes also film directors, journalists, film historians, and lay members. Already the archive holds over 20,000 reels of film, to which new titles are added at a rate of 10 to 20 a month.

The National Film Library is not, of course, alone in the field. The Museum of Modern Art in New York and the Cinémathèque Française, to mention but two, carry on similar work in their own countries, and – thanks to the institution in 1938 of the active Fédération Internationale des Archives du Film – there is now a high degree of international co-ordination, which extends beyond the Iron Curtain. The Library is, however, unique in one respect, in that it has, at Aston Clinton in Buckinghamshire, a set of vaults specially constructed for the preservation of films. These vaults, under the supervision of a Technical Officer and a laboratory staff, are kept at carefully controlled levels of temperature and humidity. The staff is mainly engaged, however, in the work of film preservation.

Cinematograph film on a nitrate base is perhaps the most ephemeral material used in any visual art. After twenty to thirty years (although age is no certain yardstick) a complex series of chemical reactions may produce from the nitrate base acidic substances which, if allowed to develop unchecked, will combine to destroy the gelatine emulsion in which the actual picture is recorded. In extreme cases the film becomes sticky and unfit for projection or further reproduction. Hence a test has been devised to check the state of all films suspected of instability. A small circle of film is punched out of the reel to be tested, and inserted into a test-tube. Since the deterioration of film can be artificially hastened by raising its temperature, the test-tube is heated to 134 degrees Centigrade. Inside the tube is test paper impregnated with alizarin red dye and moistened with glycerine and water. The volatile acid vapour generated from the hot film has the effect of bleaching the test paper; the result of this test is therefore taken as the time in minutes required for the colour change to occur.

The bulk of the films held in the archive are used prints given by the distributing company on the request of the Selection Committee. Many private collections, however, have been donated to the Library, and these may contain a certain percentage of negatives. The technical quality of the material is important, because the archive is not a viewing library in any sense; it is a collection of matrices from which any future viewing prints may be struck.

The mobilization of this vast treasure-house will present posterity with a sizeable task. A start, however, has already been made by setting up a Loan Section, which holds viewing prints of those films which no longer possess any reissue value in the commercial sense, but which nevertheless are of great importance to those interested in the history of films. They include the early work of the Lumières and Méliès, a representative selection from the one-reel period, early Westerns, Chaplin two-reelers, the great silent films of Griffith, Eisenstein, and Pudovkin, several examples of the French *avant-garde* school, and in the sound period, Sternberg's *Blue Angel* and Pabst's *Kameradschaft* from Germany. British film production is well represented, and in all there are some 500 films available on 16 mm. and 35 mm. gauges.

Distribution of the collection through the loan of prints had, however, obvious limitations, and until the National Film Theatre was opened on 23 October 1952, the Institute had been in the position of a museum rich in stock but without exhibition space.

The theatre is a handsome modern building constructed under the title of the Telecinema for the Festival of Britain 1951, during which it played programmes of three-dimensional films and large-screen television. Re-equipped as a repertory theatre with 400 seats and complete with club premises, it still retains the stereo equipment, but, more important for its purpose, the projectors on both 16 and 35 mm. gauges can exhibit old films at their proper speed and can adapt their gates to any size of frame.

The opening of the National Film Theatre was hailed by the Press with satisfaction, one Sunday newspaper claiming that this was 'the screen event of the week, month, year, and probably decade'. However that may be, after the first year of operation it was clear that both financially and from the point of view of public support the experiment had been successful. It brought the Institute into touch with a large new public of members and associates (some 25,000 at the time of writing) who are enrolled on the lines of a theatre club.

In arranging the initial programmes for the theatre the Institute had three objectives in view; first, to present a steady repertory of the acknowledged masterpieces of the screen; second, to concentrate attention on some theme of contemporary interest or importance in the cinema, and thirdly (in keeping with the traditions of the Telecinema) to demonstrate what was new and experimental. Thus two nights every week were devoted to a chronological survey of film history under the general title of *Fifty Years of Film*, four nights in each week were given to a series of studies of the work of outstanding directors or actors or else to some decisive trend in the cinema, past or present. In this category, under the heading of 'World Cinema', the Directors René Clair, Vittorio de Sica, Alfred Hitchcock, and Erich von Stroheim have each been given a season of from six to twelve weeks; the comedians of the silent screen (Chaplin, Buster Keaton, Harold Lloyd, and Harry Langdon) had a long and popular run. Other topics included a study of changing fashions in male and female film stars, the work of Ealing Studios, and a typical cinema programme of thirty years ago. Except for Saturdays, when the theatre is thrown open to the public, only members and associates are admitted. Under this arrangement the theatre has built up its own specialized audience while enjoying the full support of the film industry.

Although the Theatre is a boon to the London film-lover its value to other centres of population is of course negligible. In the provinces the work the Theatre is doing in London is carried out by Film Societies. The rise of the film society movement in Britain since the end of the war is very remarkable. In 1939 there were 18 societies, many of them veterans of seven or eight years' standing. During the war new societies sprang up to serve the special needs of war-time concentrations; many of these societies died as the population ebbed back into the peace-time pattern. In 1946, however, there were 48 societies, and since that date a sharp but steady rise has brought the number up to the remarkable figure of 230, serving an audience of perhaps 50,000 people.

In other countries the words 'film society' (or cine-club) are capable of bearing many meanings, covering at one end of the scale the frankly commercial operation and at the other a coterie of the intelligentsia. In Britain a *bona fide* film society can be only one thing: a group of people formed into a non-profit-making, non-political association for the purpose of seeing and enjoying films other than those normally accessible through the box-office.

The purpose and advantages of the non-political clause are clear, but the definition of 'non-profit-making' calls perhaps for a fuller explanation. The intention behind such a restriction is twofold: first, to ensure that there shall be no competition with the film industry proper, second, that societies should exist only for the purpose of seeing and enjoying films unallied to any financial motive on the part of the promoters. Thus no officers of a society can accept any emolument, members must pay their share by subscribing an annual sum and by booking their tickets in advance for each performance, and in the event of a society's ceasing to function, any surplus funds must be given to another film society or to some body working in the same field. This policy has proved its worth; the film industry, and especially the Kinematograph Renters' Society, has been constructively helpful in its attitude, and among the societies themselves, although finance is often a worry, it can never become a preoccupation.

The domestic affairs of the movement are controlled by two Federations, one for Scotland and one for England and Wales. Much of the credit for the successful realization of the film society scheme lies with these two bodies; standing in the background, however, the Film Institute has provided moral support and from time to time financial help. The hire of films, too, is organized for the societies through a central booking agency operated by the Institute. This unit receives from the society the programme requirements for the season and places the bookings with the renter of the library concerned, including the distribution section of the Institute itself. The service is used by the majority of societies and in the season 1952–53 the agency passed some 6,500 films through its books. Continental films which have made a reputation in their country of origin, or which have been screened in one of London's specialized cinemas, are perhaps the group of films most in demand; during 1953, for example, *Golden Marie*, *Don Camillo*, *Kermesse Heroïque*, and *Rashomon* topped the poll.

The societies themselves fall into three broad groups. First come the giants with a membership of from 1,000 to 3,000 operating in big cities and in big cinemas. Their programmes are run usually on Sundays outside cinema opening hours, and they attract an audience comparable to that of regular concert- or play-goers, which fluctuates in accordance with the appeal of the programme. Many of them, such as the lively Merseyside society, run a 16 mm. section too, organized as a study group complete with courses of lectures; but in the main the larger societies have only the loosest sort of organization of membership. Next come the bulk of the 35 mm. societies; their membership is from as few as 200 up to 1,000. These may be run on much the same lines as the larger societies, or they may be more or less closely knit round a central group of enthusiasts for whom the weekly show is as much an occasion for discussion as a chance of seeing a film. Lastly there is a smaller 16 mm. society with upwards of eighty members, often operating under difficult conditions. These are the societies whose enthusiasm can stand the test of the 16 mm. sound track, the draughty hall, and the more limited choice of films available to them.

The success of the film society movement has been largely built upon the work of a small band of enthusiasts. Such people as Forsyth Hardy and Margaret Hancock (to mention but two), themselves running flourishing societies, found time to plan and carry through the development into federation with its attendant opportunities for nation-wide participation. To-day the Federations are strengthening their structure by the development of semi-autonomous regional groups, each with a centre and a corporate life of its own.

The film society movement is one of the practical expressions of the Institute's concern to raise the standard of film going from the level of a habit to something more like serious critical appreciation. To this end the Institute also organizes a service of lectures, and runs courses for the many social and cultural groups interested in the problem. One of these, the annual course now held in conjunction with the Edinburgh Festival, is an event of some note, during which film-makers and film-goers are brought face to face to discuss their many problems of mutual interest, but the Institute has reserved its main effort in this field for the younger generation.

It is, of course, generally agreed that the best age for teaching critical appreciation of any subject is during the middle and late teens. It is known, too, that the incidence of film-going is at its highest at this age. For the whole mass of the population it is true to say that when children leave school, if 'comics' are discounted, they largely give up reading books; they do not, however, relinquish the cinema or the Television screen. The Institute has always held that the school curriculum should be adjusted to meet this situation and has been greatly heartened by the interest recently shown in film appreciation by Institutes of Education, Teachers' Training Colleges, and the like. To give up school time to a study of entertainment films may sound a little quixotic, and indeed the subject is so young as to have no generally used technique of instruction. Some teachers encourage the children to keep maps showing what films are being played at the local cinemas and encourage discussion both as a means to select the most enjoyable film and, afterwards, to evaluate its good and bad points. Most instruction is related in this way to the children's cinema-going experience, but some teachers go further and have their pupils produce films themselves. The class will be broken into syndicates, first to write a script and then, when the best script has been chosen, to prepare for its production. Producer, director, cast, and crew are appointed, and the film is made on two or three free afternoons. Then comes the test of playing it back to the whole class, and, if good enough, perhaps to an outside audience. The Institute already has a collection of more than thirty such films, some of them of quite remarkable quality, and mostly stimulated by members of the Society of Film Teachers, a vigorous body, who are the leaders amongst their colleagues in their interest in this latest addition to our school curriculum.

For its own membership the Institute provides more specialized services. In addition to the National Film Theatre, there is a small cinema theatre available in the London premises; there is an extensive book library, and a stills library of over 60,000 photographs from a wide range of films. For its members, and for the public as well, it provides an information service and publishes two journals – *Sight and Sound*, a miscellany of topical writing upon the film, and the *Monthly Film Bulletin*, a review of all current production. The Publications Department (under the general editorship of Gavin Lambert) also produces a series of indexes of the work of well-known directors, and a variety of miscellaneous pamphlets. More specialized needs are served by the Scientific Film Association and the British Universities Film Council, and in Scotland the Institute's sister organization offers a comprehensive service which includes the distribution of educational and informational films. All three bodies receive a grant-in-aid from the Institute.

In this and in other ways the British Film Institute is tackling its main task of raising the standard of public taste in films.

Note on the British Film Academy

The British Film Academy, founded in 1947, is a private organization representing the senior British film-makers. It holds frequent lectures, discussions, and screenings for its members, and it promotes the publication of books (such as *The Technique of Film Editing* by Karel Reisz) and a quarterly Journal which contains articles written mainly by film-makers for film-makers. It has also founded a number of annual awards for films, for technical achievements, and for film acting.

SELECTED BOOK LIST

1. *Film History*

A Million and One Nights. Terry Ramsaye. Simon and Schuster, 1926. A discursive but fascinating history of silent cinema written from the American point of view.

The Film Till Now. Paul Rotha. Cape, 1930. Revised edition with Richard Griffith, Vision Press, 1949. The revised edition retains Rotha's original history of the silent cinema as it was written in 1930, and adds Griffith's cogent and exciting survey of the achievement of the American and European sound film up to 1948. The Appendices include lists of the production units of a large number of outstanding films and a carefully compiled glossary of film terms.

Celluloid. Paul Rotha. Longmans, Green and Co, 1931. A sequel to the first edition of the above, entering upon the sound film.

Documentary Film. Paul Rotha. Faber and Faber, 1936. Revised 1939. Reissued with additional contributions by Sinclair Road and Richard Griffith, 1952. The reissue was for the purpose of bringing this standard work of film history up to date. The 1952 edition surveys the great enlargement of world documentary brought about by war-time and post-war production.

Movie Parade. Compiled by Paul Rotha. Studio, 1936. Revised edition by Paul Rotha and Roger Manvell, 1950. A fine collection of stills giving a pictorial history of world cinema in its various branches.

History of the Film. Bardèche and Brasillach. Translated and edited by Iris Barry. Allen and Unwin, 1938. Revised editions in French, André Martel, Paris, 1949 and 1953–4. An interesting and important history from the French point of view.

Histoire de l'Art cinématographique. Carl Vincent. Éditions du Trident, Bruxelles, 1939. A detailed history of the film from the beginnings to about 1937. Recommended.

The Rise of the American Film. Lewis Jacobs. Harcourt Brace and Co, New York, 1939. This is undoubtedly one of the few very good books on the film, but naturally limited to the achievement of America, with occasional references only to European cinema. It is both lively and authoritative. It takes the various

300

periods of the development of American film, deals first with the economic issues of the industry, next with the work of important directors who developed the art of the film, and closes with a survey of the period from the point of view of the social content of the films, both good and bad.

Georges Méliès, 1861–1938. Maurice Bessy and Lo Duca. Prisma, 1945. A lavishly illustrated study of the early French director of theatrical fantasies in film. Contains many examples of Méliès' own treatments and scripts.

Images du Cinéma français. Nicole Védrès. Les Éditions du Chêne, Paris, 1945. A survey of the development of French cinema largely by means of stills grouped under types of film, such as Burlesque, Comedy, Horror films, 'La Condition humaine', etc. An interesting and unusual book.

The Factual Film. O.U.P., 1946. One of a series of reports prepared for the Arts Enquiry by a group of anonymous experts and sponsored by the Dartington Hall Trustees in association with the Nuffield College Reconstruction Survey. Covers the development of documentary in Britain, and contains recommendations concerning the economic reorganization of the British film industry.

Twenty Years of British Film. Michael Balcon, H. Forsyth Hardy, Ernest Lindgren and Roger Manvell. Falcon Press, 1946. A fully illustrated survey of the development of British feature and documentary film, 1928–45.

Histoire Générale du Cinéma. Georges Sadoul. Éditions Denoël, Paris, from 1946. Four parts of this history of the film have so far been published between 1946 and 1954. The first, *L'Invention du Cinéma*, covers the period 1832–97; the second, *Les Pionniers du Cinéma*, the period 1897–1909. The third part, *Le Cinéma Devient un Art* (1909–20), has appeared in two volumes, *L'Avant Guerre* and *La Première Guerre Mondiale*. Of the three remaining parts two, *L'Art Muet* (1920–30) and *Les Débuts du Parlant*, are still due to appear, but *Le Cinéma pendant la Guerre* (1939–45), the first volume of the sixth part called *L'Époque Contemporaine* (1939–54) was published in 1954. This outstanding French history of the film is the most extensive yet to be undertaken, and is as much an important work of reference as it is an evaluation of the history of the development of the film as an art.

Louis Lumière, Inventeur. Maurice Bessy et Lo Duca. Prisma, Paris, 1948. An authoritative illustrated account of one of the most important single figures in the invention of motion pictures.

Le Dessin animé. Lo Duca. Prisma, Paris, 1948. An illustrated history of animated films, and a study of their technique.

Histoire encyclopédique du Cinéma, 1895–1929. René Jeanne and Charles Ford. Vol. I, 1947; Vol. II, 1952. The series of volumes which René Jeanne and Charles Ford are publishing belong to the highest level of film histories at present being produced. They give the most generous space to their subject, quote extensively from contemporary documents, and poke into the corners which less careful historians conveniently forget. Their work, like that of Sadoul and Rotha, is indispensable.

The Film. Georg Schmidt, Werner Schmalenbach and Peter Bächlin. Holbein Publishing Company, Basel, and Falcon Press, 1948. Using an original lay-out of stills, diagrams, and text, this book, originally published in German, demonstrates the aesthetic, social, and industrial factors in the cinema. English version prepared in consultation with Roger Manvell.

From Caligari to Hitler. Siegfried Kracauer. Dobson, 1947. A detailed account of the German cinema, 1919–33, written to prove the argument that national tendencies which culminated in Hitler can be traced in the cinema of this period.

Fifty Years of German Film. H. H. Wollenberg. National Cinema Series, Falcon Press, 1947. Written with emphasis on the historical and social development of the German film. The book contains a wide selection of stills.

Experiment in the Film. Roger Manvell (Editor). Grey Walls Press, 1948. Essays, historical and aesthetic, by the critics and film-makers Lewis Jacobs (America), Jacques Brunius (France), Gregori Roshal and Roman Karmen (Russia), Ernst Iros and Hans Richter (Germany), and Edgar Anstey, Roger Manvell, and John Maddison (Britain), on the development of the experimental and *avant-garde* film in these countries. Contains much historical material not previously recorded.

The History of the British Film. Vol. I, 1896–1906. Rachael Low and Roger Manvell, Vol. II, 1907–14. Vol. III, 1914–18. Rachael Low. Allen and Unwin, 1948, 1949, and 1951 respectively. An official history, sponsored by the British Film Institute, and, in the case of Vol. III, jointly by the Institute and the British Film Academy. These three volumes give an authoritative and detailed account of the origin and early development of the British film industry and of film technique as it was practised in Britain between 1896 and 1918. The history, which it was originally intended should be carried forward to the close of the silent period by Dr Low, was written under the auspices of a Research Committee under the Chairmanship of the late Cecil Hepworth.

Soviet Cinema. Thorold Dickinson and Catherine de la Roche. National Cinema Series, Falcon Press, 1948. Thorold Dickinson writes on the Russian silent cinema with a special appreciation of the editing methods used during the first phase of Soviet film technique. Catherine de la Roche discusses the sound film up to 1947, and explains the change of outlook which was brought about when the practice of socialist realism became the official policy for the arts in the U.S.S.R. This book contains the most complete collection of stills from Russian films to have been published in this country.

The Italian Film. Vernon Jarratt. National Cinema Series, Falcon Press, 1951. An illustrated history of the Italian cinema, with special reference to the origin and development of the so-called 'neo-realist' movement.

Scandinavian Film. Forsyth Hardy. National Cinema Series, Falcon Press, 1953. An illustrated history of the Swedish, Danish, and Norwegian film.

French Film. Georges Sadoul. National Cinema Series, Falcon Press, 1953. An illustrated history of the French cinema from its origins to 1950.

Charlie Chaplin. Theodore Huff. Schuman, New York, 1951; Cassell, London, 1952. A careful, analytical study of the various phases in the development of Chaplin's career; each film of importance, long and short, is described in detail. The book is refreshingly free from adulation or over-interpretation, faults which have spoiled some other comparatively recent books on Chaplin, the best of which is Robert Payne's *The Great Charlie*, in which some excellent analyses of Chaplin's films appear, well worth reading alongside those by Theodore Huff, and R. J. Minney's informative biography, *The Immortal Tramp*.

A Pictorial History of the Movies. Deems Taylor. Allen and Unwin, 1952. This volume is an enlarged edition of Deems Taylor's interesting pictorial survey of film history, originally published in the States. It is blandly assumed that American cinema is all that matters in a book carrying so universal a title.

The British Film Industry. Published by P.E.P. (Political and Economic Planning), 1952. The most complete and authoritative survey to have been made of the economic development of the British film industry – production, distribution, and exhibition. The history of the present complex situation is given, and the causes of the recurrent financial crises to which the industry is subject are analysed.

Eisenstein. A biography by Marie Seton. The Bodley Head, 1952. Marie Seton was a close friend of Eisenstein, and this brilliant and moving biography succeeds in combining a very personal portrait of one of the rare men of genius in the cinema with a careful valuation of his work and influence. The political tensions which surrounded and frustrated him are fairly presented by one who sides with Eisenstein in his great personal and public difficulties.

The World of Robert Flaherty. Richard Griffith. Gollancz, 1953. In this book Richard Griffith brings together a series of documents about Flaherty's films and film-making written mostly by Flaherty himself and by his wife, Frances. There are omissions, and the book, readable though it is, is no substitute for the biography which must eventually be written.

A Pictorial History of the Silent Screen. Daniel Blum. Hamish Hamilton, 1954. This massive collection of stills covers the history of the silent film mainly in the United States from the time of Edison.

2. *The Art of the Film*

Film Technique and Film Acting. V. I. Pudovkin. Translated by Ivor Montagu. Vision Press, 1954. Pudovkin's two books, the first originally published by Gollancz in 1929 and the second by Newnes in 1935, are essential to understanding the first phase of Soviet Russian film theory and practice. They give, together with Eisenstein's far more difficult books, the standard exposition of the once-famous Russian theories of montage (editing) and typage (the principle of casting for Russian films of the first period).

Film. Rudolf Arnheim. Faber, 1933. A comparatively early study in film aesthetics. Not easy reading, but rewarding.

Film Craft. Adrian Brunel. Newnes, 1933. The studio and scenario in working dress. A collection of many interesting comments from different participants in the collective film job.

Film Music. Kurt London. Faber, 1936. Designed rather for the musician than the layman, but of considerable general interest.

Garbo and the Night-Watchmen. Alistair Cooke. Cape, 1937. Cooke calls this a bedside book. Its bedside manner is limited to keeping the reader awake. Satiric, amusing, caustic comments by American and British critics of distinction and wit.

Designing for Moving Pictures. Edward Carrick. Studio, 1941. An excellent book on the design and structure of film sets and properties.

The Film Sense. S. M. Eisenstein. Faber, 1943. A book of essays on film aesthetics of considerable importance. See pages 75–8 on Eisenstein's theories of the film.

The Art of Walt Disney. Professor R. D. Feild. Collins, 1944. An important and detailed, as well as beautifully illustrated volume, the result of a year's academic research in collaboration with Disney's technicians. Gives a complete history of the development of Disney's technique of animation, and the organization of the studios.

Film. Roger Manvell. Pelican Books, 1944. Revised Reprints and Editions, 1944, 1946, and 1950. A general study cf the art and social influences of the film; the predecessor to the present volume in the Pelican Series.

Grierson on Documentary. Edited with an Introduction by H. Forsyth Hardy. Collins, 1946. A well-edited selection of Grierson's brilliant essays on documentary and his early reviews of feature films.

Chestnuts in Her Lap. C. A. Lejeune. Phoenix House, 1947. A collection of Lejeune's reviews written since 1936.

The Art of the Film. Ernest Lindgren. Allen and Unwin, 1948. The most complete and carefully considered account of the art and technique of the film to have been published in this country. Very highly recommended.

Composing for the Films. Hanns Eisler. Oxford University Press, New York, 1948. A devastating survey of contemporary American film music by a distinguished left-wing composer, who analyses the special conditions governing composition for the screen.

The Boys' and Girls' Film Book. Mary Field and Maud Miller. Burke Publishing Company, 1947. An excellent survey of all aspects of film-making (not omitting historical, economic, and social considerations) for intelligent older children.

Art and Design in the British Film. Edward Carrick. Dobson, 1948. A fully illustrated survey of the work of leading British art directors and designers.

Drawn and Quartered. Richard Winnington. Saturn Press, 1948. A selection of the late Richard Winnington's sharp reviews and brilliant satiric drawings of film stars from the period 1943–8.

Film Form. S. M. Eisenstein. Dennis Dobson, 1949. A series of essays on the theory of the film, selected by Eisenstein himself and edited and translated by Jay Ledya. See pages 75–8 on Eisenstein's theories of the film.

Picture. Lillian Ross. Gollancz, 1953. This book about the vicissitudes in the production of John Huston's film *The Red Badge of Courage* is described on pages 189–92 of this book.

The Technique of Film Editing. Focal Press, 1953. Written and compiled by Karel Reisz with the guidance of a committee of film-makers appointed by the British Film Academy. This book represents considerable research by Karel Reisz, who received indispensable help from a number of film-makers, British and foreign, who were prepared to analyse and reconstruct with him the process of editing which went into their films. The result is a book which is recognized internationally as a work of authority.

Cocteau on the Film. A Conversation recorded by André Fraigneau. Dennis Dobson, 1954. Cocteau, prompted by his friend Fraigneau, discusses his personal position as a poet working from time to time through the medium of film, and explains his intentions in his chief productions. A very illuminating book.

3. *Screenplays and Books about Individual Films*

The Private Life of Henry VIII. Lajos Biro and Arthur Wimperis. Edited by Ernest Betts. Methuen, 1934. A complete scenario, nicely cleaned up for the press. But useful and illuminating, as well as entertaining.

Twenty Best Film Plays; and *Best Film Plays*, 1943–44, and also 1945. Gassner and Nichols. Crown, New York. These three volumes contain American screenplays edited for the reading public including *It Happened One Night, Rebecca, The Grapes of Wrath, Little Caesar, Fury, The Life of Emile Zola, Juarez, The Good Earth, All that Money can Buy, Stagecoach, The Miracle of Morgan's Creek, The Ox-bow Incident, Hail the Conquering Hero, The Southerner*, and *Double Indemnity*. Introductions on script-writing by Dudley Nichols.

Scott of the Antarctic. David James. Convoy Publications, 1948. Written by the film's Arctic Adviser, this book is a model description of the planning and making of a film which involved considerable research and elaborate location work.

The Film Hamlet. Edited by Brenda Cross. Saturn Press, 1948. This well-illustrated book is a record of the film's production in the form of a series of essays by the people concerned with (among other aspects of the film) its casting, its camerawork, the set design and construction, the acting and editing. It is prefaced by Sir Laurence Olivier, who writes about the problems of adapting the film for the screen.

Quartet (1948), *Trio* (1950), and *Encore* (1951). Stories by Somerset Maugham, with the screenplays based upon them by R. C. Sherriff, Noel Langley, T. E. B. Clarke, Arthur Macrae, and Eric Ambler. Heinemann. It is interesting in this series of volumes to compare the screenplays with their originals, the divergencies becoming less as the success of the Maugham stories with the cinema public became more assured.

The Red Shoes Ballet. A Critical Study by Mark Gibbon. Saturn Press, 1948. An enthusiastic analysis of every element in the famous ballet sequence – music, design, choreography. Very fully illustrated.

The Third Man and *The Fallen Idol*. Graham Greene. Heinemann, 1950. The stories on which Sir Carol Reed's films were based, the first being written originally for the screen.

Three British Screenplays. Edited by Roger Manvell. Methuen, 1950. These three scripts represent broadly three stages in film-making. *Odd Man Out* is the advance screenplay as originally written, narrative and dialogue are given without the full technical breakdown; *Brief Encounter* was printed from David Lean's shooting script, with every camera set-up indicated; *Scott of the Antarctic* was a special post-production script prepared for this book, indicating every shot as it was finally edited for the film.

Que Viva Mexico! S. M. Eisenstein. Introduction by Ernest Lindgren. Vision Press, 1951. Eisenstein's notes for a script for his unfinished Mexican film are introduced and explained by Ernest Lindgren.

Making a Film. Lindsay Anderson. Allen and Unwin, 1952. This book follows in every possible detail the various phases through which Thorold Dickinson's film *Secret People* passed from scripting to the completion of production. The full shooting script of the film is included in the book.

Put Money in Thy Purse. A Diary of the film *Othello*, by Michael MacLiammoir. Methuen, 1952. A highly diverting and personal account of the production of *Othello* by Orson Welles as it was experienced by the Irish actor who plays Iago.

Diary of a Film. Jean Cocteau. Dennis Dobson, 1950. Cocteau's very personal notes on his day by day feelings whilst making *La Belle et la Bête*.

The Animated Film. Roger Manvell. The Sylvan Press, 1954. A brief history of the animated film. The artistic problems, achievements and potentialities of this special branch of film-making are discussed with special reference to the Halas and Batchelor film version of George Orwell's fable *Animal Farm*.

4. *The Film and Society*

The Film in National Life. A. C. Cameron. Allen and Unwin, 1932. 'Being the Report of an Enquiry conducted by the Commission on Educational and Cultural Films into the Service which the Cinematograph may render to Education and Social Progress.'

America at the Movies. Margaret Thorp. Yale, 1939; Faber, 1947. Margaret Thorp examines what the American film-goers want, what they get, and how the industry organizes them to want what they get.

Hollywood. Leo Calvin Rosten. Harcourt Brace, 1941. The result of a three-year investigation conducted by a team of social investigators. An astonishing collection of data about the organization, finance, and personnel of Hollywood.

Tendencies to Monopoly in the Cinematograph Film Industry. Stationery Office for the Board of Trade, 1944. A wartime study of the ramifications of the British film industry, especially in relation to the extension of power by the Rank Organization and the relationship of the British to the American film industry during the War. Other official Reports for the Board of Trade include the *Report of the Film Studio Committee* (1948) on whether or not it would be advisable for the Government itself to own studio space to let to the independent producers, the *Report of the Working Party on Film Production Costs* (1949), and the *Report of a Committee of Enquiry on the Distribution and Exhibition of Cinematograph Films* (1949).

Freedom of the Movies. Ruth Inglis. University of Chicago Press (G.B., Cambridge U.P.), 1947. Written as a report from the American Commission on Freedom of the Press, which included the film in its survey. This is an important book on the history of American film censorship and its social implications.

Essai sur les Principes d'une Philosophie du Cinéma. Vol. I. Introduction Générale. Gilbert Cohen-Séat. Presses Universitaires de France, 1946. An outstanding study of the importance of the cinema considered from the strictly philosophical and psychological points of view. This author has founded the international Filmologie movement in association with universities in France and abroad.

Sociology of the Film: Studies and Documents. J. P. Mayer. Faber, 1946. Half this book consists of documents resulting from Mayer's interviews and questionnaires and from other material coming mainly from children and adolescents. The author generalizes on various problems arising out of his analysis of this evidence. An interesting and controversial book.

British Cinemas and their Audiences. J. P. Mayer. Dobson, 1949. The text of this book is mainly extensive essays written by the readers of *Picturegoer* in answer to the author's queries on the history of their cinema-going and their taste in films. Some are rather self-conscious, but many are of great interest.

The Negro in Films. Peter Noble. Skelton Robinson, 1949. This book is a study of the Negro actor especially as he appears in the American film, and the problems involved in the racial interpretation of the Negro in the film.

Report of the Departmental Committee on Children and the Cinema. H.M.S.O., 1950. The Report to the Home Office and the Ministry of Education on the attendance of children at ordinary cinema performances and at the special club shows, the influence of films upon children and the need for certain safeguards, the production of films for children and the problem of the raising of standards in the appreciation of films.

Hollywood: The Dream Factory. Hortense Powdermaker. Secker and Warburg, 1951. An attack by an anthropologist on the alleged obsessions of the people of Hollywood. A very American book, enjoying with great thoroughness the exposure of human corruption.

Newsreels Across the World. Peter Baechlin and Maurice Muller-Strauss. UNESCO, 1952. An invaluable international survey of the newsreels – their economy, production, and contents.

Good Company. Mary Field. Longmans Green, 1952. The story of Mary Field's experiences as producer in charge of Children's Entertainment Films. The special problems of making films for youthful audiences are discussed in a manner which is both entertaining and informative.

There have been many novels written about the film industry in Britain and America. Among the more amusing and the more revealing are:

Merton of the Movies. Harry Leon Wilson.
Voyage to Purilia. Elmer Rice.
Nobody Ordered Wolves. Jeffrey Dell.
What Made Sammy Run. Budd Schulberg.
The Producer. Richard Brooks.
The Magic Lantern. Robert Carson.

5. *Television*

An annotated list of books on the subject of television appears in the author's work *On the Air* (Deutsch, 1953), a study of broadcasting in sound and vision.

The chief books giving special consideration to television are:

Broadcasting and Television since 1900. Maurice Gorham. Dakers, 1952. A history of British broadcasting.

Adventure in Vision. John Swift. John Lehmann, 1950. An account in popular terms of the development of television in Britain.

The Report of the Broadcasting Committee. Two volumes. H.M.S.O., 1949. This Report by the Beveridge Committee is the fullest account of British broadcasting to have been published. The second volume reproduces all the documents presented in evidence to the Committee by the BBC and by organizations and individuals specially interested in broadcasting.

The Great Audience. Gilbert Seldes. Viking Press, New York, 1950. An attack on the stereotyping of entertainment through film, radio, and television in the United States.

Radio, Television, and Society. Charles A. Siepmann. O.U.P., New York, 1950. The history of American radio and television. This is one of the most important books to have come from America on the social aspects of broadcasting.

The Art of Television. Jan Bussell. Faber, 1952. This book is by an experienced television producer, and would have been better titled 'The Technique of Production for Television'.

Television and Education in the United States. Charles A. Siepmann. UNESCO, Paris, 1952. A further study of the practice of television in the United States, with particular reference to various experiments in educational television.

Television: A World Survey. UNESCO, 1953. A detailed account, country by country, of the position reached in the various national television services.

6. Other Books

Secrets of Nature. Mary Field and Percy Smith. Faber, 1934. A book of great interest on the making of nature films.

Cine-Biology. J. V. Durden, Mary Field and Percy Smith. Pelican Books, 1941. A development of the subject of *Secrets of Nature* for Pelican Books.

Working for the Films. Oswell Blakeston (Editor). Focal Press, 1947. A collection of short essays on their work by experts in almost every branch of film-making. Intended for readers contemplating a career in films.

British Film Music. John Huntley. Skelton Robinson, 1947. A useful reference volume on British film music.

Reports of the Commission on Technical Needs in Press, Radio, and Film, and on *The Facilities of Mass Communication.* A series of volumes published by UNESCO in Paris, commencing 1947. This series of Reports and the Supplements which have been issued to keep them up to date are of the greatest use in bringing together statistics and details of the organization and practice of the press, the film industry, and broadcasting throughout the world.

The Uses of the Film. Basil Wright. Bodley Head, 1948. A short but valuable survey of the conditions governing motion-picture production in Britain.

Film and its Techniques. Raymond Spottiswoode. Faber, 1951. A detailed study of every technical aspect of film-making, with special reference to documentary production.

See How They Grow. Mary Field, J. V. Durden, and Percy Smith. Pelican Books, 1953. A companion volume to *Cine-Biology* devoted to plant life as it is seen by the makers of scientific films.

The Theory of Stereoscopic Transmission and its Application to the Motion Picture. Raymond and Nigel Spottiswoode. University of California Press, 1954. An advanced scientific exposition of the technical principles upon which the production and exhibition of 3–D films depend. The authors have themselves played a major part as pioneers in developing the three-dimensional film in Britain and America.

STUDIES OF INDIVIDUAL FILM
DIRECTORS

I am most grateful to Mrs Beatrice Trainor, formerly of the Library and Information Department of the British Film Institute, for her assistance in compiling the following selected list of studies of individual directors, including books and articles written by them, which have appeared in publications in the English language. Readers should also consult, of course, the leading histories of the film and anthologies of film criticism given in the preceding Book List. The following abbreviations are used in the references to the titles of certain publications:

British Film Institute Special Publications:
  Index Series: IS.
  New Index Series: NIS.
  Records of the Film: RF.
Cinema 1950, etc. (Pelican Books): *C.* 1950, etc.
Cinema Quarterly (Edinburgh): *CQ.*
*Cine-Technician (Journal of the A.C.T.): *CT.*
Close Up (Switzerland): *CU.*
*Documentary 1951, etc. (Edinburgh Film Guild): *D.* 1951, etc.
Documentary Film News (Film Centre): *DFN.*
Documentary News Letter (Film Centre): *DNL.*
*Films in Review (New York): *FR.*
Hollywood Quarterly (University of Southern California): *HQ.*
National Board of Review Magazine (New York): *NBRM.*
Penguin Film Review (Penguin Books): *PFR.*
*Quarterly of Film, Radio, and Television (University of Southern California): *QFRTV.*
The Screenwriter (Hollywood): *SC.*
Sequence (London): *S.*
*Sight and Sound (British Film Institute): *SS.*
World Film News (London): *WFN.*
The Year's Work in the Film (British Council): *YWF.*

Note: Journals and annuals marked .* are being published at present.

Asquith, Anthony. Articles by Asquith: 'The Tenth Muse Climbs Parnassus', *PFR*, 1. 'The Tenth Muse Takes Stock,' *C*, 1950. 'A Style in Film Direction,' *CT*, July–October (two issues; 1951). 'Anthony Asquith' in *NIS*, by Peter Noble.

Balcon, Sir Michael. Articles by Balcon: 'The Producer', *B.F.I. Pamphlet.* 'Film Production and Management' (British Institute of Management). Article by Thorold Dickinson in *YWF*, 1950.

Bresson, Robert. Article by Gavin Lambert, *SS*, July 1953. Also article *S* 13.

Buñuel, Luis. See books: Dali, *The Secret Life of Salvador Dali*, Julien Levy, *Surrealism* (New York, 1936), Henry Miller, *The Cosmological Eye*, and studies of *Los Olvidados* in *S* 14, and *QFRTV*, Summer 1953.

Capra, Frank. 'Frank Capra' in *NIS*, by Richard Griffith.

Carné, Marcel. 'Marcel Carné' in *NIS*, by Jean Quéval. Article by Gavin Lambert, *S* 3. Studies of several individual films in *RF* Series.

Chaplin, Charles. Books on Chaplin by Robert Payne, R. J. Minney, Theodore Huff, etc. Bibliography in Huff's book; see also *IS* (Huff). Study of *City Lights* by Rotha in *Celluloid*. 'Eisenstein on Chaplin' in *SS*, Nos. 57–58, 1946. Article by Jean Renoir, *SC*, July 1947. Study of *Limelight* by Gavin Lambert, *SS*, January 1953.

Clair, René. See book by Clair, *Reflections on the Cinema.* Article by Gavin Lambert, *S* 6.

Cocteau, Jean. Cocteau: *The Blood of a Poet* (New York, Bodley Press, 1949), *Diary of a Film*, and *Cocteau on the Film.* See also *NBRM*, February 1934, on *Le Sang d'un poète*. Article by Gavin Lambert, *S* 12. Interviews, *SS*, July 1952, August 1950.

De Mille, Cecil B. Studies in *CU*, August 1928 (early history), and *SS*, February 1951.

Dickinson, Thorold. See book *Making a Film* by Lindsay Anderson (study of *Secret People*). Thorold Dickinson: 'Search for Music' (*PFR* 2). Study of *Queen of Spades*, *C*, 1950.

Disney, Walt. See book *The Art of Walt Disney*, R. D. Feild. Article by Peter Ericsson, *S* 10.

Donskoi, Mark. Article by Catherine de la Roche, *S* 5.

Dovzhenko, Alexander. Article by Ralph Bond, *CU*, October 1930. 'My Method,' interview in *Experimental Cinema* (23 April 1934). 'Dovzhenko' in *IS*, by Jay Leyda (1947). Study of *Earth* by Paul Rotha in *Celluloid*.

Dreyer, Carl. Dreyer: *Film Style, FR,* January 1952. Articles in *HQ,* Fall, 1950, and by Dilys Powell in *Screen and Audience* (1947). 'Carl Dreyer' in *NIS,* by Ebbe Neergaard. Study of *Day of Wrath* by Roger Manvell in *RF* series.

Eisenstein, S. M. See books by Eisenstein: *Film Sense* and *Film Form;* also *Que Viva Mexico!,* introduction by Ernest Lindgren (Vision Press, 1951); Marie Seton: *Eisenstein* (The Bodley Head, 1952); *Eisenstein, 1898–1948,* booklet by the Society for Cultural Relations with the U.S.S.R., 1948; section in *Film Problems of Soviet Russia* (Bryher, Poole, 1929). See also articles by Eisenstein in *SS,* Nos 57–58, 1946, *PFR* 8, and *C* 1952.

Emmer, Luciano. Studies in *SS,* Spring 1947 and January 1951.

Fairbanks, Douglas. See books: *Douglas Fairbanks* by Alistair Cooke (Museum of Modern Art, New York, 1940) and *The Fourth Musketeer* by Ralph Hancock and Letitia Fairbanks. Article by Gavin Lambert, *S* 8.

Flaherty, Robert. See books: *The World of Robert Flaherty* (Richard Griffith); *Man of Aran* (Pat Mullen); *Elephant Dance* (Frances Flaherty). Flaherty: *My Eskimo Friends* (Heinemann, 1924); 'Comock the Eskimo', *C,* 1952; 'Robert Flaherty Talking', *C,* 1950. Profile in *New Yorker,* June 1949. 'Flaherty' in *IS* by Herman G. Weinberg. Articles in *HQ,* Fall, 1950, *SS,* October 1951 (Special Issue), *S* 14, *C,* 1952. Study of *Louisiana Story* by Helen van Dongen (Editor) in *C,* 1951.

Ford, John. 'John Ford' in *IS,* by William Patrick Wootten, 1948. Articles in *S* 2, 11, 12, 14.

Gance, Abel. Article by Francis Koval in *FR,* November 1952.

Gilliat, Sidney. Article by Catherine de la Roche. *SS,* Autumn 1946.

Grémillon, Jean. Article by Hazel Hackett. *SS,* Summer 1947.

Grierson, John. See book: *Grierson on Documentary,* edited by H. Forsyth Hardy. Articles have appeared in film journals for over a quarter of a century, more especially in *CQ, DNL, DFN,* and the annual publication of Edinburgh Film Guild, *Documentary,* 1951, etc.

Griffith, D. W. See book: *D. W. Griffith* by Iris Barry (Museum of Modern Art, New York, 1940); Four pamphlets by Seymour Stern in *IS;* special series of chapters in *The Rise of the American Film* by Lewis Jacobs. Also articles by Eisenstein and Thorold Dickinson in *SS,* November 1950 and October 1951, and tributes by Lillian Gish and others, *SC,* August 1948.

Halas, John. See books, Halas: *How to Cartoon;* Roger Manvell: *The Animated Film.*

Hitchcock, Alfred. Articles by Hitchcock: 'Direction' in *Footnotes to the Film* (Davy, 1937); 'Production Methods Compared', *CT*, November 1948. 'Hitchcock' by Peter Noble in *IS*, 1949. Articles by Lindsay Anderson in *S* 9 and by Gerald Pratley in *FR*, December 1952.

Huston, John. Picture by Lillian Ross (Gollancz, 1953). Articles by Karel Reisz in *SS*, January 1952 and by David A. Mage in *FR*, October 1952.

Jennings, Humphrey. Humphrey Jennings, a booklet of tributes by film-makers and critics edited by Dilys Powell, Basil Wright, and Roger Manvell (1951). Articles by Basil Wright, *SS*, December 1950, Nicole Védrès, *SS*, May 1951, Gavin Lambert, *SS*, May 1951, Lindsay Anderson, *SS*, April 1954.

Kelly, Gene. Article by Lindsay Anderson, *S* 14.

Korda, Sir Alexander. Article by Campbell Dixon in *Films in 1951*, *SS*, 1951.

Kurosawa, Akira. Article by Jay Leyda, *SS*, October 1954.

Lang, Fritz. 'Fritz Lang' by Herman G. Weinberg in *IS*, 1946.

Launder, Frank. Article by Catherine de la Roche, *SS*, Autumn 1946.

Lean, David. Article by Simon Harcourt-Smith in *Screen and Audience* (Saturn Press, 1947). Lean: 'Brief Encounter', *PFR* 4. Studies of *Great Expectations* and *Oliver Twist* by Roger Manvell in *RF* series.

Lorentz, Pare. Lorentz: 'The River' (Stackpole Sons, New York, 1938).

Lubitsch, Ernst. Articles in *SS*, Spring 1948, *FR*, August 1952, and *Illustrated London News* (31 January 1931). 'Ernst Lubitsch' by Theodore Huff in *IS*, 1947. Symposium by Billy Wilder and others, *SC*, January 1948.

Lye, Len. Article by Cavalcanti in *SS*, Winter, 1947–8.

Mackendrick, Alexander. Interview in 'The Film Teacher' (London), Spring 1953.

Mamoulian, Rouben. Article by Harry Allan Potamkin in *CU*, March 1930; by Francis Birrell in *New Statesman*, 26 November 1932.

Marx Brothers. See books: *The Marx Brothers* by Kyle Crichton (Heinemann, 1951); *Groucho* by Arthur Marx (Gollancz, 1954). See 'My Friend Harpo' by Alexander Woollcott in *While Rome Burns*.

Mayer, Carl. Pamphlet: *Tribute to Carl Mayer* (1947).

McLaren, Norman. Articles by McLaren: 'Stereographic Animation', *Journal of Society of Motion Picture Engineers*, December 1951; 'Notes on Animated Sound', *Q FRTV*, Spring 1953. Article by William E. Jordan on McLaren in *Q FRTV*, Fall, 1953.

Méliès, Georges. 'Georges Méliès' by Georges Sadoul in *IS*, 1947.

Metzner, Erno. Writes on *Überfall* in *CU*, May 1929; writes on set construction for *Kameradschaft* in *CU*, March 1932. Also *CU*, June 1933, on the travelling camera.

Milestone, Lewis. Article by Karel Reisz, *S* 14. Study of *All Quiet on the Western Front* by Paul Rotha in *Celluloid*.

Minnelli, Vincente. Article by Simon Harcourt-Smith, *SS*, January 1952; by Lindsay Anderson in *S* 14.

Olivier, Sir Laurence. Biography *The Oliviers* by Felix Barker (Hamish Hamilton, 1953). 'Actor, Sir Laurence Olivier' by James Morgan in 'Films in 1951', *SS*, 1951. *The Film Hamlet* edited by Brenda Cross (Saturn Press, 1948). Study of *Henry V*: *HQ*, October 1946. Studies of *Hamlet*: *HQ*, Spring 1951; *PFR*, No. 8; *RF* (by Roger Manvell).

Ophuls, Max. Article by Karel Reisz, *S* 14.

Pabst, G. W. Articles in *SS*, Summer 1933; *CU*, December 1927, March 1929, March 1932, December 1933.

Painlevé, Jean. Article by John Maddison in *SS*, August 1950.

Pearson, George. Autobiographical paper published initially in *Bulletin of the British Film Academy*, Nos. 13 and 14, 1951.

Powell, Michael. See books by Powell: *Two Hundred Thousand Feet on Foula* (Faber, 1938); Monk Gibbon: *The Red Shoes Ballet* (Saturn Press, 1948) and *The Tales of Hoffmann* (Saturn Press, 1951).

Pudovkin, V. I. See books and articles by Pudovkin: *Film Technique* and *Film Acting*; 'Stanislavski's system in the Cinema', *SS*, January 1953. 'The Actor's Work', *CU*, September 1933. 'Pudovkin' by Jay Leyda in *IS*, 1948. Articles by William Hunter in *Scrutiny of Cinema* (Wishart, 1932), in *Film Problems of Soviet Russia* (Winifred Bryher, Poole, 1929), in *CU*, October 1928, *SS*, Winter 1948, *SS*, Spring 1933, *CU*, June 1933.

Reed, Sir Carol. Two studies by Basil Wright: *YWF*, 1949, and 'Films in 1951', *SS*, 1951.

Reiniger, Lotte. See articles by Reiniger: 'Film as Ballet' in *Life and Letters To-day*, Spring 1936; 'Moving Silhouettes' in *Film Art*, Vol. 3, No. 8, 1936; *SS*, Spring 1936, 'Scissors make films'. Article by Eric Walter White, *Walking Shadows*, published by *Hogarth Press*, 1931.

Renoir, Jean. See articles by Renoir: 'I know where I'm going', *FR*, March 1952. Interview in *SS*, July 1954. Study of *La Règle du Jeu* by Gavin Lambert in *S* 11.

Richter, Hans. 'Richter' by Herman G. Weinberg in *IS*, 1946. Article by Richter: '*Avant-garde* Film in Germany' in *Experiment in the Film*.

Rochemont, Louis de. Articles on de Rochemont in *Theatre Arts Monthly*, October 1951, and in *Screen and Audience* (Saturn Press, 1947).

Room, Alexander. Article by Winifred Bryher in *Film Problems of Soviet Russia* (Poole, 1929).

Rossellini, Roberto. Articles in *Screen and Audience* (by Basil Wright, 1947), in *DFN*, May 1948, in *SS*, February 1951. Studies of *Rome Open City* and *Paisa* by Roger Manvell in *RF* series and *PFR*, No. 9.

Rotha, Paul. For numerous books by Paul Rotha, see Selected Book List.

Rouquier, Georges. Study of *Farrebique* in *RF* series by Roger Manvell.

Sica, Vittorio de. Article on neo-realism by Cesare Zavattini (*SS*, October 1953) reveals outlook behind de Sica's more important films. See also *FR*, May 1951 and May 1952.

Sjostrom, Victor. Articles in *Classics of the Swedish Cinema* (published by the Swedish Institute, 1952), and by Robert Herring in *CU*, January 1929.

Smith, Percy. Article by Grahame Tharp in *DNL*, Vol. II, No. 1 (1941). *Secrets of Nature* written with Mary Field (Faber, 1934).

Sternberg, Josef von. 'Josef von Sternberg' by Curtis Harrington in *IS*, 1949.

Stevens, George. 'Shane and George Stevens' by Penelope Houston, *SS*, October 1953.

Stroheim, Erich von. 'Erich von Stroheim' by Herman G. Weinberg in *IS*, 1943. *Hollywood Scapegoat* by Peter Noble (Fortune Press, 1950). See also *CU*, April 1928 and June 1931; *WFN*, September 1937; *CQ*, Summer 1933; *SS*, April 1953.

Sturges, Preston. Article by Peter Ericsson, *S* 4.

Sucksdorff, Arne. Articles by Peter Ericsson in *S* 7, by H. Forsyth Hardy in *SS*, Summer 1948, by Catherine de la Roche in *SS*, October 1953.

Trnka, Jiri. Article in *FR*, March 1952.

U.P.A. Cartoons. 'Animation Learns a New Language' by John Hubley and Zachary Schwartz, *HQ*, July 1946; 'Disney and U.P.A.' by David Fisher, *SS*, July 1953.

Vidor, King. Vidor: *A Tree is a Tree* (Harcourt Brace, New York, 1953). Articles in *Experimental Cinema*, February 1931 and by Curtis Harrington, *SS*, April 1953.

Vigo, Jean. 'Jean Vigo' by Joseph and Harry Feldman, *NIS*. Articles by Cavalcanti in *CQ*, Winter 1935; and by Henri Storck and P. F. Sales-Gomez on *Zero de Conduite* in *C*, 1951.

Visconti, Luchino. Article by Vernon Jarratt, *SS*, Spring 1948.

Watt, Harry. Article by Watt: 'You Start from Scratch in Australia', *PFR*, No. 9; Interview in *Film Forum*, February 1949.

Welles, Orson. *Orson Welles*, biography by R. A. Fowler, Pendulum Publications, 1946. *Put Money in Thy Purse* by Michael Mac-Liammoir on the making of *Othello* (Methuen, 1952). Articles in *Theatre Arts* (New York), September 1951, *SS*, December 1950. Gregg Toland (cameraman) on 'Realism for *Citizen Kane*', *DNL*, Vol. II, No 11 (1941). Welles: 'The Third Audience', *SS*, January 1954.

Wiene, Robert. Article by Kraszna-Krausz in *WFN*, August 1938.

Woolfe, H. Bruce. Woolfe: 'Commercial Documentary', *CQ*, Winter, 1933. See *Secrets of Nature* by Mary Field and Percy Smith (Faber, 1934).

Wright, Basil. Wright: *The Use of the Film* (Bodley Head, 1948). See above under Jennings, Reed, Rossellini. Frequent contributor to *CQ*, *WFN*, *DNL*, *DFN*, *SS*.

Wyler, William. Articles by Hermione R. Isaacs in *Theatre Arts* (New York), February 1947, and by Karel Reisz in *S* 13. Article by Wyler on *The Best Years of Our Lives*, *SC*, February 1947.

Zinnemann, Fred. The Story of *The Search*, *SC*, August 1948.

LIST OF SELECTED FILMS
AND FILM-MAKERS

The following lists give a selection of directors and those films they have made which are notable either for artistic reasons or for the part they play in the historical development of the film as a whole. They are divided into five main periods:

1. *From the Beginning of the Cinema to 1919.*
2. *The Silent Film of the Nineteen-Twenties.*
3. *The Pre-War Sound Film.*
4. *Films of the War Period.*
5. *Films of the Post-War Period up to 1954.*

I am most grateful to John Gillett of the British Film Institute for the help he has given me in the compilation of these Lists.

1. *From the Beginning of the Cinema to 1919*

1892	Work of Emile Reynaud for his *Théâtre Optique*.
1893	Films made in U.S.A. by W. K. L. Dickson for individual viewing by Kinetoscope.
1895	Skladanowski demonstrates moving pictures in Berlin.
	Public exhibition of moving pictures in Paris by Auguste and Louis Lumière begins in December.
1896	Private followed by commercial public demonstrations of moving pictures in London by Birt Acres and R. W. Paul (January to March).
	The Lumière programme opened to the public at the Regent Polytechnic in February.
	First films of Méliès and of Pathé made in Paris.
1897	G. A. Smith and James Williamson begin film-making in Britain.
	Stuart Blackton begins film-making in the U.S.A.
1898	Cecil Hepworth begins film-making in Britain.
1901	Ferdinand Zecca begins film-making in France.
1902	*Voyage à la Lune* (Georges Méliès).
	Life of an American Fireman (Edwin S. Porter).
	Will Barker makes his first film at Ealing.
1903	*The Great Train Robbery* (Edwin S. Porter).

1904 *Voyage à travers l'Impossible* (Georges Méliès).

1905 *Rescued by Rover* (Cecil Hepworth).
Victorien Jasset began film-making in France.

1906 *Le Pendu* (Max Linder).

1907 D. W. Griffith becomes a film-actor.
Louis Feuillade begins film-making in France.
The Legend of Polichinelle (Zecca).

1908 *L'Assassinat du Duc de Guise* (Calmettes and Le Bargy).
Emile Cohl begins making animated films in France.
D. W. Griffith directs his first film. Uses dramatic close-up in *Enoch Arden*.
Percy Smith begins his biological and botanical films for Charles Urban.

1909 *Transfiguration* (Cohl).
The Maccabees (Guazzoni).
The Lonely Villa and *Pippa Passes* (Griffith).

1910 Starevitch begins work in Russia.
The Thread of Destiny (Griffith, with Mary Pickford).

1911 *Quo Vadis?* (Ambrosio.) The first version in Italy of this subject.)
George Pearson begins work in Britain.
Urban Gad begins work in Denmark.
Thomas Ince begins work in the U.S.A.
The Lonedale Operator (Griffith).

1912 *Man's Genesis* and *The Massacre* (Griffith).
La Reine Elizabeth (Mercanton, with Sarah Bernhardt).
Mack Sennett produces the first Keystone Comedy in the U.S.A.
Abel Gance begins film-making in France.
Mauritz Stiller begins film-making in Sweden.

1913 *Cabiria* (Pastrone).
Mario Caserini and Arturo Ambrosio both make separate versions of *The Last Days of Pompeii* in Italy.
Feuillade begins the *Fantômas* series in France.
Cecil B. de Mille begins film-making in the U.S.A.
Victor Sjöstrom begins film-making in Sweden.
The Expedition of Captain Scott to the South Pole (Ponting).
The Student of Prague (Stellan Rye. First version of this subject to be made in Germany).

1914 *Judith of Bethulia* (Griffith).
Charles Chaplin makes his first film for Keystone.
Typhoon (Ince).

The Perils of Pauline (Louis Gasnier).

1915   *Birth of a Nation* (Griffith).

Carmen (De Mille).

Essanay Series (Chaplin), including *The Champion* and *The Tramp*.

1916   *Intolerance* (Griffith).

Carmen, The Fireman, The Vagabond, The Count, The Pawn-shop (Chaplin).

Judex (Feuillade).

Protozanov makes his first film in Russia.

Germaine Dulac makes her first film in France.

1917   *Easy Street, The Cure, The Immigrant* (Chaplin).

Jacques Feyder begins film-making in France.

Pat Sullivan begins Felix the Cat series.

1918   *Shoulder Arms* (Chaplin).

Hearts of the World (Griffith).

Carmen (Ernst Lubitsch in Germany).

Marcel l'Herbier begins film-making in France.

1919   *Broken Blossoms* (Griffith).

Sunnyside (Chaplin).

Male and Female (De Mille).

Blind Husbands (Stroheim).

Arne's Treasure (Stiller).

Madame Dubarry (Lubitsch).

J'Accuse (Gance).

La Fête Espagnole (Germaine Dulac and Louis Delluc).

The Cabinet of Dr Caligari (Robert Wiene).

Among the stars made famous by their American films were Lillian Gish, Mary Pickford, Florence Turner, Theda Bara, Mabel Normand, Pearl White, and Alla Nazimova; Charles Chaplin, Douglas Fairbanks, Francis X. Bushman, William Farnum, H. B. Warner, William S. Hart, Earle Williams, Fatty Arbuckle, Harry Langdon, Wallace Beery, Tom Mix, John Bunny, Ford Sterling, Ben Turpin, Chester Conklin, and the Keystone Cops. In Britain the chief stars included Alma Taylor, Chrissie White, Stewart Rome, Henry Edwards, Ivy Close, and Fred Evans (Pimple).

2. *The Silent Film of the Nineteen-Twenties*

ASQUITH, ANTHONY: Shooting Stars, 1928. Cottage on Dartmoor, 1929.

THE FILM AND THE PUBLIC

BERGER, LUDWIG: Cinderella, 1923.

BUNUEL, LUIS: Un Chien Andalou, 1928.

CAPRA, FRANK: Long Pants, 1927 (with Harry Langdon).

CAVALCANTI, ALBERTO: Rien que les Heures, 1926.

CHAPLIN, CHARLES: The Kid, 1921. The Pilgrim, 1923. A Woman of Paris, 1923. The Gold Rush, 1925. The Circus, 1928.

CHRISTENSEN, BENJAMIN: Hekson, 1921.

CLAIR, RENÉ: Entr'acte, 1924. The Italian Straw Hat, 1927. Les Deux Timides, 1928.

CRUZE, JAMES: The Covered Wagon, 1923.

VON CSEREPY: Fridericus Rex, 1923.

DELLUC, LOUIS: Fièvre, 1922. La Femme de Nulle Part, 1922.

DE MILLE, CECIL B.: The Ten Commandments, 1923. King of Kings, 1927.

DOVZHENKO, ALEXANDER: Arsenal, 1929. Earth, 1930.

DREYER, CARL: The Passion of Joan of Arc, 1928.

DULAC, GERMAINE: The Seashell and the Clergyman, 1927.

DUPONT, E. A.: Vaudeville, 1925 (in association with Erich Pommer).

DZIGA-VERTOV: The Man with the Movie-Camera, 1928.

EISENSTEIN, S. M.: The Battleship Potemkin, 1925. October (Ten Days that Shook the World), 1928. The General Line (The Old and the New), 1929.

ERMLER, F.: The Fragment of an Empire, 1929.

FAIRBANKS, DOUGLAS: The Three Musketeers, 1920. Robin Hood, 1922. The Thief of Bagdad, 1924. Don Q, Son of Zorro, 1925. (These films made with the assistance of various directors.)

FEYDER, JACQUES: Thérèse Raquin, 1927. Les Nouveaux Messieurs, 1928.

FLAHERTY, ROBERT: Nanook of the North, 1920–21 (released 1922). Moana, 1923–4 (released 1926). Tabu, 1928–9 (released as a sound film 1931).

FORD, JOHN. The Iron Horse, 1924.

GALEEN, HENRIK: The Student of Prague, 1926.

GANCE, ABEL: La Roue, 1922. Napoléon, 1927.

GRIERSON, JOHN: Drifters, 1928.

GRIFFITH, D. W.: Way Down East, 1920. Orphans of the Storm, 1921.

GRUNE, KARL: The Street, 1923.

HITCHCOCK, ALFRED: The Ring, 1927.

INGRAM, REX: The Four Horsemen of the Apocalypse, 1921.

KEATON, BUSTER: The Navigator, 1925. The General, 1926. The Cameraman, 1928. (These films made with the assistance of various directors.)

KING, HENRY: Tol'able David, 1921.

KINUGASE, TEINOSUKE: Crossways, 1929.

KIRSANOFF, DIMITRI: Ménilmontant, 1924.

LANG, FRITZ: Destiny, 1921. Dr Mabuse, 1922. Siegfried, 1924. Metropolis, 1927. The Spy, 1928.

LEGER, FERNAND: Le Ballet mécanique, 1924.

L'HERBIER, MARCEL: Eldorado, 1921. Le Feu Mathias Pascal, 1925.

LENI, PAUL: Waxworks, 1924.

LLOYD, HAROLD: Safety Last, 1923. The Freshman, 1925. (These films made with the assistance of various directors.)

LUBITSCH, ERNST: Sumurun, 1920. The Marriage Circle, 1924. Forbidden Paradise, 1924. The Patriot, 1928.

METZNER, ERNO: Überfall, 1929.

MONTAGU, IVOR: Bluebottles, 1928.

MURNAU, F. W.: The Last Laugh, 1924 (with Karl Mayer). Sunrise, 1928. Tabu, 1929 (with Robert Flaherty).

NIBLO, FRED: Ben Hur, 1926.

PABST, G. W.: The Joyless Street, 1925. Secrets of the Soul, 1926. The Love of Jeanne Ney, 1927. Pandora's Box, 1929.

PUDOVKIN, V. I.: Mother, 1926. The End of St Petersburg, 1927. Storm over Asia, 1928.

REINIGER, LOTTE: The Adventures of Prince Achmed, 1926.

RENOIR, JEAN: La Fille de l'eau, 1924. La Petite Marchande d'allumettes, 1928.

ROACH, HAL: Laurel and Hardy Comedies.

ROOM, ALEXANDER: Bed and Sofa, 1927. The Ghost that Never Returns, 1929.

RUTTMANN, WALTHER: Berlin, 1926.

SJÖSTROM, VICTOR: The Wind, 1928.

VON STERNBERG, JOSEF: Salvation Hunters, 1925. Underworld, 1927. The Docks of New York, 1928. The Last Command, 1928.

STILLER, MAURITZ: The Atonement of Gosta Berling, 1923.

VON STROHEIM, ERICH: Foolish Wives, 1921. Greed, 1923. The Wedding March, 1927. Queen Kelly, 1928.

SUMMERS, WALTER: The Battle of Falkland and Coronel Islands, 1928.

TRAUBERG, L.: The New Babylon, 1929 (with G. Kozintsev).

TURIN, VICTOR: Turksib, 1928.

VIDOR, KING: The Big Parade, 1925. The Crowd, 1928.

VIGO, JEAN: A propos de Nice, 1930.

WOOLFE, H. BRUCE: Zeebrugge, 1921 (with A. V. Bramble). Secrets of Nature (photographed by Percy Smith), 1921.

Among the famous stars of the period were Greta Garbo, Mary Pickford, Nazimova, Asta Nielsen, Betty Balfour, Vilma Banky, Alice Terry, Blanche Sweet, Mae Marsh, Pauline Frederick, Lillian Gish, Marie Dressler, Constance Talmadge, Colleen Moore, Clara Bow, Louise Brooks, Joan Crawford, Gloria Swanson, Pola Negri, Norma Shearer, Norma Talmadge; and John Gilbert, Buster Keaton, Harold Lloyd, Harry Langdon, Douglas Fairbanks, Rudolph Valentino, Emil Jannings, John Barrymore, Jean Hersholt, Charlie Chaplin, Clive Brook, Thomas Meigham, Richard Barthelmess, Monty Banks, Ronald Colman, Antonio Moreno, Ramon Novarro, Lon Chaney, Walter Forde, Will Rogers, Adolphe Menjou, Earle Fox, Roy d'Arcy, Rod la Rocque, Lew Cody, William Powell, Erich von Stroheim.

3. *The Pre-War Sound Film*

ALEXANDROV, GRIGORI: Jazz Comedy, 1934. Volga-Volga, 1938.

ANDERSON, JOHN MURRAY: King of Jazz, 1930.

ANSTEY, EDGAR: Enough to Eat, 1936.

ASQUITH, ANTHONY: Tell England, 1930. Pygmalion, 1938 (in association with Leslie Howard).

BACON, LLOYD: The Singing Fool, 1928. 42nd Street, 1933.

BARTOSCH, BERTHOLD: L'Idée, 1934.

BEAUMONT, HARRY: The Broadway Melody, 1929.

BLASETTI, ALESSANDRO: 1860, 1933.

BROWN, CLARENCE: Anna Christie, 1930.

BROWN, ROLAND: Quick Millions, 1931.

BUNUEL, LUIS: L'Âge d'or, 1931. Land without Bread, 1932.

CAMERINI, MARIO: Gli Uomini che Mascalzoni, 1932 (with Vittorio de Sica).

CAPRA, FRANK: American Madness, 1932. It Happened One Night, 1934. Mr Deeds Goes to Town, 1936. You Can't Take it with You, 1938.

CARNÉ, MARCEL: Drôle de drame, 1937. Quai des Brumes, 1938. Le Jour se lève, 1939.

CAVALCANTI, ALBERTO: Coalface, 1935 (in association with John Grierson).

CHAPLIN, CHARLES: City Lights, 1931. Modern Times, 1936.

CLAIR, RENÉ: Sous les Toits de Paris, 1929–30. A Nousla liberté, 1931. Le Million, 1931. Le Quatorze Juillet, 1932.

COCTEAU, JEAN: Le Sang d'un poète, 1931.

CUKOR, GEORGE: Camille, 1937.

DE MILLE, CECIL B.: The Plainsman, 1937.

DENIS, ARMAND: Dark Rapture, 1938.

DIETERLE, WILLIAM: The Story of Louis Pasteur, 1936. Life of Emile Zola, 1937. Blockade, 1938. Juarez, 1939.

DISNEY, WALT: First cartoons with sound, 1928. Snow White and the Seven Dwarfs, 1938.

DONSKOI, MARK: The Maxim Gorki Trilogy, 1938–40.

DOVZHENKO, A.: Shors, 1939.

DREYER, CARL: Vampyr, 1931.

DUVIVIER, JULIEN: Poil de carotte, 1932. Un Carnet du bal, 1937. Pépé le Moko, 1937.

DYKE, W. S. VAN: The Thin Man, 1934.

DZIGA-VERTOV: The Three Songs of Lenin, 1934.

EISENSTEIN, SERGEI M.: Alexander Nevski, 1938.

EKK, NIKOLAI: The Road to Life, 1931.

ELTON, ARTHUR: Housing Problems, 1935 (assisted by Edgar Anstey).

FEYDER, JACQUES: La Kermesse héroique, 1935.

FLAHERTY, ROBERT: Industrial Britain, 1932 (in association with John Grierson). Man of Aran, 1933. Elephant Boy, 1937. The Land, 1939.

FLEMING, VICTOR: Gone with the Wind, 1939.

FORD, JOHN: The Informer, 1935. Stagecoach, 1939. Young Mr Lincoln, 1939.

FORDE, WALTER: Rome Express, 1933.

HAWKS, HOWARD: Scarface, 1932.

HITCHCOCK, ALFRED: Blackmail, 1929. The Man Who Knew Too Much, 1934. The Thirty-Nine Steps, 1935. Secret Agent, 1936. The Lady Vanishes, 1938.

HOLLERING, GEORGE: Hortobagy, 1936.

KORDA, ALEXANDER: The Private Life of Henry VIII, 1933. Rembrandt, 1936.

LAMPRECHT, GERHARD: Emil and the Detectives, 1931.

LANG, FRITZ: M, 1931. The Testament of Dr Mabuse, 1933. Fury, 1936. You Only Live Once, 1937.

LEGOSHIN, VLADIMIR: The Lone White Sail, 1937.

LEROY, MERVYN: Little Caesar, 1931. I am a Fugitive from a Chain Gang, 1932. They Won't Forget, 1937.

LITVAK, ANATOLE: Mayerling, 1935. Confessions of a Nazi Spy, 1939.

LORENTZ, PARE: The Plow that Broke the Plains, 1936. The River, 1938.

LUBITSCH, ERNST: The Love Parade, 1930. Trouble in Paradise, 1932. Ninotchka, 1939.

LYE, LEN: Colour Box, 1935. Rainbow Dance, 1936.

MACHATY, GUSTAV: Ekstase, 1933.

MAMOULIAN, ROUBEN: Queen Christina, 1934.

MARX BROTHERS: Animal Crackers, 1932. Duck Soup, 1933. A Night at the Opera, 1936. A Day at the Races, 1937.

MENZIES, WILLIAM CAMERON: Things to Come, 1935.

MILESTONE, LEWIS: All Quiet on the Western Front, 1930. Front Page, 1931. Of Mice and Men, 1939.

MINKIN, ADOLPH: Professor Mamlock, 1938 (with G. Rappoport).

OPHULS, MAX: Liebelei, 1932.

PABST, G. W.: Westfront, 1918, 1930. Kameradschaft, 1931.

PAGNOL, MARCEL: La Femme du boulanger, 1938.

PAINLEVE, JEAN: The Seahorse, 1934.

PETROV, VLADIMIR: Peter the Great, Parts I and II, 1938–9.

POWELL, MICHAEL: The Edge of the World, 1937.

PTUSHKO, ALEXANDER: The New Gulliver, 1934.

PUDOVKIN, V. I.: Deserter, 1933.

REED, CAROL: Bank Holiday, 1938. The Stars Look Down, 1939.

REINIGER, LOTTE: Carmen, 1933. Papageno, 1935.

RENOIR, JEAN: La Chienne, 1931. Toni, 1934. Les Bas fonds, 1936. La Grande Illusion, 1937. Partie de campagne, 1937. La Marseillaise, 1938. La Bête humaine, 1938. La Règle du jeu, 1939.

RIEFENSTAHL, LENI: The Blue Light, 1933. The Olympic Games of 1936, 1938.

ROACH, HAL: Laurel and Hardy Comedies.

ROCHEMONT, LOUIS DE: The March of Time. Commenced 1935.

ROMM, MIKHAIL: Lenin in October, 1937. Lenin in 1918, 1939.

ROTHA, PAUL: Contact, 1933. Shipyard, 1935. The Face of Britain, 1935. The Fourth Estate, 1939.

SAGAN, LEONTINE: Madchen in Uniform, 1931.

SANDRICH, MARK: Top Hat, 1935.

SANTELL, ALFRED: Winterset, 1936.

TRIVAS, VICTOR: War is Hell, 1931.

UCICKY, GUSTAV: Morgenrot, 1932.

VASSILIEV BROTHERS: Chapayev, 1934.

VIDOR, KING: Hallelujah, 1929. Our Daily Bread, 1934. The Citadel, 1938.

VIGO, JEAN: Zéro de Conduite, 1933. L'Atalante, 1934.

VON STERNBERG, JOSEPH: The Blue Angel, 1930. The Scarlet Empress, 1934.

WATT, HARRY: Night Mail, 1935 (with Basil Wright). North Sea, 1938.

WELLMAN, WILLIAM: The Public Enemy, 1931. A Star is Born, 1937. Nothing Sacred, 1937.

WOOD, SAM: Goodbye, Mr Chips, 1939.

WRIGHT, BASIL: Song of Ceylon, 1935.

WYLER, WILLIAM: Dodsworth, 1936. Dead End, 1937.

The famous stars of the period include Bette Davis, Irene Dunne, Madeleine Carroll, Deanna Durbin, Constance Bennett, Tallulah Bankhead, Greta Garbo, Norma Shearer, Joan Crawford, Marlene Dietrich, Katherine Hepburn, Mae West, Jean Harlow, Myrna Loy, Carole Lombard, Gracie Fields, Merle Oberon, Jean Arthur, Ginger Rogers, Rosalind Russell, Claudette Colbert, Shirley Temple; and Edward G. Robinson, James Cagney, Gary Cooper, Spencer Tracy, Paul Muni, Charlie Chaplin, William Powell, Leslie Howard, Fred MacMurray, Cary Grant, Melvyn Douglas, the Marx Brothers, Laurel and Hardy, W. C. Fields, Maurice Chevalier, Charles Laughton, Will Rogers, Herbert Marshall, Fredric March, Wallace Beery, Bing Crosby, Fred Astaire, Victor McLaglen, Conrad Veidt, Clarke Gable, George Arliss, Charles Ruggles, Franchot Tone, Humphrey Bogart, Robert Montgomery.

Stars of the French cinema included Michele Morgan, Arletty, Danielle Darrieux, Françoise Rosay; and Raimu, Jean Gabin, Louis Jouvet, Michel Simon, Harry Baur, Charles Boyer, Fernandel, Sacha Guitry.

4. Films of the War Period (1939–45)

ASQUITH, ANTHONY: We Dive at Dawn, 1943. The Way to the Stars, 1945.

AUTANT-LARA, CLAUDE: Douce, 1943. Sylvie et la fantôme, 1945.

BECKER, JACQUES: Goupi mains rouges, 1942. Falbalas, 1944–5.

BLASETTI, ALESSANDRO: Four Steps in the Clouds, 1942.

BOULTING, J. and R.: Pastor Hall, 1940. Thunder Rock, 1942.

BRESSON, ROBERT: Les Anges du péché, 1943. Les Dames du Bois de Boulogne, 1944.

CAPRA, FRANK: Meet John Doe, 1941. Why We Fight Series, 1943–44.

CARNE, MARCEL: Les Visiteurs du soir, 1942. Les Enfants du Paradis, 1943–44.

CASTELLANI, RENATO: Un Colpo di Pistola, 1941.

CAVALCANTI, ALBERTO: Went the Day Well? 1942.

CHAPLIN, CHARLES: The Great Dictator, 1940.

CLAIR, RENÉ: I Married a Witch, 1943. It Happened Tomorrow, 1944.

CLEMENT, RENÉ: La Bataille du Rail, 1945.

CLOUZOT, HENRI-GEORGES: Le Corbeau, 1943.

CUKOR, GEORGE: The Philadelphia Story, 1941.

DICKINSON, THOROLD: Gaslight, 1940. Next of Kin, 1942.

DIETERLE, WILLIAM: All That Money Can Buy, 1941.

DISNEY, WALT: Pinocchio, 1940. Fantasia, 1940. Dumbo, 1941.

DONSKOI, MARK: The Rainbow, 1944.

DOVZHENKO, ALEXANDER: The Battle for the Ukraine, 1943.

DREYER, CARL: Day of Wrath, 1943.

EISENSTEIN, SERGEI: Ivan the Terrible, 1944–5.

FORD, JOHN: The Grapes of Wrath, 1940. The Long Voyage Home, 1941. They Were Expendable, 1945.

FREND, CHARLES: San Demetrio, London, 1943.

GENDELSTEIN, A.: Lermontov, 1944.

GILLIAT, SIDNEY: The Rake's Progress, 1945.

GREMILLON, JEAN: Le Ciel est à vous, 1944.

HITCHCOCK, ALFRED: Shadow of a Doubt, 1943. Lifeboat, 1944.

HOLMES, J. B.: Merchant Seamen, 1941. Coastal Command, 1942.

HOWARD, LESLIE: The First of the Few, 1942.

HUSTON, JOHN: The Maltese Falcon, 1942.

JACKSON, PAT: Western Approaches, 1944.

JENNINGS, HUMPHREY: Listen to Britain, 1941. The Silent Village, 1943. Fires Were Started, 1943. Diary for Timothy, 1945.

KLINE, HERBERT: The Forgotten Village, 1944.

LANG, FRITZ: Hangmen Also Die, 1943. The Woman in the Window, 1944. Scarlet Street, 1945.

LAUNDER, FRANK (with GILLIAT, SIDNEY): Millions Like Us, 1943.

LEAN, DAVID: In Which We Serve, 1942 (with Noel Coward). This Happy Breed, 1944. Brief Encounter, 1945.

LINDTBERG, LEOPOLD: The Last Chance, 1945.

LUBITSCH, ERNST: Heaven Can Wait, 1943.

MASSINGHAM, RICHARD: Short trailer films for Government Departments.

MCLAREN, NORMAN: Short animated films in Canada from 1941.

MILESTONE, LEWIS: A Walk in the Sun, 1945.

MINNELLI, VINCENTE: Meet Me in St Louis, 1944. Under the Clock, 1945.

OLIVIER, LAURENCE: Henry V, 1944.

POWELL, MICHAEL: 49th Parallel, 1941. The Life and Death of Colonel Blimp, 1943.

PUDOVKIN, V. I.: General Suvorov, 1941.

REED, CAROL: Kipps, 1941. The Way Ahead, 1944. The True Glory, 1945 (with Garson Kanin).

RENOIR, JEAN: The Southerner, 1945.

ROTHA, PAUL: World of Plenty, 1943. Land of Promise, 1945.

SERVICE UNITS: Desert Victory, 1943. Tunisian Victory, 1944.

DE SICA, VITTORIO: Teresa Venerdi, 1941. The Children are Watching Us, 1943.

SJOBERG, ALF: Frenzy, 1944.

STEVENS, GEORGE: Talk of the Town, 1942.

STURGES, PRESTON: Christmas in July, 1940. The Lady Eve, 1941. Sullivan's Travels, 1942. Hail the Conquering Hero, 1944.

SUCKSDORFF, ARNE: Trut, 1944.

TAYLOR, DONALD and ELDRIDGE, JOHN: Our Country, 1945.

TENNYSON, PEN: The Proud Valley, 1940.

VISCONTI, LUCHINO: Ossessione, 1942.

WATT, HARRY: Target for To-Night, 1941. Nine Men, 1943.

WELLES, ORSON: Citizen Kane, 1941. The Magnificent Ambersons, 1942.

WELLMAN, WILLIAM: The Oxbow Incident, 1943. The Story of G.I. Joe, 1945.

WILDER, BILLY: Double Indemnity, 1944. The Lost Weekend, 1945.

WYLER, WILLIAM: The Letter, 1940. The Little Foxes, 1941. Memphis Belle, 1943.

The popular stars of the period include Bette Davis, Vivien Leigh, Olivia de Havilland, Greer Garson, Irene Dunne, Joan Fontaine,

Anna Neagle, Betty Grable, Margaret Lockwood, Ingrid
Bergman, Hedy Lamarr, Jane Wyman, Anne Baxter, Rosalind
Russell, Judy Garland, Barbara Stanwyck, Constance Cummings,
Ida Lupino, Mary Astor, Loretta Young, Paulette Goddard,
Gene Tierney, Katherine Hepburn, Claudette Colbert, Lana
Turner, Rita Hayworth; and Thomas Mitchell, James Stewart,
David Niven, Burgess Meredith, Laurence Olivier, Leslie Howard,
Robert Donat, Fredric March, Charles Laughton, Henry Fonda,
Bing Crosby, Bob Hope, Orson Welles, Charles Chaplin, Gary
Cooper, Claude Rains, Walter Pidgeon, Cary Grant, Herbert
Marshall, James Cagney, John Mills, Ray Milland, Eric Portman,
Edward G. Robinson, Humphrey Bogart, Spencer Tracy, Joseph
Cotten, John Garfield, Clark Gable, Anton Walbrook, Charles
Boyer, Errol Flynn, William Powell, George Sanders, Gene
Autry, Mickey Rooney, Robert Taylor, John Wayne, Robert
Young, Tyrone Power, Fred MacMurray, Alan Ladd, Lionel
Barrymore, Victor Mature, Van Heflin, Fred Astaire, Stewart
Granger.

5. *Films of the Post-War Period (1945–54)*

ALLEGRET, YVES: Une si jolie petite plage, 1948. Les Orgeuil-
leux, 1953.

ANTONIONI, MICHELANGELO: Cronaca di un Amore, 1950.

ASQUITH, ANTHONY: The Browning Version, 1951.

AUTANT-LARA, CLAUDE: Le Diable au Corps, 1947. Occupe-toi
d'Amélie, 1949. Le Blé en Herbe, 1953.

BAN, FRIGYES: A Piece of Earth, 1949.

BARDEM, J. A.: Comicos, 1953.

BECKER, JACQUES: Antoine et Antoinette, 1947. Rendezvous de
Juillet, 1949. Édouard et Caroline, 1951. Casque d'Or, 1952.
Ali Baba, 1954.

BENEDEK, LASZLO: Death of a Salesman, 1952.

BOULTING, J. and R.: Seven Days to Noon, 1950.

BRESSON, ROBERT: Journal d'un Curé de Campagne, 1951.

BROWN, CLARENCE: Intruder in the Dust, 1949.

BUNUEL, LUIS: Los Olvidados, 1950. El, 1952. Robinson Crusoe,
1953. Cumbres Borrascosas, 1954.

CAPRA, FRANK: State of the Union, 1948.

CARNÉ, MARCEL: Les Portes de la nuit, 1946. Thérèse Raquin,
1953.

CASTELLANI, RENATO: Sotto il Sole di Roma, 1948. E Primavera, 1949. Due Soldi di Speranza, 1952. Romeo and Juliet, 1953–4.

CAVALCANTI, ALBERTO: Caiçara, 1950. O Canto do Mar, 1953.

CAYATTE, ANDRE: Les Amants de Verone, 1948, Nous sommes tous des assassins, 1952.

CHAPLIN, CHARLES: Monsieur Verdoux, 1947. Limelight, 1952.

CLAIR, RENÉ: La Beauté du Diable, 1949. Les Belles de nuit, 1952.

CLEMENT, RENÉ: Les Maudits, 1947. Jeux interdits, 1952. Knave of Hearts, 1954.

CLOUZOT, HENRI GEORGES: Quai des Orfèvres, 1947. Le Salaire de la peur, 1953.

COCTEAU, JEAN: La Belle et le Bête, 1946 (with CLEMENT, RENÉ). Les Parents terribles, 1948. Orphée, 1950.

CORNELIUS, HENRY: Passport to Pimlico, 1949. Genevieve, 1953.

COUSTEAU, J.: Paysages du silence, 1946.

CRICHTON, CHARLES: Hue and Cry, 1947. The Divided Heart, 1954.

CUKOR, GEORGE: Born Yesterday, 1950. Pat and Mike, 1952. A Star is Born, 1954.

DASSIN, JULES: The Naked City, 1948.

DEARDEN, BASIL: The Captive Heart, 1946. The Blue Lamp, 1949.

DELANNOY, JEAN: La Symphonie pastorale, 1946. La Minute de vérité, 1952.

DICKINSON, THOROLD: The Queen of Spades, 1948. The Secret People, 1951.

DICKSON, PAUL: The Undefeated, 1950. David, 1951.

DISNEY, WALT: Cinderella, 1949.

DMYTRYK, EDWARD: Farewell, My Lovely, 1946. Crossfire, 1947. Give Us This Day, 1949.

DONEN, STANLEY: Seven Brides for Seven Brothers, 1954.

DONSKOI, MARK: The Village Teacher, 1948.

DOVZHENKO, ALEXANDER: Michurin, 1947.

EMMER, LUCIANO: Isola della Laguna, 1948. Paradiso Perduta, 1948. Domenica D'Agosto, 1950. Picasso, 1954.

ENGEL, ERICH: The Blum Affair, 1949.

FERNANDEZ, EMILIO: Maria Candelaria, 1946.

FLAHERTY, ROBERT: Louisiana Story, 1948.

FORD, ALEXANDER: Five Boys from Barska Street, 1954.

FORD, JOHN: My Darling Clementine, 1946. Wagonmaster, 1950. The Quiet Man, 1952. The Sun Shines Bright, 1953.

FRANJU, GEORGES: Sang des bêtes, 1949. Hotel des Invalides, 1952. Le Grand Méliès, 1953.

FREND, CHARLES: Scott of the Antarctic, 1948. The Cruel Sea, 1952.

GERASSIMOV, SERGEI: The Young Guard, 1948. The Country Doctor, 1952.

GOSHO, HEINOSUKE: Four Chimneys, 1952. A Hotel at Osaka, 1954.

HALAS, JOHN: Many animated films. Animal Farm, 1954.

HAMER, ROBERT: Kind Hearts and Coronets, 1949. Father Brown, 1954.

HATHAWAY, HENRY: The House on 92nd Street, 1946. Fourteen Hours, 1951.

HEYER, JOHN: The Back of Beyond, 1953.

HITCHCOCK, ALFRED: Strangers on a Train, 1951. Rear Window, 1954.

HUSTON, JOHN: Treasure of Sierra Madre, 1947. We Were Strangers, 1949. The Asphalt Jungle, 1950. The Red Badge of Courage, 1951.

JACKSON, PAT: White Corridors, 1951.

JAKUBOWSKA, WANDA: The Last Stage, 1948.

JENNINGS, HUMPHREY: Family Portrait, 1951.

KAZAN, ELIA: Boomerang, 1947. Viva Zapata!, 1952.

KEENE, RALPH: Cyprus is an Island, 1946. Nelungama, 1953.

KELLY, GENE (with DONEN, STANLEY): On the Town, 1950. Singin' in the Rain, 1952.

KING, HENRY: Twelve O'Clock High, 1950.

KINUGASA, TEINOSUKE: Gate of Hell, 1953.

KLAREN, GEORG: Wozzeck, 1947.

KUROSAWA, AKIRA: Rashomon, 1950. Ikiru, 1952. The Seven Samurai, 1954.

LAMORISSE, ALBERT: Crin Blanc, Cheval Sauvage, 1953.

LATTUADA, ALBERTO: The Mill on the Po, 1950. Luci del Varieta, 1951 (with FELLINI, F.). The Overcoat, 1952.

LEAN, DAVID: Great Expectations, 1946. Oliver Twist, 1947. The Sound Barrier, 1952. Hobson's Choice, 1954.

LEE, JACK: Children on Trial, 1946. The Wooden Horse, 1950.

LITVAK, ANATOLE: The Snake Pit, 1948.

MACKENDRICK, ALEXANDER: Whisky Galore, 1949. The Man in the White Suit, 1951. Mandy, 1952. The Maggie, 1953.

MCLAREN, NORMAN: Begone Dull Care, 1949 (and other short animated films). Neighbours, 1952.

MALAPARTE, CURZIO: Cristo Proibito, 1951.

MANKIEWICZ, JOSEPH L.: Letter to Three Wives, 1949. Julius Caesar, 1953.

MASSINGHAM, RICHARD: Pool of Contentment, 1946. They Travel By Air, 1948. What a Life, 1949 (and other short films).

MENOTTI, GIAN-CARLO: The Medium, 1951.

MEYERS, SIDNEY: The Quiet One, 1948.

MINNELLI, VINCENTE: The Pirate, 1948. Father of the Bride, 1950. An American in Paris, 1951. The Bad and the Beautiful, 1952. The Band Wagon, 1953.

MIZOGUCHI, KENJI: The Lady O'Haru, 1952. Tale of the Pale and Mysterious Moon after the Rain, 1953. Sansho Dayu, 1954.

OLIVIER, LAURENCE: Hamlet, 1948.

OPHULS, MAX: Letter from an Unknown Woman, 1948. La Ronde, 1950. Le Plaisir, 1952.

POWELL, MICHAEL (with PRESSBURGER, EMERIC): The Red Shoes, 1948. The Small Back Room, 1949. Tales of Hoffmann, 1951.

PUDOVKIN, V.: Harvest, 1952–3.

RAY, NICHOLAS: They Live by Night, 1949.

REED, CAROL: Odd Man Out, 1947. The Fallen Idol, 1948. The Third Man, 1949.

RENOIR, JEAN: The River, 1950–51. The Golden Coach, 1952.

ROSSELLINI, ROBERTO: Rome, Open City, 1945. Paisa, 1946. Amore (two parts), 1948.

ROSSEN, ROBERT: Body and Soul, 1947. All the King's Men, 1949.

ROTHA, PAUL: The World is Rich, 1948. World without End, 1953 (with Basil Wright).

ROUQUIER, GEORGES: Farrebique, 1944–6. Le Sel de la terre, 1950.

SANDERS, DENIS: A Time Out of War, 1954.

DE SANTIS, GUISEPPE: Caccia Tragica, 1947. Bitter Rice, 1949.

SHINDO, KANETO: The Children of Hiroshima, 1953.

DE SICA, VITTORIO: Sciuscia, 1946. Ladri di Biciclette, 1949. Miracolo a Milano, 1951. Umberto D, 1952. L'Oro di Napoli, 1954.

SJÖBERG, ALF: Miss Julie, 1950.

STAUDTE, WOLFGANG: The Murderers are Amongst Us, 1946. Der Untertan, 1951.

STEMMLE, R. A.: Berliner Ballade, 1949.

STEVENS, GEORGE: A Place in the Sun, 1951. Shane, 1952–3.

STORCK, HENRI: Rubens, 1949.

STURGES, PRESTON: Unfaithfully Yours, 1948.

SUCKSDORFF, ARNE: People in the City, 1946. A Divided World, 1948. Indian Village, 1951. The Great Adventure, 1952–3.

TATI, JACQUES: Jour de fête, 1949. Les Vacances de M. Hulot, 1953.

TETZLAFF, TED: The Window, 1948.

TRNKA, JIRI: The Emperor's Nightingale, 1949. Song of the Prairie, 1951. Old Czech Legends, 1953. A Drop too Much, 1954.

VEDRÈS, NICOLE: Paris 1900, 1948. La Vie commence demain, 1950.

VISCONTI, LUCHINO: La Terra Trema, 1948. Bellissima, 1952. Senso, 1954.

WATT, HARRY: The Overlanders, 1946.

WEISS, JIRI: Stolen Frontiers, 1947.

WELLES, ORSON: Macbeth, 1948. Othello, 1951–2. Mr Arkadin, 1954.

WILDER, BILLY: Sunset Boulevard, 1950. Ace in the Hole, 1951.

WISE, ROBERT: The Set-Up, 1949.

WRIGHT, BASIL: Waters of Time, 1951. World without End, 1953 (with Paul Rotha).

WYLER, WILLIAM: The Best Years of our Lives, 1947. Carrie, 1952. Roman Holiday, 1953.

ZAMPA, LUIGI: Vivere in Pace, 1946.

ZINNEMANN, FRED: The Search, 1948. The Men, 1950. Teresa, 1951.

U.P.A. (United Productions of America) Cartoons.
    (Executive Producer: Stephen Bosustow.)
    Work includes the Mr Magoo Series, Gerald McBoing-Boing, Madeline, Rooty-Toot-Toot, A Unicorn in the Garden.

The popular stars of the period include Vivien Leigh, Anne Baxter, Olivia de Havilland, Mary Astor, Barbara Stanwyck, Jennifer Jones, Ingrid Bergman, Jane Wyman, Judy Garland, Irene Dunne, Teresa Wright, Agnes Moorehead, Rita Hayworth, Gene Tierney, Betty Hutton, Jane Russell, Elizabeth Taylor, Marlene Dietrich, Ava Gardner, Katherine Hepburn, Ida Lupino, Marilyn Monroe, Yvonne de Carlo, Ginger Rogers, Linda Darnell, Vera-Ellen, Susan Hayward, Shelley Winters, Anna Neagle, Celia Johnson, Ann Todd, Jean Simmons, Margaret Lockwood,

Margaret Leighton, Glynis Johns, Mai Zetterling, Anna Magnani, Hildegarde Neff, Googie Withers, Michèle Morgan, Danielle Darrieux, Gina Lollobrigida, Edwige Feuillère; Victor Mature, Bing Crosby, Fredric March, Bob Hope, Danny Kaye, Gregory Peck, Orson Welles, Zachary Scott, Edward G. Robinson, Joseph Cotten, Montgomery Clift, the Marx Brothers, Van Heflin, Van Johnson, Humphrey Bogart, Frank Sinatra, Douglas Fairbanks Jnr., Anton Walbrook, Gene Kelly, John Wayne, Spencer Tracy, Marlon Brando, Jose Ferrer, Kirk Douglas, Walter Pidgeon, Dana Andrews, Claude Rains, Richard Widmark, Rex Harrison, Richard Attenborough, Michael Wilding, John Mills, Cedric Hardwicke, Trevor Howard, Michael Redgrave, Robert Newton, David Niven, Charles Laughton, Peter Ustinov, Richard Todd, Ralph Richardson, Jack Hawkins, Alec Guinness, Robert Donat, James Mason, Dirk Bogarde, Laurence Olivier, Leo Genn, Vittorio de Sica, Aldo Fabrizi, Michel Simon, Jean Marais, Jean-Louis Barrault, Pierre Fresnay, Louis Jouvet, Serge Reggiani, Maurice Chevalier, Jean Gabin, Gérard Philipe, Jacques Tati, Fernandel, Pierre Brasseur.

INDEX

Titles of films are in italics; those of books within quotation marks.

INDEX

343

INDEX